FOUNDING A BALKAN STATE

Albania's Experiment with Democracy, 1920–1925

OCTOBER 2012
To my dear
friend NESS GASHI.
I have enjoyed our
many adventures!

ROBERT

ROBERT C. AUSTIN

Founding a Balkan State

Albania's Experiment with Democracy, 1920–1925

UNIVERSITY OF TORONTO PRESS
Toronto Buffalo London

ISBN 978-1-4426-4435-9

Library and Archives Canada Cataloguing in Publication

Austin, Robert C. (Robert Clegg), 1964–
Founding a Balkan state : Albania's experiment with democracy,
1920–1925/Robert C. Austin.

Includes bibliographical references and index.
ISBN 978-1-4426-4435-9

1. Albania – Politics and government – 1912–1944.   2. Albania – Foreign
relations – 1912–1944.   3. Albania – History – 1912–1944.   4. Noli, Fan
Stylian, 1882–1965.   5. Democracy – Albania – History.   I. Title.

DR973.A98 2012   949.65′02   C2012-903009-0

University of Toronto Press acknowledges the financial assistance
to its publishing program of the Canada Council for the Arts
and the Ontario Arts Council.

 Canada Council   Conseil des Arts
for the Arts   du Canada

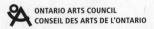 ONTARIO ARTS COUNCIL
CONSEIL DES ARTS DE L'ONTARIO

University of Toronto Press acknowledges the financial support of the
Government of Canada through the Canada Book Fund
for its publishing activities.

Contents

Illustrations follow page 84.

Preface

This book deals with the process of nation and state building in Albania between 1920 and 1925. It was in this period that the fundamental goals and directions of the new state were most hotly contested and Albania engaged in a political debate that proved to be the exception in the twentieth century, with some telling implications for Albania in the future. After the Congress of Lushnjë in 1920, which established the basis for a national government, Albania embarked on a path that for some leaders promised prosperity, a break with the Ottoman past, and modernization through democracy. Despite lacking many of the internal preconditions that would ensure success, as well as facing some extraordinary external obstacles, a small coterie of political leaders set out on the road toward democracy with vigour and optimism. However, by 1925, the forces that offered something new were in a retreat, and political pluralism collapsed. Albania slid into dictatorship, as well as into economic and political dependence, under Ahmed Zogu, first as president in 1925, then as self-proclaimed king in 1928. Because of the intensity of the debate, this period is unique as the zenith in Albania's pre–Second World War political life, and as such it amounts to a missed opportunity in need of further scholarly inquiry.

The main spokesman of a republican, modernized, and democratized Albania was Bishop Fan S. Noli, who arrived in Albania in 1920 from the United States determined to uproot the legacy of five hundred years of Ottoman rule. Emerging as the leading spokesman of a new Albania, Noli is the focal point of this book. Why Fan Noli and his brief rule as prime minister in 1924? Although by no means apparent at the time, Noli's temporary victory represented a lost opportunity to alter the central tenets of Albania's domestic and foreign policies as he undertook

to radically transform Albanian society on all levels. Within the wider
post–Paris Peace Conference Balkans, Albania faced the very same problems that confronted the entire region. All the Balkan states struggled
with key questions of political and social reform after the First World
War, and all slipped into various forms of dictatorship or authoritarianism. The Albanian manifestation of this trend sheds important light
on why reform failed not only in Albania but elsewhere in the Balkans.
Equally important, this study also helps us to better understand the very
nature of democratic transitions in both historical and contemporary
contexts.

During his six months as prime minister, Noli confronted the main
obstacles to a complete break with the past and the creation of a Western-
style parliamentary government. The principal goals of this study are to
uncover the causes of Albania's internal chaos in the years following the
war, the roots of Noli's 'revolution,' the evolution of his program, and
the reasons for its subsequent collapse. Readers will note that Ahmed
Zogu, a key spokesman of the ruling class, also plays a fundamental role
in this book. Noli and Zogu emerged as symbols for the main political currents at the time, although Zogu did his best to masquerade as
a reformer since, for him, reform was something you threatened but
never implemented. Noli and his friends in the United States came to
stand for reform and a 'European' Albania, while Zogu chose to defend
the conservative order and ruled by classic divide-and-rule tactics, taking constant advantage of the incompleteness of the Albanian national
awakening.

In addition to exploring the domestic side of Albania's struggle for a
new political order, foreign policy is also vital to understanding Albania.
For the most part, Albania's twentieth-century history has been shaped
by outside powers. The period between 1920 and 1925 is one of the few
instances when Albania was not totally dependent on one Great Power
or another for survival but was instead looking for foreign support. As a
result, while domestic problems were severe, problems outside the state
were far more intense and often served to shape the domestic agenda.
Political leaders still needed to define Albania's place in the Balkans and
the wider European political context. Borders were in dispute, minorities needed to be defended, and Albania, by far the poorest and weakest
of the Balkan states, needed financial and other support if it was to make
a serious start at state and nation building.

If a new political and social order was to be implemented, someone
else was going to have to pay for it. Political instability and the failure of

Noli were not solely the result of internal contradictions and the hopeless legacy of Ottoman rule, which left hardly any infrastructure. Albania's neighbours, Greece and Yugoslavia, played pivotal roles in shaping the domestic path of Albania. Equally important was the role of the Great Powers, the 'international community' in contemporary parlance, especially Great Britain and the United States, which were in a position to aid Noli and the reformers. The League of Nations, which for Noli was a potential saviour, also had the opportunity to shape events. Since Albania subsequently emerged as an almost silly 'Ruritania' or even 'Slaka' with an exotic self-proclaimed king dependent on Mussolini's Italy, Noli's somewhat independent or even renegade foreign policy is instructive as to the wider problems faced by small states.

I have tried to rely as much as possible on what was then new access to primary sources in Albania and the United States. To that I have added the published collections from Great Britain and the League of Nations. Western historiography on the period is limited, owing to the legacy of Albania's extraordinary isolation during the communist period (1944–91), and there is no single monograph dealing with the early 1920s. Western literature tended to focus on Zog, both as president and later king. Bernd J. Fischer's *King Zog and the Struggle for Stability in Albania* remains one of the best books on the period, along with Jason Tomes's more recent *King Zog: Self Made Monarch of Albania*. Both devote little space to the period prior to Zogu's final seizure of power in late 1924. Albanian communist-era historiography is extremely weak. The Noli interregnum and the period that preceded it served only communist political purposes. There was never a critical approach. Secondary literature was often repetitive and politicized, viewing 1924 as a 'bourgeois democratic' revolution and suggesting Noli was almost without flaws. For Albania's hard-line Marxist-Stalinists, June 1924 was February 1917 in Tsarist Russia.

The communist interpretation is certainly part of the picture. There was a battle between liberal-minded reformers, such as Noli, and status-quo conservatives found in the elite that Albania inherited from the Ottoman Empire. However, severe ideological restrictions on Albania's communist-era historians meant that other factors were ignored. These included disintegrative religious and regional trends, the role of the Albanians in the United States and Kosovo, and the military. As to the eventual collapse of Noli's government, communist historiography blames this almost exclusively on outside powers. This was an ideologically driven conclusion meant to serve the needs of a country perpetually under siege that was so much part of communist rule in Albania. Post-communist historiography has started to note Noli's mistakes and offer a more nuanced approach, but the idea that foreign powers shaped and continue to shape the course of events resonates still in Albania and elsewhere in the region.

The chapters of this book are chronological. I begin with a brief introductory survey of Albania from 1878 until 1920. Chapter 1 introduces the reader to the bleak economic, political, and social context of Albania both before and after the First World War. It also introduces the main political players and the emerging contest inside and outside of Albania. Chapter 2 looks at the gradual unification of the forces opposed to the Islamic ruling class and the origins of Noli's revolution, which became apparent in the fall of 1923 and the spring of 1924. Chapter 3 analyses the dilemmas faced by Noli and his government after seizing power in June 1924. The next three chapters deal exclusively with the international context of the period. Chapter 7 examines the last days of Noli's rule, the return of Zogu, and the end of Albania's democratic phase. Chapter 8 is a conclusion.

I am grateful to a number of people. The University of Toronto's then Centre for Russian and East European Studies (CREES) and its director, Robert Johnson, provided travel funds so that I could live and work in Albania in the early 1990s. My first two visits to Albania were made possible by the intervention of Paskal Milo and Fatos Tarifa. I owe them a great deal. Inside Albania, I have too many friends to list. It is enough to say that everyone I met helped me. Special thanks to Lindita Bubesi, Spiro and Maria Dede, Nasho Jorqagi, and Petrit and Margaret Nathanaili. Outside Albania, I benefited from the insights of Elez Biberaj, Bernd Fischer, Nicholas Pano, and Louis Zanga. My old friend Mark Biondich read this book so many times and always gave sound advice. More recently, the role of the Centre for European, Russian, and Eurasian Studies (CERES) has been crucial in providing a great place to work. I am especially grateful to Professor Jeffrey Kopstein, the Centre's director. The late Professor Peter Brock was both a great mentor and editor who pointed the way ahead from dissertation to book. Financial support for publication came from CERES and a number of Albanian-American friends. Special thanks to Sergio and John Bitici in New York for helping bring supporters together to provide the remaining financial support.

Finally, my wife, Maureen, always stood by me. I dedicate this book to her and our lovely children, Andrew and Kate.

Robert C. Austin, Toronto

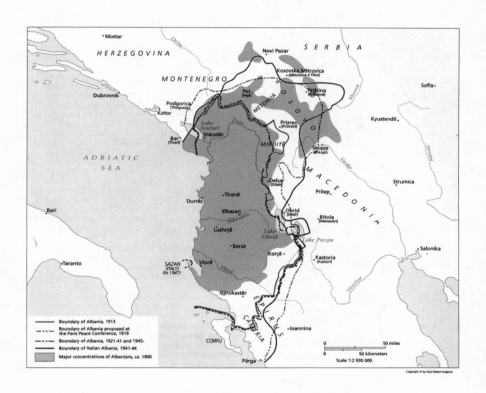

Albania in the twentieth century. C Paul Robert Magocsi, *Historical Atlas of Central Europe* (Toronto: University of Toronto Press, 2002), p.166. Used with permission.

FOUNDING A BALKAN STATE

1

Internal and External Challenges

While most Albanian political leaders in the early 1920s were careerists without a commitment to a defined program, there were also politicians and organizations with a long-term vision for Albania. Foremost among them were Fan Stylian Noli and Ahmed Bey Zogu, both of whom emerged as young and determined leaders of the new Albania. While not apparent from the outset, it was the conflict between these two that helped to define the political struggle from 1920 until Zog emerged triumphant in late 1924. This was a conflict between two types of politicians in Albania at the time: those who obtained their political experience during Ottoman rule, such as Zogu; and those, like Noli, who either had no experience or had gained it outside Albania.

Noli was by no means an ordinary Albanian politician. Prior to 1920, he had spent almost no time in Albania. Born in 1882 in Ibrik-Tepe (Qyteze in Albanian), an Albanian village in Ottoman Thrace, he was educated in a nearby Edirne [Adrianople] gymnasium.[1] He was an Ottoman citizen, who spoke Albanian at home and Greek at church and in school. Between 1900 and 1903, Noli lived in Greece, where he worked as a translator and actor, before travelling to Egypt to take a position as a grammar school teacher and church cantor. In 1906, at the age of twenty-four, he travelled to the United States and began to work in earnest for the Albanian national cause. Arriving in New York City, he first went to Buffalo, took a job at a lumber mill, and then moved on to Boston, where in July 1906 he began working for the first Albanian newspaper published in the United States, *Kombi* (The Nation), with Sotir Peci, also destined to play a role in making a new Albania. After a falling-out with Peci, Noli took a job operating a machine that stamped labels on cans. He finally found his calling in religion, although his decision to become a priest was primarily patriotic.[2] In 1908, in New York, he was consecrated as an Orthodox deacon, by Bishop Platon of the Russian Orthodox Church, apparently under suspect circumstances.[3] As a result, to quote one British observer, Noli found himself 'in the happy position of being his own spiritual chief.'[4] Hoping to eliminate Greek influence within the Albanian Orthodox Church, he focused his early activities on translating the church liturgy into Albanian and establishing an independent Albanian Orthodox Church. The latter he considered as vital to Albania's evolution into a unified nation and as a major blow to the supporters of the Greek 'Great Idea.'[5]

In 1908 he began studies at Harvard University, earning a bachelor of arts degree in 1912. He also engaged in extensive political activity, working as editor of the Albanian-American newspapers *Dielli* (The Sun) and *The Adriatic Review,* and playing an active role in Vatra (The Hearth), an organization of Albanian Americans based in Boston, which he founded with the U.S.-based Albanian leader Faik Konica in 1912.[6] In 1911, he visited the Orthodox Albanian communities in Bulgaria, Ukraine, and Romania, and by 1912, with the proclamation of independence, Noli had become an established journalist and writer in addition to being the leader of the Orthodox Albanian community in the United States. A true citizen of the world and a cosmopolitan, in addition to speaking Greek and Albanian, Noli was also conversant in English, Turkish, Arabic, and French.

His career as a diplomat began with the Albanian declaration of independence in 1912. Between 1912 and 1915, he was active in promoting the Albanian national cause throughout Europe. He made his first visit to Albania in 1913. Returning to the United States in 1915, he was elected president of the Vatra association, and transformed that organization into an active promoter of Albanian issues in the United States. In 1918, he attended the Washington Congress of Oppressed Nations and used the opportunity to explain to President Woodrow Wilson the unhappy plight of his homeland. Noli's experience in the United States exposed him to Western forms of governance, and his association with Albanian Americans, most of whom were from southern Albania, convinced him that democracy could be established in Albania.

His subsequent return to Albania in November 1920, initially as Albania's delegate to the First Assembly of the League of Nations and later as a representative in the Albanian parliament,[7] armed him with experience in the Albanian political environment. Nevertheless, in Albania he remained a neophyte and never seemed at home in its political atmosphere. Unlike the country's conservative forces, who favoured maintaining the social and economic status quo, Noli called for extensive reforms, especially land redistribution, which would have broken the control of the landowners and liberated the peasants. Arguing that the country lacked unity on all fronts, he felt that only the organization of the peasantry would allow Albania to overcome the disintegrative trends that plagued the country.[8] Noli's program, which emerged in bits and pieces, gradually transformed him into the major symbol for those who wanted radical change.

As a politician, Noli was something of an enigma. He left only vague reminiscences of his experiences, and his autobiography devotes little space to his career in politics. His grand vision for Albania was clear, but he seemed to lack the patience required to establish a connection with the people he hoped to liberate. Aside from calls for sweeping reforms and an end to what he perceived as feudalism, he lacked a concrete agenda to implement his plan. Arriving late in Albania, lacking his own political base, and spending the vast majority of his career abroad arguing Albania's case at the League of Nations and elsewhere, Noli never really established a grassroots movement. His political impact was primarily limited to the Orthodox south. As one observer noted, Noli was an international Albanian figure prior to becoming a national one.[9] Judging from his own writings, he considered his most important legacy to fall within the realm of the Albanian Orthodox Church.

However vaguely, it was early in his political career that Noli had already identified the roots of what he dubbed the Albanian sickness: one was internal; the other, external. The internal 'disease' was represented by Albanian landlords who controlled the key political and economic positions, wielded enormous power over the peasantry, and were determined to retain the socio-economic status quo. Noli loathed the continued dominance of this Ottoman ruling class and believed that the Albanian people first needed to be liberated from the old order. The external 'disease' was modern post–First World War imperialism exemplified in the expansionist policies of Serbia, Greece, and Italy.[10] Noli understood that Albania's independence was insecure in the face of the territorial ambitions of these neighbours. For Noli, Albania needed a benefactor, which he hoped would be the League of Nations, to provide Albania with security and financial assistance while the country embarked on reforms.

Noli had also identified, in a rather obtuse way, what he called the five anarchies that hindered the quest for national integration: religious, social, moral, patriotic, and ideological. More concretely, he declared that Albania had four faiths (Sunni Islam, Bektashi Islam, Catholicism, and Albanian Orthodox), but none had ever reached the hearts of a 'pagan people.' His special concern was always the impact that Albania's diverse religious make-up would have on national unity, and he noted that religious unity had been important for other Balkan nations such as the Greeks and Serbs. For him, as long as Albanian Orthodox citizens were under the control of the Greek Patriarchate and Moslems were under the influence of Turkey, there could be little progress. Social anarchy existed because Albania had not even developed so much as a class structure and, he wrote, there were no real classes of beys, peasants, or bourgeoisie. 'A peasant,' Noli wrote, 'is more a bey than a bey, and a bey is more a peasant than a peasant.' There was moral anarchy because 'the dog does not know his master'; patriotic anarchy because 'inside of one day as if by magic a traitor can be made patriot and patriot made a traitor'; and ideological anarchy because Albanian ideals were in the dark.[11] Only by eliminating the five anarchies, along with what he called 'land-lordism' and modern imperialism, could Albania move forward.

Noli, along with many Orthodox Christians, hoped that Albanian independence would usher in a new era in which the new state would emerge as something other than the Ottoman province it had been. As noted, in terms of prosperity and progress, the south was ahead of the north. The south paid more than its share of the country's tax burden, and it was only natural that many southerners hoped 'that they would get influence in the public affairs of the country, which would in some measure be proportionate to their culture and to the economic importance of their provinces.'[12] In the aftermath of the Lushnjë Congress, Noli gradually became the voice of the disgruntled southerners, who not only resented their lack of influence in Tirana but were growing intolerant of the continued dominance of Moslem beys in government and administration and the failure to initiate substantive change. These southerners, armed with what they believed to be a superior economic, political, and cultural experience, felt that they deserved to be the rulers of modern Albania.

The other important Albanian leader was Ahmed Bey Zogu. From the onset of the First World War until the Italian invasion in April 1939, Zogu was the key figure in Albania by virtue of his influence among tribesmen in the central region of Mati, a zest for intrigue, boundless energy, and an extraordinary thirst for power.[13] Zogu was born in 1895 in Burgajet, in Mati, and his forefathers had ruled the region as tribal chieftains for five hundred years. After the death of his father in 1903, he went to study in

Istanbul (Constantinople) and later entered an Ottoman military school. He returned to Albania in 1912 to lead his tribe in a revolt against the centralizing trends of the Young Turks. The independence proclamation in 1912 opened up new opportunities for Zogu. When Ismail Bey Qemal established a provisional government (prior to the selection of William of Wied as prince) and called a national congress, Zogu was in attendance representing the Mati district.

While Noli was abroad lobbying for support for the Albanian cause during the First World War, Zogu earned a reputation as one of the country's most able soldiers, battling Bulgarian, Serbian, and Montenegrin troops. His success in uniting the Albanians caused concern in Vienna as it was feared Zogu might succeed in re-establishing an independent Albania during the war and joining the Entente. In the spring of 1916, he was 'invited' to Vienna in hopes of getting him out of the way in Albania. This was his first visit to a Western capital, and he was dazzled.[14] While Zogu's wartime experiences came to an end, his stay in Vienna brought other rewards; he studied Western politics and was able after the war to add 'western constitutionalism to his collection of political doctrines.'[15] This, coupled with his military prowess, ensured that he was destined to become a major figure in interwar Albania.

Despite the fact that his formative experiences came during Ottoman rule and although he had limited knowledge outside the Balkans, in the aftermath of the Lushnjë Congress Zogu appeared as a voice of reform and westernization. However, his policies, in the long run, were often at odds with his stated intentions. Even after achieving complete dominance in Albania in January 1925, Zogu continued to cloak his authoritarian tendencies with progressive slogans and cited Mustafa Kemal Ataturk as his role model. No doubt Ataturk found this news troubling given the extent of reform in Turkey and the near total absence of reform under Zogu. Early in his career, Noli had been taken in by Zogu's calls for modernization and westernization and believed that despite the fact that he was both a bey and a clan chief, Zogu had abandoned his ties to the country's landowners.[16] As the product of a completely different environment from Zogu's, Noli was determined to reform all levels of Albanian society. Zogu, on the other hand, paid lip service to notions of reform but had a long-term vision for Albania that differed considerably from Noli's. If Noli became known for being stubborn and inflexible,[17] Zogu was recognized as a man driven by relentless opportunism and a lack of concern for political scruples.[18]

Zogu used the period after the war to lay the foundations for an implementation of his vision for Albania, which was the antithesis of Noli's.
Since the question of selecting a type of government remained open
until 1925, and since Zogu would eventually assume the mantle of self-
proclaimed king in 1928, he already had that ambition in mind in the
early 1920s.[19] Faik Konica suggested later that Zogu may have become
a monarchist in 1916 while in Vienna for the coronation of Emperor
Charles. 'It is interesting to speculate,' Konica wrote, 'whether the pag-
eantry of Emperor Charles's coronation might not have been responsible for firing the imagination of the young mountaineer and for turning
his thoughts to a coronation of his own some day. Strangely enough,
when he returned to Albania at the close of the war, he started on the
road to becoming a king.'[20] Unlike Noli, who was a republican, Zogu
thought that, given the tribal nature of Albanian society, a monarchy better suited the Albanian mentality. Zogu later argued that the Albanians'
'very mentality was such as did not permit full understanding of the ideals of a republican state. For them, patriotism and love of country could
mean nothing unless there was some living man to personify it to them:
the true Albanian is at heart a monarchist.'[21]

However, during the years when the question of monarchy was most
hotly debated, Zogu was a republican for one simple reason: had Albania
converted to a monarchy, he was not among the candidates for king.
The monarchists either hoped to attract a new sovereign from Europe
or supported the return of Wied. Zogu first needed to impose his complete dominance on Albanian political life before he would be able to
impose what he identified as the natural order of things in Albania.
Zogu, unlike Noli, knew both his country and people well, and was a
master manipulator who could shift with the trends of the time. He
'played his cards skilfully, shifting back and forth between traditional
and progressive ideas.'[22] He was first and foremost an opportunist whose
primary consideration was power. As such, realpolitik, particularly in
relations with Albania's neighbours and his lack of zeal for border revision, was the hallmark of his program. He also understood the regional
cleavages of the country, and possessing considerable influence within
his tribe, which with 23,000 people was Albania's largest, he always had
an army to call on. Unlike Noli, who sought a unified Albania through
reform, Zogu often followed the Ottoman example of divide and rule
and used the disintegrative trends in the country for his own ends.

Yet while the struggle between the old and new orders, which in many
ways emerged as a struggle between Noli and Zogu, was an important

issue in the period, it is not enough to explain the roots of the political upheaval in the early 1920s or Fan Noli's seizure of power. On the surface there was a battle between near-feudal landlords and an Albanian variant of liberalism, but this picture is limited and fails to probe the complicated cleavages that existed in Albania, especially among its liberal groups.[23] While there was a determination among liberals to break the power of the Islamic aristocracy, the question of the extent of the desired reform was subject to considerable debate. The form of government in Albania was also a major point of contention; supporters of monarchism or republicanism were to be found in both camps. Some forces were pro-communist, while others were merely liberal in outlook, seeking strong ties with Great Britain, France, and the United States. Others hoped that Italy would emerge as the benefactor of the country. Finally, Albania remained a divided country with regional allegiances having an important impact on developments, and these often took precedence over political programs.

It was only in early 1921 that the broad outlines of a political system were established when elections were called for a new national council or parliament to replace the unelected officials put in place after the Lushnjë Congress.[24] While Albania's first elections were intended to be for a constituent assembly, and not a parliament, voting for the former was postponed pending final delimitation of borders. The decision of the Lushnjë parliament to hold elections for a parliament, as opposed to a constituent assembly, was not in keeping with the Lushnjë statutes and angered many patriots, especially those who hoped for the emergence of a democratized Albania or wanted to see the key questions facing the state settled once and for all. Making matters worse, on 5 December 1920 the unelected parliament passed an electoral system that left power firmly in the hands of those who had designed the system: the traditional Islamic aristocracy. Voting was to be indirect and conducted in two rounds. In the first round, based on census data from ten administrative districts (prefectures),[25] every 500 males selected one delegate; the delegates subsequently elected a 75-member parliament of deputies from a list of candidates which was usually drawn up to give the designers of the system the upper hand. There was one deputy for every 12,000 citizens. This system made the voter a mere spectator in the process, and indirect voting, at least in the Albanian case, was ripe for corruption. It was especially despised by the country's emerging liberal elements for being inherently undemocratic and serving the interests of the landowners.

Two parties emerged that reflected the low level of political development and the importance of personalities over policies: the Popular
Party (Partia Popullore) and the Progressive Party (Partia Përparimtare).
Outside these labels were nominal independents and cliques who tended
to shift with the political breeze, hoping to secure the benefits of office
and political power. While their labels were certainly derived from those
employed in established democracies and were supposed to denote a commitment to westernization, neither was a political party in the Western
sense with well-defined programs and mass organizations.[26] Both parties
championed almost identical programs calling for political and economic
reform, mass education, and economic development. Such agendas, however, never went beyond slogans, and it was essentially the personalities in
the party leaderships that shaped membership and party policy.

The Popular Party was the larger party and tended to represent both
conservative and liberal opinion, as evidenced by the membership of
both Fan Noli, who was the party's first leader, and Ahmed Bey Zogu.
The party was generally more reform-minded; it sought a state developed along modern lines, was hostile to the continued dominance of the
beys, included many intellectual and democratic elements, and was correspondingly well represented in southern Albania. The Roman Catholic
minority, who tended to play a moderating role in Albanian politics,[27]
also preferred the enlightened program of the Popular Party but largely
remained outside the party due to the presence of Zogu, whose increasing influence they had come to fear.[28]

The Progressive Party was more or less the party of the beys and represented the interests of central Albania, where large landowners held sway.
Essentially in favour of the status-quo, its platform was more 'distrustful
of the masses, preferring to stick to national and social traditions.'[29] The
party was dominated by Shefket Verlaci from the central town of Elbasan,
one of Albania's largest landowners, who was bitterly opposed to any land
reform. It also included members of the Kosovo Committee (established
to protect the rights of the Albanian majority in Kosovo or ensure the
inclusion of Kosovo in Albania), among them Azem Bejta, Bajram Curri,
Hoxha Kadriu, and Hasan Prishtina, who had identified Ahmed Zogu as
pro-Serb, given his obvious distaste for shouldering the Kosovo cause.[30]
However, membership in any one party was not carved in stone, and
organizations or individuals shifted allegiance quite quickly, depending
on circumstances and prospects of personal gain. With the exception of
Noli and his closest supporters, few Albanian politicians were dogmatic
in their adherence to one solution or another.

Outside the loose framework of political parties, which had achieved nothing in terms of integrating the wider population, a number of more grassroots organizations, primarily defined by religion or region, took shape. These organizations were primarily progressive in outlook and sought to challenge the dominance of the Moslem landowners. They included the highly progressive Atdheu (Fatherland) organization, Bashkimi (The Union), the Kosovo Committee, Vatra (The Hearth), and Ora e Maleve (Hour of the Mountains). The Vlorë-based Atdheu was first organized by the young radical Avni Rustemi in the spring of 1921. Atdheu's official agenda was to promote the liberation of the peasantry, improve the educational system, and to seek the overall enhancement of Albanian cultural life.[31] Rustemi, born in 1895 in Libohova, was a student activist who, in June 1920, assassinated the wartime Albanian leader Esad Pasha Toptani, who had first undermined Wied and after the war been a serious rival for power to the government established at Lusnhjë. After his quasi-acquittal by a Paris court, which accepted the defence argument that the murder was a crime of national passion sanctioned by a whole people, Rustemi paid a single one-franc fine, returned to Albania as a national hero, and set about organizing the country's democratic forces. He focused his efforts on a potentially radical youth organization. It was a club of young Albanian intellectuals committed to a democratized and leftist Albania. Atdheu eventually came under pressure from the government and was shut down by government decree after only fourteen months in existence.

Atdheu was re-created in the fall of 1922 as the Tirana-based Bashkimi organization, which later had offices in Vlorë and Durrës. Bashkimi, although not a political party, emerged as the most progressive organization in the country. Later a pillar of support for Noli, it called for the eradication of the landowning class through land confiscation. It did not rule out the use of force to achieve that goal.[32] In a 1924 pamphlet, Bashkimi outlined the purposes of the organization, which included, among its twelve points, strengthening national equality, the creation of a classless society, a war on foreign propaganda injurious to the fatherland, support of desirable customs, war on any vice that might injure the morality and health of the people, fighting against female slavery, and the improvement of women's conditions.[33] While statistics on Bashkimi's membership are not available, Rustemi's main aim was to recruit the country's youth, and his organization evidently grew considerably in this period.

The aforementioned Vatra organization was also liberal in outlook and emerged as a key source of support for Noli, especially in terms of finance. It was established in 1912, with Faik Konica as its first general secretary and Noli as one of its key members. In the aftermath of the First World War, Vatra and the Albanian-American community as a whole played a vital role in Albanian political developments, gathering support for an independent Albania in both Britain and the United States. Vatra also acted as a government in exile for Albania during the war. After the Lushnjë Congress, Albanian Americans became a key source of support for political reform and westernization. Vatra was somewhat exclusionist, promoting a vision of Albania that reflected the needs, education, and experiences of Orthodox Albanians; it tended toward a hierarchic view of Albanian society, with Orthodox Albanians at the top. The influence of the Albanian-American community was the result of three factors: a growth in numbers, due to ongoing emigration; extensive political freedoms that other branches of the Albanian diaspora lacked; and, finally, the presence of very distinguished patriots such as Konica and Noli.[34] As noted, emigration to the United States in the first decade of the twentieth century was primarily Orthodox Tosk. Of these, some twenty to thirty thousand Albanians, like Noli, returned home during1919-25 to take part in building the country.[35]

Despite the relatively small size of the Albanian-American community, its two leading personages – Konica and Noli – transformed it into the most influential Albanian community abroad. Like Noli, Konica supported an activist stance on the homeland. He was a committed modernizer who believed that Albania had to abandon the legacy of Ottoman rule and install a Western-style parliamentary government. Born into a prestigious bey family in 1876 in Konitsa, in what is now part of northern Greece, Konica studied in Istanbul, France, and the United States, where he earned a master of arts degree in literature from Harvard in 1912. He started working for Albanian independence in Belgium in 1897, and in 1902 he transferred his activities to London. As the publisher of the journal *Albania,* founded in 1897 in Brussels, Konica had earned a name as one of the country's leading activists. In 1907 the journal fell on hard times and suspended publication. Owing to Noli's initiative, Konica arrived in Boston in 1909 to assume the editorship of the Albanian-American paper *Dielli,* then the organ of Besa-Besen, an Albanian-American organization established in 1908.[36] *Dielli* later became the official voice of Vatra.

After 1921, Vatra and *Dielli* were extremely anti-bey; they called for a westernized and republican Albania and focused their efforts in the southern town of Korçë. *Dielli* became known for its biting editorials and political cartoons portraying the post–Lushnjë Congress governments as corrupt, elitist, and neglectful of the needs of the Albanian peasants. While many in the Albanian-American community would have preferred Vatra to remain outside internal Albanian politics, Konica, who was made president of Vatra in 1921, felt that the American-Albanian community had both a vested interest in developments in the homeland and the financial resources to promote the democratization of the political system. Under his editorship, throughout the early 1920s, *Dielli* became one of Zogu's greatest enemies and led an all-out attack on what Konica identified as the 'former tools of Turkey' that dominated the Albanian governments.[37] In 1921, Vatra declared that it had

> opened warfare against Albania's internal enemies, against those who are enemies of freedom ... Albania has fallen into bad hands, into those who never wished for her welfare ... The majority of those who now fill government positions were formerly tools of Turkey and have always tried to skin the poor. Vatra is not going to surrender its struggle until it wipes away the injustices committed in Albania against the people. Vatra is going to strive, as it has always done, for a civilized and cultured Albania.[38]

To expand its efforts, in October 1922 Vatra began publishing a weekly in Korçë, *Shqiptari i Amerikës* (The Albanian American), with Konica as editor and another progressive, Hasan Bitincka, as manager. Under the tutelage of Noli and Konica, *Shqiptari i Amerikës* was a vocal critic of Zogu and the landowners.[39]

While Vatra and its subsidiary counted on winning over Orthodox Albanians in the south, progressive forces emerged from the Catholic minority in the northern town of Shkodër. Ora e Maleve, a group of Catholic clerics, included noted patriots Luigi and Shuk Gurakuqi. It was also a bastion of anti-Zogist activity and was disturbed by the continued dominance in Tirana of Moslem landowners. Its newspaper, also called *Ora e Maleve*, began publishing in April 1923 and was the voice of reform, defending the interests of the Shkodër prefecture. Luigi Gurakuqi, who served as a deputy from Shkodër from 1921 until 1924, was one of the leading lights of the Albanian intelligentsia. In 1908, he had taken part in the Monastir Congress, which established an alphabet for the Albanian language; in 1912, he attended the proclamation of independence and was named minister of education in Qemal's provisional government. In the aftermath of the Lushnjë Congress, Gurakuqi emerged as the key spokesman of the Catholic community. Like southern Orthodox Albanians, the

Catholic minority of the north also felt that from an economic, political, and cultural point of view, Shkodër was the most developed part of the country and thus deserved a far greater say in governance. The Catholic minority, although primarily progressive in outlook, first and foremost promoted a regional and clericalist agenda. Like the Orthodox Tosks, they too possessed a hierarchical view of Albanian society, one which put themselves at the top in terms of culture and education. What facilitated cooperation between Orthodox and Catholic Albanians was not necessarily agreement on just how the new state should look, but a shared assessment that the continued dominance of the beys was unacceptable.

The fact that Albania's borders, rather than following ethnic lines, were the product of geopolitical concerns, ensured that Albanians eager for border revision would play an important role in the political struggle. Serbia essentially conquered Kosovo in 1912-13, and Albania's then borders had left over 500,000 Albanians living in western Macedonia, Montenegro, and Kosovo.[40] In the war's aftermath, it was simply assumed that Kosovo was an integral part of Serbia.[41] The Kosovo question has been an on-again-off-again dilemma for successive Albanian governments since 1913. What is most important is that it was only between 1920 and 1924 that Albania actually had a Kosovo policy. In the aftermath of Noli's departure, Zogu adopted a 'hands-off' policy, while Albania's later communist rulers were happy to ignore it. For many Albanians, especially those in the northeast, who had had their trade and other links with the towns of Prishtina and Prizren in Kosovo severed when borders were drawn, there was a strong desire for national unification. Also, Belgrade's policy, which was aimed at Serbianization after five centuries of foreign rule, manifested itself in multiple injustices and abuses. The period between 1920 and 1925 stands out as by far the worst period for Albanians in Serbia prior to the policies of the regime of Slobodan Milosevic between 1989 and 1999.

The interwar experience of the Albanians in the new Yugoslavia was decidedly horrific. On paper, they enjoyed the same rights as other 'Yugoslavs,' but the reality on the ground was totally different. Although Yugoslavia had reluctantly signed the Treaty for Protection of Minorities in 1919, pledges meant nothing, especially the ones related to access to language. The denial of language rights was coupled with large-scale colonization by Serbs, and the confiscation of Albanian land had one simple goal – to alter the ethnic balance in Kosovo by encouraging migration to Albania and Turkey. By 1930, there was not a single Albanian-language school in Kosovo.[42] In a 1921 petition to the League of Nations, the

Albanian community in Serbia alleged that since 1918, some 12,371 people had been killed and 22,000 imprisoned.[43] Belgrade's attitude toward the Albanians was never disguised. The Serbian delegation in Paris initially refused to sign any minority protection treaties, essentially because they believed that the Albanians were simply inferior.[44] The chief of the Serbian Military Mission in Paris suggested that the 'uncivilized' people of Albania were not ready for independence and that Yugoslavia should be awarded northern Albania in order to civilize the region.

The Kosovo Committee and the Kaçak movement were the direct result of Serbian policy. The Kosovo Committee, fundamentally a clandestine resistance movement, which drew its membership from both sides of the border, was formed in 1918 to promote a more aggressive Albanian policy on Kosovo. Its maximalist goal was unification of all Albanians in what has become known as ethnic or Greater Albania.[45] Its minimalist goal was Yugoslav adherence to minority rights commitments. It was progressive in the sense that it would have welcomed assistance from the Soviets to achieve its ends and would stop at nothing to eliminate Zogu, who was the 'sworn enemy of all Kosovar rebels and irredentists.'[46] Its minimum goals were Yugoslavia's adhesion to the rights of its Albanian minorities as stipulated by the post-war minority treaties, while its long-term ambition was the annexation to Albania of the territories primarily inhabited by Albanians.[47] Its leadership, especially Azem Bejta, Bajram Curri, Hasan Prishtina, Zia Dibra, and Hoxha Kadriu, were men who had little use for diplomacy and preferred armed action. It had fundamentally two enemies: the government in Belgrade, which they maintained was waging a war on the Albanian community; and politicians in Tirana who preferred a hands-off policy in the region. The Kosovo Committee, and the Kaçak movement it directed, played a vital role in the 1920-4 period since it offered the main military challenge to Zogu, and its membership was battle-hardened. The group's size is difficult to ascertain, although Serbian sources suggest that at the war's end, Prishtina and Curri had three thousand men on the Albanian side of the frontier ready to 'liberate' Kosovo.[48]

Albania's disastrous financial predicament also had important implications for developments. After the war, Albania was a state only in name. League of Nations commissioners noted in 1922 that while the essential elements of a prosperous, politically and economically independent state were there, much work remained to be done. Albania was 'still in a situation similar to that of several Balkan countries immediately after their liberation from Turkish domination.'[49] There was virtually no transportation system: less than 200 kilometres of paved roads, and no modern port. Vast parts of the north were accessible only by foot, and there was no motorized traffic (the entire rolling stock in the 1920s consisted of three Fords left behind by a U.S. relief mission).[50] As to forces to preserve internal order and guard against external threats, Albania had an army that consisted of roughly eight battalions of gendarmerie with 400 men each, three infantry regiments of 2,000 men, and one engineer battalion of 600 men. It had no air or naval forces.[51]

The main problem was that in order to begin the process of state building, Albania needed a domestic source of stable income, international loans, and foreign investment, but none of these were possible without political stability. Throughout the early 1920s, successive League of Nations observers had noted the extremely unsatisfactory state of Albania's financial situation. Professor Albert Calmes (Luxembourg), on behalf of the League, noted in 1921 that Albania's economic life depended on agriculture but its economic system and methods of cultivation were primitive, leading to Albania being forced to import foodstuffs.[52] Calmes added that the most urgent needs were the construction of roads, the development of agriculture, draining of marshes, a campaign against malaria, establishment of a bank of issue, and prospecting for mineral wealth, especially coal and oil.[53] The national budget was perpetually in arrears and there was a severe balance of payments problem.[54] Like many observers, Calmes suggested that Albania obtain a loan to start work on the many challenges. Another League observer noted that without a loan, Albania would have little chance of retaining its independence.[55] External hopes aside, Albania had few steady sources of domestic revenue. Income tax stood at only 6 per cent for even the highest earners, tax inspectors were routinely bribed, and only a quarter of income was even declared.[56]

Despite the fact that so many observers were on record as supporting a loan for Albania, the loan never materialized. As a result, there was tremendous competition within Albania for the meagre resources available, leaving the state treasury perpetually bare. The quest for a share of the budget was most profound in the army, and it wound up exerting considerable influence over Albania's political destiny. The military often suffered from a lack of funds, and in order to maintain its loyalty, the government provided it with incentives where possible. Attempts were made to create an organized, Western-style army that was completely de-politicized. However, as events were to prove, this aim was for the most part thwarted, and Albania's military hierarchy emerged as both careerist and politicized.[57] Zogu, as minister of interior in the first Lushnjë government, tended to focus limited financial resources on the gendarmerie, which was attached to his ministry. The League's financial advisor to Albania concurred with Zogu's preference for the gendarmerie and suggested the army's outright abolition in order to lessen the budget deficits.[58]

As a political culture was taking shape inside Albania, the first elections to the parliament, which were held between February and March 1921, provided limited internal stability. The 75-member chamber, which opened on April 5, was divided almost evenly between members of the Popular and Progressive Parties. A new parliament meant little as events outside Albania were of paramount concern. If Albania faced many domestic challenges in terms of state and nation building, its external problems were far more threatening. While there were certainly different solutions on offer by Albania's leaders, they could all at least agree that Albania should exist as an independent country. This was not the case outside, as Italy, Greece, and Serbia had not been reconciled to the notion of an independent Albania. The ability of its neighbours to interfere in domestic political affairs was enhanced by domestic turmoil – the result of Albania's regional and religious cleavages – financial instability, and the simple fact that Albania was by far the weakest of the Balkan states. Even the struggle to eliminate or at least reduce the dominance of the landowners was bound to have implications outside Albania as it encouraged the belief that Albania was a Moslem state. Greece and Yugoslavia could thus champion themselves as defenders of the Catholic or Orthodox minorities.

None of Albania's neighbours were happy with Albanian independence in 1912/13, and feelings did not improve when Albania re-emerged in 1920. Greece, Yugoslavia, and Italy rejected the 1913 borders, and all three used the Peace Conference as an opportunity to reopen the question of Albania's right to exist as an independent state. While Italy sought paramount influence in Albanian affairs, Greece and Yugoslavia had defined territorial agendas. By far the greatest problem was the wartime Treaty of London (1915) between the Entente powers and Italy, which provided for the partition of most of the country. Italy was promised the strategic port of Vlorë and the island of Sazan off Vlorë's coast, while northern Albania was assigned to Serbia and Montenegro. The treaty envisioned the creation of a tiny and neutralized Albania to be represented by Italy in foreign affairs.[59] Making matters worse, in July 1919 the Italian and Greek governments had concluded

an agreement pledging support for the other's claims to Albanian territory. Albania's position in Paris was weak. However, vital support came
from U.S. president Woodrow Wilson, who denounced the Treaty of
London as inconsistent with the principle of self-determination. This
stand, which subsequently elevated Wilson to the position of saviour of
Albania and established the basis for the very pro-American sentiments
of so many Albanians, increased American political capital and opened
the door for a strong U.S. presence in Albania. Despite support from
Wilson, both Greece and Yugoslavia continued to press for changes to
Albania's southern and northern borders. The former sought annexation of what Greeks refer to as northern Epirus (to denote continu-
ity with the Greek province), while the latter demanded the cities of
Shkodër and Durrës.[60]

Given the potential threat to Albanian sovereignty from neighbouring states, Albanian leaders, especially Noli, attached great significance
to membership in the League of Nations. Noli possessed an extraordinary faith in the organization and its promise of a new world order.
Acceptance into the League, Noli believed, would provide a source of
much-needed financial aid, but the promise of international action to
defend the integrity of states also appealed to Albanians who felt under
constant threat from their neighbours. In hindsight, it's apparent that
Noli, and others who always placed external issues above internal ones,
incorrectly assessed the League as the key defender of Albania's territorial integrity.

The task of defending Albania's interests at the League fell to Fan
Noli. This was not his first major task as an emerging Albanian statesman. Both during and after the war, on behalf of Vatra, he was already
an articulate defender of Albania's right to renewed independence.[61]
His experience at the League not only left a lasting impression on him
but also increased his stature back home and elevated him to the first
rank among Albanian leaders. It also provided him with a measure of
recognition abroad. The *Manchester Guardian* remarked that Noli was 'a
man who would have been remarkable in any country. An accomplished
diplomat, an expert in international affairs, a skillful debater, from the
outset he made a deep impression in Geneva. He knocked down his
Balkan opponents in a masterly fashion, but always with a broad smile.'[62]
After his arrival in Albania in November 1920, Noli was immediately sent
on this vital diplomatic mission by the government. Noli later argued
that he was chosen for this position because he spoke both English and
French.[63] However, it probably had more to do with the fact that some

patriots, especially Sotir Peci, who had worked with Noli in the United States, distrusted the all-too-progressive bishop and were eager to keep him out of Albania for as long as possible.[64]

Albania's acceptance into the League was by no means considered a *fait accompli,* and diplomats undertook extensive lobbying in the months following the Congress of Lushnjë, focusing efforts on support from Great Britain. In a February 1920 appeal to Prime Minister Lloyd George, the Albanian Foreign Ministry called the proposed partition of Albania at the hands of the London Treaty 'a denial of justice' and hoped that British representatives at the Peace Conference 'would not permit this outrage.'[65] Noli made a personal appeal to the League, calling for the confirmation of Albanian independence with its 1913 borders intact.

The key spokesman of the Albanian cause in Great Britain was the aristocratic Aubrey Herbert, a member of the British House of Commons, and it was on him that Noli focused his efforts. In 1913, Herbert founded the London-based Albanian Committee to help the Albanian delegation negotiate with the Great Powers in the aftermath of the First Balkan War and the proclamation of independence. So profound was Herbert's role in defending Albanian rights that he was twice offered the Albanian throne.[66] Although he declined the position, Herbert, who worked closely with Albanian Americans, was nominated by Vatra to act as representative to the Paris Peace Conference. As a tireless promoter of the Albanian cause, Herbert earned a very prominent place in the hearts of Albanian patriots, and helped to create and sustain the belief that only Great Britain was a disinterested promoter of the Albanian cause. In October 1920 he wrote Noli that he would seek support for Albania in the British House of Commons and that he would argue Albania's case at the British Foreign Office. He told Noli that he had had a very satisfactory talk with Harold Nicholson, then first secretary in the British Foreign Office's Central Department, who was very open to the suggestion that Albania should be recognized at once. According to Herbert, Nicholson was also reassuring about the Greeks and the Serbs, in terms of their quest for substantial revision of Albania's southern and northern frontiers.[67]

Armed with the support of Herbert, who undertook to use his influence at all levels of the British government, Albania's admission to the League was due to be considered by the First Assembly in Geneva on 15 November 1920. The commission to study Albania's entry into the League consisted of delegates from Canada, Italy, Poland, France, and

Czechoslovakia. Opposition to the country's entry came from several quarters: the most vocal from the Greek and Yugoslav governments, which still hoped to gain territorial concessions. Because of Albania's peculiar status, in that the country existed but its borders were not yet delimited, talk focused on postponing the decision until the border question was resolved.

However, support for the Albanian cause came from both South Africa and Canada, no doubt acting at Great Britain's behest. The South African delegate, Lord Robert Cecil, who was profoundly influenced by Herbert, disagreed with a French proposal to postpone the decision and argued that 'Albania should be admitted because she presented all the conditions of a nation perfectly constituted.'[68] While a decision was in fact postponed, the League finally admitted Albania on 17 December 1920 with 35 ayes and 7 abstentions. In his speech to the League Assembly, Noli revealed not only his satisfaction at Albania's entry into that body, but also his own firm beliefs in the League's new mandate:

> Edmund Burke exclaimed once in the House of Commons: Alas, the age of chivalry is gone. What happened here yesterday when Albania was admitted to the League of Nations convinced me that Burke was mistaken. When I saw yesterday champions from all corners of the earth standing up in defense of that abandoned child of Europe, champions from Africa and America; from Asia and Europe; when I saw our neighbours – neighbours like all European neighbours – generously cast their vote in our favour, with my eyes dimmed by tears and a lump rising in my throat, I felt like shouting with all the power of my lungs: Nay, the age of chivalry is not gone.[69]

Noli left the League with a feeling of considerable accomplishment. He felt that Albania's acceptance into the League was his greatest diplomatic success.[70]

Noli had the misplaced sense that the League was the bastion of progressivism and that the world had embarked on a new era of international relations in which small nations like Albania could not only survive, but thrive. As he remarked in another speech:

> And yet, even though the League of Nations is a dream, a utopia that makes sceptics smile or laugh, the League must stand as an ideal representing the noblest aspirations of mankind, in defiance of grotesque military glory. It must stand as a solemn reaffirmation of the world's longing for peace.[71]

As it turned out, Noli's expectations of the League's ability to provide cash for Albania and defend its security were as exaggerated as was his assumption that Great Britain was a disinterested promoter of Albanian interests, willing to stand up for the country in the face of Italian, Greek, and Yugoslav territorial demands. These false beliefs haunted Noli for the rest of his political career by clouding his judgment of Albania's position in world affairs, thus affecting his ability to adopt a foreign policy that realistically accorded with its position in the Balkans. Noli suffered from an Albano-centric view of the world, which was made worse by his stint at the League. He tended to exaggerate the Great Powers' and the League's commitment to actively aid in the implementation of radical social reform, as well as their willingness to act as allies in Albania's often tedious regional disputes.

After Albania's admission to the League of Nations, definitive frontiers needed to be established. This battle lasted until 1925, posed severe challenges for the new state, and created friction with Albania's neighbours. With valuable diplomatic experience from the League, Noli undertook to remain in Geneva for most of 1921 to argue Albania's case. During the ensuing year, Noli's attitude toward Albania's neighbours hardened, and he became reluctant to make any concessions to either the Yugoslavs or Greeks when he finally obtained power. Albania's goal was simple: the restoration of her 1913 borders. Albania's pre-war borders were the result of two agreements: the July Conference of Ambassadors in London and the December Florence Protocol. The former established Albania as a neutral state, while the latter delimitated Albania's southern border. Work on Albania's other frontiers was postponed by the outbreak of the First World War.

Stern opposition to restoration of the 1913 borders again came from Greece, Yugoslavia, and Italy, and Noli focused his efforts on winning the support of Great Britain. The situation was extremely complex. On the one hand, cooperation between Italy and Greece on Albanian territorial spoils had collapsed with the August 1920 expulsion of Italian troops from Albania and Italy's subsequent recognition of Albania.[72] Yugoslavia, on the other hand, was still pushing for certain rectifications of Albania's northern frontier and continued to occupy key parts of northern Albania. The Greeks argued, among other things, that the Florence Protocol of 1913 was no longer valid since Albanian neutrality in the war had been abrogated by Esad Pasha Toptani's declaration of war against the Central Powers and therefore the question of borders could be re-examined. The Greeks and Yugoslavs were in agreement that Albania's 1913 borders had perished along with the demise of the form of government previously established and that all agreements needed to be reopened. The Yugoslavs argued that since the Treaty of Sevres (between the Entente and Turkey in August 1920, which established Turkey's post-war borders) stipulated that Yugoslav frontiers to the south and with Italy should be fixed subsequently, Albania's 1913 frontier was therefore not sacrosanct.[73]

The Greek and Yugoslav positions being identical, the two countries employed similar tactics designed to prove that Albania and the Albanians were not ready for self-government. Foreshadowing later attempts in the late 1990s to tarnish the Albanians, many attacks focused on the fact that a very large percentage of Albanians were Moslems. To this, Yugoslavia added its already well known position in Kosovo: the Albanians were uncivilized. Noli, therefore, was forced to fight on two fronts, defending both Albania's borders and the country's right to exist as an independent state. Both Yugoslavs and Greeks tried to use the lack of religious unity in the country to their advantage by fomenting opposition to what they dubbed a Moslem government, serving the interests of a Moslem land-owning class. For the Greek government, the presence of a tiny Greek minority in southern Albania was an excellent device for maintaining pressure on the government. The Yugoslavs sought to manipulate the Catholic minority in the north by highlighting the predominance of the Moslem landed aristocracy in Tirana. Noli, exasperated by Greek and Yugoslav hostility, met each attack with evidence of the secular nature of the Albanian government: Albania had a cabinet with representatives from all three religions. He asked a League Council session in June 1921 if there was 'anywhere in the world' with 'less [religious] fanaticism than in Albania.'[74] Shifting the focus from Albania's minority policy to the position of Albanians living in Greece and Serbia, he added that the million or so Albanians living in Kosovo did not have a single school, while the only Serbian village in Albania, Vraka, with a mere hundred inhabitants, had a school. The same, he argued, could be said about the Greeks: whereas in Çameria,[75] the Albanians had no schools, 'the small Greek minorities in Southern Albania possess several Greek schools.'[76]

As to giving up territory either to Greece or to Yugoslavia, Noli out-lined his attitude in June 1921 in Geneva:

The Albanian nation has suffered cruelly from the unjustifiable dismember-ment of which the country was a victim in 1913. The vast districts of Kossovo

and the districts of Dibra, Hotti, Gruda, Plava and Gussinje, with a population of more than a million Albanians, have been annexed to Serbia and
Montenegro as a result of political manoeuvres; the same fate has befallen
the Albanian region of Chameria [Cameria], which has been annexed to
Greece. Albania cannot endure to be further manipulated. The surrender
of even the smallest part of her territory would, to her, be equivalent to the
renunciation of her very existence.[77]

Noli's emotional but not altogether unreasonable position was to have
a profound effect later as he attempted to foster cooperation with
Albania's neighbours. In Geneva he had learned that the satisfaction of
Greek and Yugoslav demands was no easy task.

To counter the combined weight of Greek and Yugoslav pressure at
the League in the summer of 1921, Noli again sought support from
Great Britain. The small but important Albanophile group, embodied by
the Anglo-Albanian Society, which included Aubrey Herbert and Edith
Durham,[78] did extraordinary work in promoting the Albanian cause.
Outside of this group, Noli also tried to influence figures such as Major
Julian Barnes and Major Harold Temperley,[79] both of whom held important positions in the Conference of Ambassadors, which in the end was
charged with solving Albania's outstanding territorial issues.[80] Albania's
grip on its 1913 borders was by no means firm, and had it not been
for some poorly timed manoeuvres by the Yugoslavs, a much smaller
Albania might well have emerged. In September 1921 it appeared
that Britain was preparing to support at least part of the Yugoslav and
Greek positions. In a letter of September 8 from Temperley to Barnes,
Temperley, who supported some modifications in the 1913 borders in
Belgrade's favour, noted that despite criticism from the Anglo-Albanian
Society, Great Britain was trying to obtain the best decisions under the
circumstances.[81] Temperley went on to note that no one doubted that
Serbia was 'legally entitled to possession of all the territory they held
in 1913' and that Greece was twice promised the southern provinces
of Gjirokastër and Korçë (northern Epirus) and that these promises
had imposed a 'moral obligation from which it is difficult to escape.'[82]
He concluded that under the circumstances 'it was very rare for one
State [Great Britain] to have done so much for another as we have for
Albania for entirely disinterested reasons and, if you compare Wilson's
similar support of Yugoslavia to restrain Italian claims there, you will
find, I believe in the end, that we have done far better for Albania.'[83]

In his reply to Temperley, Barnes reiterated his belief that Albania's 1913 borders should be maintained and that any changes could only be undertaken on the basis of compensation.[84] He also appealed to Temperley not to neglect the fact 'of honest men morally outraged by having to sign a document handing over districts to Serbia inhabited exclusively by their countrymen, which have never been legally acquired by Serbia, and where abominable excesses have been committed by Serbian troops.'[85] Barnes also kept Noli well aware of the British position and advised him on September 19 that Temperley was 'sincerely and honestly doing all he can to help Albania, and that in so far as he has recommended or sanctioned any modifications to the 1913 borders [he] has done so in the honest conviction that he was getting the best for Albania in the present difficult circumstances.'[86] Barnes advised Noli that in the event Albania could not secure any reconsideration of the recommendations proposed by the Conference of Ambassadors, he should 'agree to an immediate settlement rather than leave the matter open. Leaving the matter open is extremely dangerous and I sincerely believe that prudence at the present moment is our best counsellor.'[87]

The discussion of Albania's borders shifted from the League to the Conference of Ambassadors. Representatives from France, Great Britain, Italy, and Japan convened in early November 1921 in Paris to finally settle Albania's borders. When the Conference arrived at a decision on November 9, it was a product of some haste. The brief establishment of an independent republic in the northern region of Mirdita in July 1921 made the finalizing of Albania's frontier imperative. With Yugoslav military assistance, Catholic chieftain Marka Gjoni sought to create an independent republic under Yugoslav auspices. Gjoni's justification for separation from Albania was the Tirana government's 'Young Turkish' tendencies and its hostility to Catholic religious liberty. Gjoni appealed to the Yugoslav government to take the required steps to secure the recognition of the Mirdita Republic.[88] Belgrade clearly hoped that unrest in northern Albania would ensure that its claims to the region would find support. In Geneva, Noli was confronted by accusations from the Yugoslav delegation that the Tirana government was a tool of the Moslem landowners, that the government in Tirana could not maintain control over the entire country, and that there were two governments in Albania. Midhat Frashëri, as part of Albania's League delegation, noted that the 'Tirana government is not a Mohammedan government. Its cabinet comprises representatives from all Albanian religions.'[89]

The Yugoslav delegate to the League, M. Jovanovic, stated that it was doubtful that the 'Tirana government' deserved recognition as the government of all Albania. He added that the League should consider dispatching a commission to Albania in order to determine who ruled.[90] In keeping with the Yugoslav premise that all previous decisions on Albania's borders required re-examination, Jovanovic argued that Albania's status as a state, and correspondingly a League member, was thrown into doubt with the establishment of the Mirdita Republic.[91] In Jovanovic's argument, Albania's admission to the League was premature since it was based on the mistaken belief that there was a de facto government. The Mirdita episode proved that 'there is not only one de facto Government, but two; unanimity of the people, therefore, does not exist.'[92] Great Britain rejected Yugoslavia's position and, through the League Council, demanded its withdrawal from the disputed region on November 7. The intervention of Great Britain was vital because it ended Yugoslav support for Gjoni. Great Britain, which in November recognized the Albanian government de jure, advised League secretary General Eric Drummond that the Council should consider taking measures against Yugoslavia under Article 16 of the Covenant.[93] Charged with disarming the rebels within Albania was Ahmed Zogu. Although allegedly suffering from malaria with a temperature of 105 degrees, Zogu set out for Mirdita, where, without bloodshed, he restored peace and order.[94]

Just days after the demand for Yugoslav withdrawal, the Conference of Ambassadors handed down a decision that upheld the 1913 boundaries. Certain rectifications in the northwest, around Shkodër, and in the southeast, around Lake Ohrid, were made in Yugoslavia's favour.[95] The decision pleased nobody: Yugoslavia still sought changes in the north; Greece remained steadfast that southern Albania was ethnically Greek; and Albania was once again left with more citizens outside of its borders than within. Nevertheless, Noli and the Albanian delegation were prepared to heed Barnes's advice and accept the decision. While Albania now had internationally recognized borders, the Conference gave special powers to Italy. Arguing that a violation of either the frontiers or the independence of Albania would constitute a danger to Italy, which claimed special interests in Albania, the maintenance of Albanian independence was entrusted to the Italians.[96] Both decisions angered Noli and had important implications for his future career. Since the question of borders was by no means closed, it ensured that Noli would remain steadfast in his hostility toward both Greece and Yugoslavia and in his belief that Albania could not make any more territorial sacrifices. Noli, who did not feel Italy's new-found role was in Albania's best interests, realized that Albania's independence could only be guaranteed by a power without territorial ambitions in the region. Great Britain, in addition to supporting Albania's entry into the League, was credited with an important role in shaping Albania's borders. Its forceful stance on the Mirdita uprising was also important. Given the circumstances, it was not surprising that Noli's early diplomatic experience had given him the sense that Great Britain, alone of the world's Great Powers, was prepared to defend Albania without ulterior motives.

In the aftermath of the Lushnjë Congress of January 1920, Albania experienced an exciting and lively debate on fundamental political, economic, and social issues. A political culture was taking shape, albeit still at a very early, rudimentary stage; Albania had had its first parliamentary elections. However, the main goals of the Lushnjë Congress, which were to decide on a permanent form of government and draft a new constitution through an elected constituent assembly, had not been fulfilled. The decision to hold elections to a parliament, as opposed to a constituent assembly, further postponed these questions. Despite the establishment of a parliamentary facade through elections in 1921, little had been done to decide the fundamental questions facing the country. Political parties were formed, but they possessed no mass base of support, offered nearly identical programs, and made little effort to broaden their appeal to the wider population. Politics remained the domain of the landowning aristocracy. Other political organizations appeared, although most were regional or religious in outlook, indicating that much remained to be done in terms of creating national unity and eliminating the disintegrative trends that had hindered Albania's national awakening in the years prior to the First World War.

As for the battle between progressives and status-quo conservatives, this too was taking shape. The Bashkimi and Vatra groups emerged as the main pillars of a new Albania. Noli, who was usually abroad, had not yet become a serious political figure inside Albania, although he had gained a reputation as an able and skilled diplomat, having served Albania well at the League. Albania's conservatives remained the ruling class and were determined to maintain the traditional system of landownership, which meant that Albania was the only country in Europe that was still primarily feudal. Outside these rigid parameters were a number of other groups vying for influence. These included careerists, the marginalized Catholic and Orthodox fringes, Kosovar irredentists, and those merely motivated by a desire to assert greater influence in Tirana.

Internal instability was very much exacerbated by external problems, which is why close attention has been paid in this chapter to Albania's unfavourable external predicament. In order to make a serious attempt at state building, Albania desperately needed a financial benefactor who could provide support. But financial assistance would not be forthcoming until Albania had established internal stability and border issues had been solved. Noli's international experience, whereby he had secured membership in the League and resolved a good deal of outstanding territorial issues, led him to overestimate the foreign commitment to Albania's development. This would prove to be a costly mistake. A benefactor was also required to preserve Albania's fragile independence. Neither Greece nor Yugoslavia was well disposed to the re-creation of an independent Albania, and both used whatever means possible to foment disorder in order to prove to the world that Albanians were not capable of self-government. Despite international agreement on the majority of Albania's frontiers, both states still pushed for changes. The question of Kosovo was also crucial and destined to become of great significance in the months leading up to Noli's seizure of power. Since Kosovo represented a major source of potential instability for Belgrade, a government in Tirana that could be counted on to ignore the Kosovo question was required. Both Greece and Yugoslavia had an interest in promoting chaos, which would call into question Albania's right to independence and thus reopen the question of frontiers. Albania's neighbours sought, at the least, to keep Albania weak enough that it could not make serious claims to border revisions in its favour or pursue the issue of minority rights with vigour.

2
Creating a Revolutionary Situation

Between April 1921 and June 1924, Albania's internal political climate changed substantially, and the conflicts that had been taking shape in the immediate aftermath of the Lushnjë Congress became more intense. Increasing power drifted to Zogu, who came to be respected by the outside world as possibly the only Albanian politician who could maintain internal stability. As Zogu's power increased, Noli's prestige diminished, and as early as March 1922 Noli appeared to be a spent political force. However, Zogu's increasing control over Albanian political life did not go unchallenged as the number of his enemies within Albania continued to increase. As events unfolded prior to June 1924, Noli reappeared as a formidable political force, while Zogu faced the most serious obstacles to date in his struggle to control Albania.

Major events inside Albania caused this fundamental realignment of Zogu's and Noli's political fortunes. Elections for a constituent assembly, finally held in the fall/winter of 1923, angered many who saw them as yet another step toward a dictatorship by Zogu. Moslem landowners retained the upper hand in the corridors of power, a situation which alienated reformers like Noli, Vatra, and Bashkimi. The progressive-minded Catholic and Orthodox fringes remained marginalized. Financial instability continued unabated as Albania still vainly sought a loan and foreign investment. Kosovar irredentists remained opposed to Zogu because he ignored their cause altogether. It would take the combined effect of these factors, along with a set of well-timed murders, to create the necessary conditions for Zogu's temporary eclipse and Noli's triumph in June 1924. If Zogu had obtained his influence by opportunism, realpolitik, vengeance, and sheer hard work, as will become clear later on, Noli's success was ultimately more superficial.

The parliament, which convened in April 1921, remained outside the political battle that emerged. After all, a parliament was intended to come after a constituent assembly, not before. Legislative achievements were meagre, no substantive investment was attracted, and no loans were offered, as parliament remained hopelessly stalled by conflict between the Popular and Progressive Parties. Upon his return from Geneva in 1921, Noli took his seat in the parliament as Vatra's representative. Although the parliament was a mere facade, Noli distinguished himself there as a skilled debater:

> He was in a position to lecture on democracy, availing himself of a cultural background matched by that of very few colleagues. He could adorn his speeches with quotations from great authors, or spice them with anecdotes that sent his colleagues into roaring laughter.[1]

However, the parliament meant little as the main struggle was at the cabinet level, with competing interests fighting to gain control over the key positions and the luxuries that political office would bestow.

While cabinets changed regularly throughout 1921, the primary development thereafter was Zogu's increasing influence, which engendered a level of stability at the cabinet level in 1922. Zogu, who had been named interior minister in the first Lushnjë government of Sulejman Bey Delvina, was temporarily in the political wilderness following the formation of a new cabinet in November 1920.[2] His main achievement subsequently had been quelling the strife in Mirdita during the fall of 1921. After a period of intense political instability throughout the fall and winter of 1921, owing partly to the crisis in Mirdita and an attempt by Kosovo Committee leader Hasan Prishtina to take control of the cabinet, in December four cabinets were formed in the span of eighteen days.[3] After the political chaos ended, Zogu returned to the foreground again as interior minister in Xhafer Ypi's cabinet of December 24. Fan Noli, owing to his success at the League, his skill as a diplomat, and good contacts abroad was named foreign minister.

As interior minister, Zogu, at least in the opinion of many outside observers, brought internal stability, the only cost being an increase in authoritarianism. This was a price most of the Great Powers were willing to pay in a country where expectations were incredibly low – democracy was a nice idea, but the outside powers were always willing to sacrifice pluralism for stability. Indeed, between the end of 1921 and Zogu's eventual resignation in March 1924, Albania had only two cabinets and one set of relatively free and fair elections for a constituent assembly in the autumn of 1923. However, at the same time, events between 1922 and early 1924 served to bring together hitherto diverse interests in a concerted attempt to rid the country of Zogu's influence. It was neither a single issue nor a particular event that united Zogu's divided opponents but the cumulative effect of nearly two years of his rule, which had highlighted the vast problems still to be solved.

While a political battle between progressive and conservative forces had become part of the picture following the Lushnjë Congress, progressives were not Zogu's major threat. Fan Noli had yet to emerge as the country's leading progressive spokesman, and, until March 1922, he appeared willing to tolerate Zogu's influence. Kosovar irredentists, however, were not as patient, and it was Zogu's conflict with them that provoked the final break between Zogu and Noli. Owing to his continued lack of zeal on the Kosovo question and the widely held assumption that he had struck some kind of bargain with the Serbs, Zogu's relations with the Kosovo Committee were strained. Zogu recognized that a normalization of relations with Belgrade was in the interests of stability and viewed the Kosovo Committee as the major obstacle to that end. Zogu reflected the dominant trend in twentieth-century attitudes of Albania toward Kosovo, which placed emphasis on occasional public denouncements of Serb rule there but little else. Zogu never considered Kosovo a serious issue.

As interior minister, Zogu had undertaken a much-needed program of disarmament in order to establish a semblance of political stability in the country; as long as armed groups could form and march on Tirana, Zogu's position was not secure. While disarmament was a useful and necessary agenda, Zogu's program was selective, leaving his own supporters in Mati armed while moving against traditional enemies in and around Shkodër and among members of the Kosovo Committee. Zogu's detractors alleged that he undertook the move against his enemies in the Kosovo Committee with the aid of Yugoslav/Serb agents eager to see the end of support for the Kosovo cause from Albanian soil. Zogu's activity provoked an armed uprising by some northern tribes led by Bajram Curri and Elez Jusufi.[4] By March 1922 a rebel contingent led by Curri, Zia Dibra, and Jusufi sat just outside Tirana demanding Zogu's resignation.

Faced with rebellion, Noli, then in Rome, submitted his resignation as foreign minister, citing Zogu's dictatorial tendencies, the reactionary policies of the government, and the failure to move toward a constituent assembly.[5] While the entire cabinet and most of the deputies fled to the central town of Elbasan, Zogu remained and tried to defend Tirana on his own. His cause would have almost certainly been lost had it not been for the crucial intervention of British representative Harry Eyres, who convinced the rebels to withdraw.[6] Had he wanted, Zogu could have secured the premiership, but instead he decided to resurrect the previous cabinet and maintain himself as interior minister. Noli returned to Albania from Rome with the intention of removing himself from politics; he resigned his membership in the Popular Party and dedicated himself to questions related to the formation of an autocephalous Albanian Orthodox Church. Noli's effort culminated in the Berat Congress of 1922 and the founding of the Albanian Autocephalous Orthodox Church.[7] For the next eighteen months, Noli was in the political wilderness, while Zogu's fortunes were on the rise.

Zogu continued to use his position in the Interior Ministry to consolidate his power, initiating an aggressive agenda to root out potential enemies. Subsequently, a flood of anti-Zogists fled abroad or into exile in the mountains of the northeast.[8] As the wave of arrests went much deeper than merely the arrest of those responsible, the campaign against participants in the March 1922 rebellion backfired and served to lend credence to the notion that Zogu's aspirations were dictatorial. Nevertheless, Zogu faced no unified opposition, and in December 1922 he supplemented his post as interior minister with the premiership.[9] Zogu, at the age of twenty-six, had thus become the country's most powerful politician. He managed to maintain his hold on the premiership for over one year (December 1922 to March 1924) – a considerable feat given the legacy of political instability he inherited. His tenure, however, was characterized by an increasingly intense battle with the main centres of resistance to his rule. If hitherto Zogu's primary challenge came from disgruntled Kosovars,[10] then his tenure as premier witnessed the gradual unification of a diverse number of groups opposed to his vision for Albania.[11] Despite his declaration that he intended to establish a 'fully civilized Western state,' his actions, which included plans to marry the daughter of Shefket Vërlaci, undermined his claims.[12] Vërlaci was one of the country's largest landowners and leader of the pro-bey Progressive Party.

It was only in the summer of 1923 that Zogu's opponents received their first legal chance to challenge his position, when elections were finally called for the long-awaited constituent assembly. Postponed repeatedly, the elections were designed ostensibly to decide the fundamental questions of the state's structure. The first round of voting was to take place in September, and the second round in December. The constituent assembly would both function as a parliament and draft a new constitution to replace the Lushnjë statutes. The type of government, republic or monarchy, was a central question. After fulfilling this agenda, the assembly was expected to resign before new elections were held for a regular parliament.

Because of growing discontent in the south, rivalry with Zogu, and pressure from Faik Konica, Noli returned from self-imposed exile to challenge Zogu and, in September 1923, create the Korçë-based Liberal Party. Only then did Noli finally emerge as the key organizer of the southern progressive forces lined up against Zogu. The political structure established at the time of the 1921 elections, represented by the Popular and Progressive Parties, diversified, and new forces emerged. Reform-minded southerners and the Catholic community in the Shkodër region took to the field with new organizations, hoping to undercut the influence of the remnants of the Popular Party and the Progressives. Zogu, who like Noli had been a member of the Popular Party, chose not to ally himself with reform-minded politicians like Noli and created a type of government party. As was so often the case in the past, Zogu championed himself as the guarantor of order and stability.

The country's progressive challengers, drawn from Bashkimi, supporters of Vatra in the United States and elsewhere, and former Popular Party members, presented a wide array of programs. Their unity was only due to their hostility to Zogu's continued dominance. These groups eventually campaigned together as the Opposition Party, which included Noli's Liberals, the Gjirokastër-based Democrats, Ora e Maleve from Shkodër, and the Vlorë-based National Democrats. Bashkimi, ostensibly not a political party, did not put forth candidates, although its leader, Avni Rustemi, was a candidate in the prefecture of Kosovo (Kukes). While communist historiography has blamed the lack of unity on the poor development of the Albanian bourgeoisie;[13] the reality was more complicated. Regionalism was perhaps the biggest problem, as the opposition was a collection of groups lacking support beyond their religious or regional constituencies.[14]

With profound doubts about the system of indirect voting, the progressives gathered around Noli sought to impose a new electoral law to replace the December 1920 regulations, which stipulated that voting was to be conducted in two rounds.[15] Noli's supporters argued a new electoral law would ensure an end to fraud and halt what they identified as

Zogu's march toward dictatorship. The first pre-electoral battle revolved around the type of voting: direct or indirect. The opposition was united in the belief that direct voting was more democratic and would ensure not only a more representative assembly, but also their victory by ending corruption in the second round. Given a free and direct vote, progressives argued, the peasant masses would surely dismiss their oppressors. The opposition also called for a broadening of the franchise to include women, and the neutralization of the army and gendarmerie. Noli, arguing that Albania needed to make a fresh start, also pushed hard for a political amnesty for those who had been charged with political offences as a result of the March 1922 rebellion. However, no concessions were made: parliament never considered the amnesty, and the battle for a new electoral law was lost in a parliamentary vote. With the opposition already disgruntled and feeling that the government possessed the upper hand, Albania entered a fierce electoral contest in the fall of 1923, which not only underlined the deep polarization in the country but also gave every indication that it was on the verge of revolution.[16] While questions of the type of government Albania was to have and the location of the capital city were in dispute, the main cleavage was between reformers and conservatives. In the middle sat a mass of undecided politicians, prepared to swing either way depending on the election's outcome or waiting for financial or other incentives from the main contenders.[17]

Deep-seated differences among progressives were the major obstacle to unseating Zogu. Moreover, these groups had only appeared with the call for elections to the constituent assembly, and none had more than superficial influence. Noli's Liberals called for the 'retention of the four-man regency council, universal voting rights in secret, full independence of the judiciary, a constitution that guaranteed fundamental freedoms of speech, press and property, constitutional guarantees against dictatorship, occidental [Western] ... administration and a simplification of the government bureaucracy.'[18] As to the eventual type of government, the Liberals felt that this should be decided by the Albanian people in a referendum. The Democrats possessed a similar agenda, calling for vigorous agrarian reform and a fight against monarchist ideas. This group included some of the country's leading progressives, among them Bashkimi leader Avni Rustemi, Konstandin Boshnjaku, and Stavro Vinjau.

The organization Ora e Maleve remained monarchist in orientation, and some members still felt bound to Prince Wied. Since Ora e Maleve was a Catholic organization, its position was essentially regional

and clerical in outlook. Its members argued that Shkodër was suffering under Zogu's rule and that his government was consistently anti-
Catholic.[19] A major part of this group's agenda was the naming of
Shkodër as the capital since Tirana was perceived as only an interim
choice, and Luigi Gurakuqi became the key defender of that position. For historical, cultural, and economic reasons, Gurakuqi argued,
Shkodër would have been a far more suitable location than the other
main contenders. Through intense coverage in the Shkodër press, the
argument took shape, while southern newspapers tried to counter the
momentum to move the capital northward. Claiming that with the long-
awaited arrival of a constituent assembly the selection of a capital was of
vital importance, Gurakuqi and others argued that, given the low levels
of urban development in other towns, Shkodër was the natural choice.
Pointing to historical reasons, this group added that Shkodër was the
old capital of the Kingdom of Illyria and remained the biggest and most
important city in contemporary Albania.[20] From an economic point of
view, Shkodrans emphasized that the city was located on a lake, not far
from the sea, and that Shkodër already possessed an established position
in the Balkan economy.[21] Challenging this argument, the Vlorë-based
Politika newspaper, which favoured Vlorë as the new capital, argued that
Shkodër was a poor choice because it was too close to the border with
a 'Slav aggressor state' and as such would be in almost constant danger.
The anti-Zogist forces were thus torn by regionalism.

Zogu avoided commenting on this issue, remained above the regional
controversies, and called for discipline, good government, and slow but
steady progress. However, he could not resist taking advantage of the
regional cleavages and the hostility to Noli that predominated among
the Greek minority. Hoping to undercut Noli's profound influence in
the south, Zogu's government party was 'lending its support' to candidates who spoke Greek and who were 'affiliated with the Greek speaking
population.'[22] The Greek minister in Durrës was also using his influence
to secure votes for Zogu.[23] Zogu's official statements portrayed the opposition, not incorrectly, as divided, declaring that Albania's first need was
discipline and stability.[24] Zogu's supporters also argued that Noli and
his supporters had little more to offer than criticism at a time when the
people wanted action. Noli's experience in the United States was also
used against him by the government, which declared that although Noli
knew America well, he had not studied the realities of Albania. As to its
own program, the government called for much of the same as the opposition, including a republican and parliamentary form of government,

and a centralized state administration. However, it offered no comment on the question of land reform.

Zogu could count on the support of northeastern Albania and the central plains. In the former, his tribal connections were strong, and in the latter, the bastion of Albanian landlordism, Zogu's platform of stability over reform found a receptive audience. Noli based almost his entire campaign on winning over the discontented southerners in the districts of Korçë and Gjirokastër. In an extensive speaking campaign, Noli delivered one invective after another against the government. Borrowing extensively from Western notions of democracy, he called repeatedly for a 'government of the people, from the people, for the people'[25] and attacked Zogu's claim that he was a 'westernizer,' declaring instead that his heart was 'oriental.'[26] In August 1923, while campaigning in Gjirokastër, Noli told the crowd his party wanted to elevate the Albanian people, 'not enslave them.' 'We want,' he said,

> to respect people, freedom and the dignified traditions of the Albanian people. We want to give people freedom, not tyranny. We want to regulate state finances with savings and not destroy the state with bribes and taxes. We want to build and not break. We want to give the main importance to agriculture, health and education.[27]

Noli was also on the regional bandwagon promoting the interests of the south over the north, even declaring that the new constituent assembly should be moved to Vlorë.[28] His pleas for reform and democracy masked a deep-seated belief that if Albania was to modernize and develop along Western lines, it would have to have a government of southerners.

Zogu took Noli to be a very serious opponent. The Interior Ministry kept a close watch on Noli's activities in the south, while Zogu stressed that the activities of the opposition were undermining political stability and would thus prevent the arrival of much-needed foreign capital and loans. Reports from the south stressed that the population was still behind the government, but that Noli was making serious headway. Prefectural reports suggested that Noli's speeches there were greeted with indifference, even in Korçë, and that after his campaigning in Bilisht, crowds had shouted 'Long live the government and down with the traitors.'[29] However, the opposition media portrayed a different picture altogether. Instead of Noli being greeted by hostility and indifference, press reports suggested that his reception throughout the south was entirely positive, with Noli receiving enthusiastic audiences and being welcomed with shouts of 'Long live Fan Noli.'[30] Judging from the paranoia that seized both Zogu and the Interior Ministry, it seems that Noli had a tremendous impact on southerners. Zogu's directives to his prefects had an air of panic. Although he tried publicly to portray a situation that was under control, the reality was different. One prefect even went so far as to suggest that a new secret police be formed to monitor Noli's activities.[31]

Despite claims of electoral fraud by the opposition parties, the outcome of the election proved to be an accurate representation of Albania's political climate: neither group secured a majority.[32] After the second round of voting on December 27, in the 102-seat assembly, opposition candidates took 39 seats and Zogu could count on 44. These 44 supporters were not devout Zogists and needed convincing from Zogu. Using his connection with Progressive Party leader Shefket Vërlaci, Zogu gained the support of the conservative beys, who hoped that he would leave their privileges intact.[33] The remaining independents, led by K. Kota and E. Frashëri, who were primarily conservative beys, were persuaded to join forces with Zogu, giving him a majority in the assembly and allowing him to retain the post of prime minister. In any case, Zogu's cabinet was built on a shaky foundation.

The election results also revealed important regional cleavages, with opposition forces succeeding primarily in the country's southern and northern fringes. Noli's group secured 4 of 15 seats in the district of Korçë, 5 of 14 in the district of Berat, 5 of 6 in the district of Vlorë, and 7 of 16 in Gjirokastër district. The opposition also took all the seats in the districts of Shkodër and Kosovo.[34] In addition to doing well in Korçë, Berat, and Gjirokastër, Zogu's forces had nearly complete control over the districts of Dibra, Elbasan, and Durrës. Southern Orthodox Christians voted for Noli's group in the hope of getting the influence their advanced cultural and economic position warranted. Shkodrans voted out of the desire to secure their dominance in Albanian affairs, while the Moslem beys in central Albania, in league with the northern chieftains, largely prevailed by appealing to the traditional conservatism that permeated those regions. The election's regionalist outcome was in fact recognized by Albania's progressive forces, and the elimination of this factor was to become a battle-cry of Noli's supporters in the months that followed his seizure of power.[35]

The opposition forces were outraged at the results and argued that their good showing in the first round of voting should have given them a majority when the delegates selected the assembly. Indirect voting, so their argument went, had cheated them of victory. *Dielli* proclaimed that the outcome of the second round was 'because the government used force, terrorized the delegates and representatives and used religious propaganda.'[36] Albanian communist historiography has long maintained that, owing to indirect voting and the legacy of corruption in elections, the outcome was unrepresentative of the real situation. It suggests that Noli's opposition forces should have won the contest. According to this interpretation, the simple fact that the opposition did not win a single seat in areas like Berat, Durrës, and Elbasan, the bastion of Albanian landlords, which would have correspondingly possessed a mass of disgruntled peasants eager for land, is cited as the key evidence of electoral manipulation.[37] However, this charge makes one altogether dangerous assumption: that the mass of landless peasantry was eager for land reform and willing to go to the polls to break the chains of the Moslem landowners. As Noli was to learn later, the peasantry was not a group that embraced radical change, meaning that it was possible that they chose to stand by the status quo. Moreover, Moslem peasants, regardless of their desperate economic circumstances, could more easily identify with Moslem landlords than with Orthodox liberals. Noli claimed later that only in central Albania, where the influence of the landowning beys was most felt, was there any real demand for land reform. When he spoke about agrarian reform to the peasants, they were so terrorized by the beys, their uniform answer was: 'Please, do not create problems for us.'[38] Also, since so broad a number of groups ran under the banner of the opposition, voters were confused, and the lack of a unified program among the opposition undercut its influence. Lastly, the progressive agenda, embodied especially in Noli's party, appealed only to the relatively small middle class.

Nevertheless, in terms of financing, there seems to be a stronger case for suspecting electoral manipulation. Vatra was the key source of financing for Noli's party. In fact, throughout the fall of 1923, Konica worked tirelessly to raise funds for Noli. Zogu allegedly benefited from the support of outside powers, including Greece, Yugoslavia, and Italy.[39] These countries possessed good reasons to interfere: Greece hoped to obtain a more advantageous position on unresolved territorial issues, and disliked Noli's intensely activist position on church matters; Yugoslavia had come to appreciate Zogu's indifference on the Kosovo question, and was worried about a potential triumph of an opposition which included individuals more inclined to an aggressive stance on the issue; and Italy sought economic concessions and hoped to re-establish its influence in Albania.

Belgrade preferred Zogu over any other potential Albanian ruler because of his strained relations with Kosovar irredentists. Moreover, Yugoslavia had an important agent in Albania, Ceno Bey Kryeziu from Gjakovë, who was also Zogu's brother-in-law. Kryeziu's role as an active promoter of Serbian interests during the election is unclear, but in the aftermath of Zogu's removal from power in June 1924, he was vital in opening political doors for Zogu in Belgrade. Albanian opposition forces widely distrusted him, especially the Kosovar irredentists. In the long run, Zogu's continued association with Kryeziu undermined his position considerably.[40] Italy's position is even less transparent, owing to its wavering attitude in Albanian affairs. At the outset of the Albanian political battle, Italy was prepared to support the opposition forces, as the country's leading Italophiles were in that camp. However, Italy was willing to exploit the potential to gain on both sides and, according to the British minister in Albania, provided financial aid to Zogu. In his report, Eyres suggested that Zogu sold a worthless piece of land to Italian interests for some 300,000 lira and that the sale was a mere pretext for the transfer of money which was to be used in the electoral battle.[41]

Despite complaints from the opposition, the elections provided a result that was in keeping with the political reality. Moreover, even before the elections had taken place, Zogu's opponents had decided that the electoral system would give victory to status-quo forces. The opposition therefore rejected the results outright and decided that Zogu's removal from office required alternative measures. The newly elected assembly convened on 21 January 1924. It attempted to move on the important questions, hoping to reach a final decision on the form of government, decide on the location of a capital, and finally adjourn for elections to a new parliament. However, the opposition was not interested in moving on these issues. As a result, the assembly remained incapable of meeting the country's problems head-on.[42]

Noli and his allies first sought to encourage the government to recognize that the opposition had done well in the elections and that the new situation required a new cabinet. Noli even declared that if their demands for senior positions in a new cabinet were not met, they would 'quit Tirana and leave the situation in the hands of the army.'[43] Zogu retained the cabinet he formed in December 1922, and he chose repression as a means to undercut the opposition's influence. His main preoccupation continued to be the key opposition centres in Vlorë, Korçë, Krumë,[44] and Shkodër, and he sought continued vigilance from the country's prefects in observing the movements of his opponents. Zogu targeted especially the activities of the Vatra organization, banning the organization's newspaper and closing its office in Tirana, despite appeals from Konica.[45]

An attempt on 23 February 1924 on Zogu's life both intensified the crisis and created the opportunity to impose a conciliatory cabinet to forestall further polarization. While the attempted assassination has been interpreted as a political act undertaken by a member of Rustemi's Bashkimi organization, it was in fact little more than a blood-feud attack which all sides later exploited for their own benefit.[46] According to Zogu, his assailant, Beqir Walter, was a 'half-witted youth'[47] from Mati who undertook to shoot the prime minister as he entered parliament. The episode began as the assembly was trying to elect a speaker, with the opposition and government finding no cause for common ground. Noli's description of events is worth quoting in full:

> At 3 p.m., when Petro Poga, the temporary Speaker, called the meeting to order, several revolver shots were heard outside the hall. Two bullets whizzed passed Fan Noli's nose and hit the desk of the speaker ... A minute later Ahmed Zog [Zogu] entered the hall limping, with his left hand bleeding and a revolver in his right hand.[48]

Noli went on to note that Zogu was accompanied by a coterie of armed bodyguards, who confronted an armed opposition; Noli claimed that he was virtually the only unarmed person in the assembly hall.[49] Nevertheless, while the opposition later interpreted Walter's attempt on Zogu 'as the first shot of the revolution,' Noli considered it a blood-feud crime, noting that in accordance with custom, Walter told Zogu to 'remember me to my uncle.'[50] However, since Walter was a stutterer, it took him some time to get the pronouncement out, and, according to Noli, the 'short delay saved Zog.'[51]

Zogu took the matter in stride. Soaked in blood from three wounds, he entered the assembly and announced that 'such things happen often – we cannot tell when or where – and therefore let us take the matter calmly.'[52] Hoping to maintain order in the country, on that same day Zogu advised the country's prefectures that while he had been shot three times by a man from Mati, the constituent assembly was beginning its work and calm had returned.[53] Walter, in the meantime, had locked himself in a toilet, and despite coaxing from opposition deputy Ali Kelcyra, refused to surrender and 'commenced singing patriotic songs as he shot through the doors.'[54]

While Walter was later jailed, the assassination attempt was not without important implications. As it was later attributed to Albania's young radicals, it did little to enhance the image of the Bashkimi organization in foreign circles, for it lent the impression that it condoned political assassination as a means to promote change. Since the Bashkimi organization was a pillar of Noli's June seizure of power, he could not help but be associated with a group of individuals whom some powers, especially Great Britain, had denounced as dangerous radicals. More importantly, it temporarily removed Zogu from the forefront of the political arena. On February 25, citing the need to recover from the bullet wounds, Zogu submitted his resignation as prime minister and began working against his opponents from an unofficial position.

Zogu maintained some influence as he managed to put together a cabinet under the leadership of Shefket bey Vërlaci, his prospective father-in-law, and according to the U.S. minister in Tirana, U. Grant-Smith, 'one of the two richest men in the country.'[55] This was another lost opportunity to install a compromise cabinet that might have appeased the opposition. The opposition had hoped this would be the case and argued for the selection of Sami bey Vrioni as prime minister, as he had some influence with the beys and was well regarded by progressives. Regardless, the chance for compromise was lost as Zogu's coalition defeated a vote of confidence for Vrioni.[56] The new cabinet again represented only one of the country's interests: the landowning beys. Vërlaci assumed the posts of both prime minister and minister of interior. The new cabinet included another large landowner, Illias bey Vrioni, as foreign minister, Myfid bey Libohova as justice minister, Mustafa Aranita as war minister, and Koco Kota as minister of public works. With the exception of Kota, who was nominally an independent, all the other figures could be counted on to support Zogu's vision.

With Vërlaci in power, Albanian progressives considered his cabinet even more reprehensible than its predecessor. Some thirty members of the opposition, including Noli, Gurakuqi, Bahri Omari, and Ali Kelcyra, denounced the new cabinet as a tool of Zogu.[57] *Shqiptari i Amerikes* cynically declared that a 'bey from Elbasan forms a democratic government' and that the battle which was raging was not personal, as the government claimed, but a class war – 'democracy versus feudalism, liberalism versus conservatism, and nationalism versus reactionism.'[58] Disappointed with the formation of a government by one of the country's largest landowners, Vatra representative Faik Konica resigned his seat in the assembly in mid-March, stating that the elections were held under governmental threats and that the assembly did not represent the people.[59] The opposition paper *Ora e Maleve* proclaimed 'new government, old situation,'[60] but Luigi Gurakuqi, a member of the opposition (albeit more moderate when compared with the likes of either Rustemi or Noli), added that the country had 'a desperate need for calm, especially because the financial and economic situation was critical.'[61] Grant-Smith echoed Gurakuqi's assessment of the situation, citing the litany of problems already apparent, including the attempt on Zogu's life, the resignation of the government, the stripping of the treasury, and the decision that the constituent assembly was to function almost solely as a regular parliament and neglect the mandate for a new constitutional order. In Grant-Smith's opinion, it was a 'record which adds further proof, were any needed, of the small capacity of the Albanians for self-government.'[62]

If the installation of Vërlaci was a triumph for conservatives, his government did offer some compromises. He pledged to meet some of the opposition's demands, especially their calls for a general amnesty for political prisoners and those expelled from the country for their political activities. The Vërlaci government also tried to appease Vatra by lifting the ban on the distribution of *Dielli*. However, opposition forces continued to harp on the presence of Ceno Kryeziu in Tirana and remained adamant that this alleged tool of Belgrade's anti-Albanian machinations be expelled from Albania. The military, growing impatient with continued chaos and the fact that their salaries were months in arrears, made its position clear to Grant-Smith, who reported that a 'well-known officer' had informed him that 'he and his colleagues caused the political leaders to be warned that unless they arrived at a compromise and formed a [new] government within a reasonable time, the army would take charge and place a representative in each ministry.'[63]

Any hopes of substantive cooperation were unlikely as both sides hardened their positions and the internal situation went from bad to worse. By March 1924 the government had two determined opponents: progressive forces gathered around Noli and the Kosovar Committee. From March onwards, developments drew more and more support to opponents of the government. While arguments raged in Tirana over the formation of a new cabinet, the country's northern periphery confronted a severe famine that required League assistance to alleviate. On March 7 the government addressed an appeal to the League Council that stated 'in consequence of the ravages caused by the Great War, followed by two successive bad harvests, the mountainous regions of north and north-eastern Albania with a population of about 200,000, had been reduced to a state of famine.'[64] The League provided some assistance, sending an envoy, Eugene Pittard of France, to oversee the relief effort, and calling for donations from member countries.[65] The most severely affected regions were the prefectures of Dibra, Kosovo, and Shkodër. In a report of April 28, Pittard noted that the situation was disastrous and that there was a desperate need for more assistance.[66] Pittard added that while the situation had improved in the Dibra prefecture, in the Kosovo and Shkodër regions the inhabitants were 'consuming the seed which they had ready for their spring and summer sowings and [were] selling the last of their livestock in order to purchase grain.'[67]

While the famine intensified hostility to the Tirana government in areas where the opposition was already strong, the ongoing financial crisis was making matters worse. Throughout the late winter and early spring of 1924, the country was bankrupt since no foreign concessions had been granted and no loan given. This created havoc both inside and outside the country and served to help swing the army to the side of the opposition. The League's financial advisor to Albania had already made some rather severe austerity recommendations, particularly regarding the army and gendarmerie, which were by no means well received by these ministries, which were accustomed to receiving the lion's share of Albania's meagre resources.[68] The support of the army, which was also facing a severe fiscal crisis, was vital to the government's survival. Military leaders needed regular supplements to ensure loyalty to the government, and Tirana was simply incapable of either paying off commanders or keeping the army supplied at anything above bare subsistence. For Albania's legations abroad, the situation was especially tense as the country's representatives could barely afford to make ends meet. Memo after memo arrived from abroad describing the most ridiculous of situations. Tefik Mborja, Albania's charge d'affaires in Rome, wrote that he could not pay the rent on his apartment and that the situation was an affront to the dignity of Albania.[69] Albania's permanent secretary to the League, Benoit Blinishti, advised Tirana in early January that his financial situation was critical.[70] Aside from these essential expenses, the costs associated with the delimitation of borders and later challenges by the Yugoslavs on questions of territory stretched the state's resources to the limit.

However, while the government faced daunting challenges in terms of meeting the day-to-day demands of being a state, it was a string of murders that served to temporarily unify the government's opponents and give the go-ahead for a revolutionary seizure of power. According to both communist-era historians and Western specialists, Zogu hoped that by creating chaos he could move toward imposing a state of emergency that would allow him to use strong-arm tactics against the opposition and deal with them once and for all.[71] However, the chaos that dominated the month of April did not benefit Zogu, but rather Noli's faction. Two acts of murder in less than three weeks were used to discredit the government.

The first was the murder of two U.S. citizens, G.B. De Long, a forty-nine-year-old native of New York, and R.L. Coleman, a sixty-five-year-old California financier, who on April 6 had been ambushed near Kruje on their way to Shkodër and shot dead. The reaction from the U.S. press and government was severe, and the Albanian government was especially concerned about the implications of the murders. Foreigners traditionally enjoyed the protection of the *besa,* which was a pledge of honour exempting foreigners from harm, and as such the two Americans should have been untouchable. Besides this, the government could ill afford the adverse press, which portrayed Albania as a savage backwater rife with thieves and murderers. Such accusations of lawlessness played directly into the hands of Albania's neighbours, who had all along argued that the Albanians were not ready for self-government but instead preferred anarchy. News of the shootings spread fast, and before long the international media had picked up on the notion that either current or former members of the government had been involved. The government did its best to head off a barrage of criticism: the Albanian Foreign Ministry instructed the consulate in New York to present condolences to the American government; Albanians demonstrated in sympathy in front of the U.S. legation; the assembly observed five minutes of silence; and shops closed on April 8 as a show of respect. Finally, in notes to consulates abroad, the foreign minister stated that 'energetic measures' were underway to apprehend the assassins and that 'the indignation of the entire population [was] indescribable.'[72]

Just who was responsible for the crime remains unclear. At the outset, U.S. officials in Tirana seemed to think that the crime was political, 'and possibly foreign in its origin and was misdirected against Americans by the blundering of the tools [fools?] although it has been made vital political capital by internal factions.'[73] Some elements of Noli's faction tried to place the blame squarely on Zogu's shoulders. In the Albanian embassy in Rome, Tefik Mborja felt that Zogu had orchestrated the murders, 'primarily with the hope of convincing the public at large that without him in power, public safety ceased.'[74] Such accusations, however, reflected both the Albanian zest for conspiracy theories and a political agenda; it is doubtful that Zogu would have ordered the murder of foreigners. While one cannot implicate the opposition in the murders, its interests were best served by creating havoc within the country and distrust abroad by trying to attribute the murders to Zogu's orders.[75]

Although it is doubtful that Zogu was responsible, and there is not enough evidence to implicate the Yugoslavs, Greeks, or the opposition, the murders did have important implications for Albania. The opposition argued that it was further proof that the government could not maintain law and order and that, therefore, it was responsible for the deaths. In trying to blame Zogu, the opposition also hoped to increase its political capital, as owing to the traditional position of foreigners in Albania, even the suggestion that Zogu would violate accepted tribal custom undermined his credibility considerably. For the government, it was an opportunity to impose a state of emergency, which was not used to bring the murderers to justice, but instead to crack down on the opposition. Martial law was proclaimed in the Durrës prefecture at the instigation of the assembly, although seventeen deputies (including Noli and Gurakuqi) abstained for fear that the government 'might misuse the power placed at its disposal' and because they anticipated that 'innocent persons would be made to suffer.'[76] The murder had an important impact on the course of U.S.-Albanian relations, for it soured the U.S. attitude toward both Zogu and the Vërlaci government, and ensured that at the outset of Noli's tenure as prime minister he would enjoy American support.[77] While two Albanians, Veysel Hidri and Sefer Hajdar Bega, were arrested, the United States was extremely critical about the slowness of the investigation.[78]

Faced with an increasingly tense situation, Vërlaci's cabinet again undertook to meet some of the opposition demands. A major victory for stability came when on April 17 Shkodër leader and opposition member Luigi Gurakuqi entered the cabinet as finance minister. Gurakuqi joined the cabinet in the hope of heading off a crisis that he knew would throw the country into chaos, possibly inviting foreign intervention. He had other motives too: he continued to champion the cause of Shkodër as capital, while also maintaining his commitment to making Albania a monarchy and recalling Prince Wied to the throne. While both he and Noli shared hostility to Zogu and the continued dominance of the Moslem beys, Gurakuqi was prepared to make certain tactical compromises to preserve order in the country, and his presence in the Vërlaci cabinet gave it considerable legitimacy, especially among the reform-hungry

Catholic population around Shkodër. Unlike Noli, whose imp the long run got the better of him, Gurakuqi shared with Zo understanding of Albania's predicament and was more willing to follow a slower path toward his vision of a new Albania.

However, Gurakuqi's entry into the government did not assuage the demands of Noli's faction. Since the opposition was adamant that a political amnesty be granted for those who had participated in the March 1922 and January 1923 rebellions, a heated battle for the legislation took place in the assembly. The government refused, as an amnesty would ensure the return to Tirana of the government's most dangerous opponents, such as Curri, Prishtina, and Dibra. Claiming obstructionist tactics, on April 17 Noli's faction, which included Sulejman Delvina, Bahri Omari, and Sami Vrioni, withdrew from the assembly, thus leaving it without a quorum, and headed for more friendly territory in Vlorë. Politically, the country was at a virtual standstill.

With Noli and his entourage holding out in Vlorë and the government rejecting compromise, the disparate centres of resistance finally found a pretext for unity: the shooting on April 20 of Bashkimi leader Avni Rustemi.[79] The murderer, Isuf Reci, who was a supporter of Esad Pasha, was avenging Rustemi's 1920 assassination of Esad Pasha in Paris.[80] However, the opposition again placed the blame squarely on Zogu's shoulders.[81] Three factors could be used to implicate Zogu in the murder: Esad Pasha was his uncle, and he sought blood vengeance; Rustemi's organization had been wrongly implicated in the February assassination attempt; lastly, Rustemi was a dangerous radical who enjoyed considerable nationwide support from progressive groups and especially among the youth. His political program, embodied in Bashkimi, was directed solely against the country's ruling class. Zogu denied any part in the murder and instead noted that the assassination was orchestrated by the revolutionaries.[82]

While some school children in Albania even today will tell you that Zogu had Rustemi killed, it is unlikely that he played any part in the murder. While Zogu was related to Esad Pasha, he certainly did not mourn his uncle's passing since he had been the major obstacle to Zogu's own success. As for the other two possibilities, Zogu really did not need Rustemi out of the way. While it is true that Zogu was concerned about Rustemi and that the Interior Ministry kept a close eye on Rustemi's every move throughout early 1924, Zogu was too shrewd to move against such a widely respected national patriot when his hold on power was so fragile or to provoke the unification of his hitherto fragmented opponents.

Secondly, Rustemi was due to leave shortly for the United States on a three-month leave of absence to work with the Albanian-American community in hopes of finding economic support for the Bashkimi organization. The leave had been approved unanimously by the assembly, and he had already set about obtaining a visa for the United States.

Regardless of who was responsible, Rustemi's murder radically transformed the situation. The opposition was steadfast in its attempt to attribute the murder to Zogu, even though they jumped to that conclusion for purely political reasons. Noli later noted in his autobiography that Rustemi's murder was 'the cause for the beginning of the revolution against Ahmed Zogu,'[83] and this assessment has been widely accepted by communist and post-communist historians.[84] Grant-Smith also noted that the 'occasion of the death of Avni Rustem [*sic*] was seized upon by the members of the opposition to launch a revolution which they appear to have been plotting for some time.'[85] Since it was assumed that Zogu was responsible, either directly or indirectly, it was a signal to the opposition that Zogu was planning to physically eliminate his opponents. It is also true that the highly impatient forces around Noli were looking for a pretext to move against the government and force either new elections or revolutionary change. The withdrawal from the assembly of Noli's group alone was not enough to force change. The murder of Rustemi was the kind of justification that the anti-government forces were looking for, and they exploited it to the fullest.

Country-wide reaction to Rustemi's death was palpable. The opposition press was quick to denounce Zogu's alleged complicity in the assassination. *Drita* declared that Zogu was definitely responsible since he sought blood,[86] and even the Italian legation in Durrës suspected the hand of Zogu in the crime.[87] Halim Xhelo, an active member of both Atdheu and Bashkimi, declared that Zogu should be condemned as a murderer and, 'as a traitor, should be hanged.'[88] Some one hundred telegrams of condolence and protest poured in from throughout the country; the people of Rustemi's hometown declared that the assassination of Avni Rustemi was 'a blow against Albanian idealism';[89] and *Politika* compared the young patriot to the nineteenth-century poet and national awakener Naim Frashëri and to Albania's founder, Ismail Qemal.[90]

The opposition forces, emboldened by the growth of anti-government sentiment resulting from Rustemi's murder, moved to confront Vërlaci's government head-on. After a brief ceremony in Tirana, where Ali Kelcyra delivered a moving eulogy, Rustemi's body was transported to the opposition stronghold of Vlorë for a massive funeral and rally attended by some five to ten thousand people. On April 28, Noli denounced the government in the harshest terms, stating that 'anti-nationals' were in power, that the people could expect nothing from the government or assembly, and that the government felt no compunction about ambushing and murdering patriots like Rustemi.[91] On May 1, following days of speeches and other manifestations of anti-government sentiment, the main funeral took place. The Vlorë assemblists added that they could not return to Tirana because of the dangerous situation there. Some twenty-six members of the assembly were present, including Ali Kelcyra, Sulejman Delvina, Noli, and Gurakuqi, as well as members of the Bashkimi organization and some five thousand peasants.[92] Speech after speech denounced the continued influence of Zogu and his complicity in Rustemi's murder.

Noli declared that the 'opposition had unmasked the crimes of the current government, that the current regime was intent on enslaving the Albanian people under a feudal dictatorship,' and that the victory of liberalism would 'signify great progress on the road of civilization and the economic development of the Albanian people.'[93] The opposition media, especially *Politika*, declared that Zogu was acting against the interests of the nation, that he was a tool of the Serbs, and that as the country's next Esad Pasha, he was determined to make Albania a Serb province.[94] Ali Kelcyra, in a highly charged speech, stated that the country was 'in a most dangerous time today because Ahmed Zogolli [Zogu] sits in Tirana like a wild monster, working against the nation in cooperation with foreign agents. He is a tool of Serbia, and is trying to dismember the nation and make it into a Serbian province.'[95] In the aftermath of the funeral, Noli and his supporters resolved to overthrow the government by force, if necessary.[96]

The now Vlorë-based opposition made a key demand upon the country's Regency Council and appeared willing to return to Tirana if it was met. Since the funeral had ended with a public declaration by the opposition of Zogu's responsibility for Rustemi's murder, it demanded that action be taken against him. Furthermore, in the event of the government being unable to fulfil this fundamental obligation, it should resign since its actions had proven that it was incapable of protecting the lives of citizens and guests. The second part of the ultimatum demonstrates how much importance the opposition attached to ending Belgrade's alleged interference. It called for the removal of Ceno Bey Kryeziu, who, according to the opposition, had come from Yugoslavia to work for the 'destruction of the Albanian state.'[97] The ultimatum went on to state that the government's continued tolerance of Ceno Bey Kryeziu and 'his band of mercenaries constituted an unconstitutional and anti-national act according to clauses of the [Lushnjë] statute that speak of the inviolability of Albanian territory and the non-infringement of that territory from armed foreign forces. The continued infringement of the statute has authorized and obliged the people to apply Article 127 of the Statute for the defence and rescue of the Fatherland.'[98]

The demand for Kryeziu's removal was a reflection of the need to win over the Kosovar irredentists. It is also interesting to note that while communist historiography interpreted Noli's seizure of power as a revolution against 'feudalism,' the ultimatum stated nothing about the social injustices then so prevalent in Albanian society. This in itself indicates that from the very beginning of the all-out confrontation with the government the opposition did not possess a defined agenda to eradicate the feudal landlords. Instead, by linking Zogu and the government to assassination and foreign interference, it could count on a broader base of support, since the majority of the assembly members who gathered in Vlorë were not altogether committed to a social revolution. Rather, they simply wanted the removal of Ahmed Zogu and his minions. Only progressive elements like Noli and the Bashkimi organization were thinking along the lines of a social revolution.

The government undertook what it called an 'aggressive investigation' to find Rustemi's murderer. The assembly observed five minutes of silence in his honour, and then issued a lengthy counter-proclamation denouncing the activities of the opposition faction. It also declared that Ceno Bey Kryeziu was little more than a Kosovar living in Albania, and that continued chaos would ensure the dissolution of the country by inviting foreign intervention, either from Italy, which under the terms of the Conference of Ambassadors was the guarantor of Albanian independence, or neighbouring states eager to expand. At the same time, Vërlaci's government initiated a wide-scale crackdown on opposition media that were trying to exploit Rustemi's death. As always, of particular concern were *Politika, Shqiptari i Amerikes,* and *Ora e Maleve* as the Ministry of the Interior ordered the Justice Ministry to take whatever action was necessary to undermine the impact of these papers. The government also advised the Interior Ministry to keep close tabs on people suspected of being anti-government or 'elements that trouble the people and disturb the peace of the country.' Of particular concern were the unemployed.[99]

The atmosphere following the rally in Vlorë was tense, and an Italian diplomat reported that 'the internal situation was gloomy and precarious.'[100] The U.S. legation reported that only the future would tell if compromise between the factions was possible.[101] The situation continued to worsen throughout the month of May, with a steady stream of ultimatums finding their way to Tirana as more and more regions of the country began supporting the opposition position. The Vlorë prefect reported to the Interior Ministry that he was deeply concerned regarding developments and the growing strength of the opposition, as prior to Rustemi's murder the opposition had not been unified.[102]

A major setback for the government came on May 13 when Gurakuqi and two other ministers resigned from the cabinet, leaving a purely Moslem cabinet comprised of members of the traditional ruling class.[103] Gurakuqi later returned to Shkodër to rally Shkodrans against the Tirana government. He called for the assembly to move there, and it is apparent that in the days prior to his departure, the assembly had engaged in a heated battle over the location of the capital.[104] Gurakuqi's departure from the Vërlaci cabinet was a major victory for the opposition since a patriot of this stature, and one noted for his patience, was giving up all hope of change in Tirana under the current government. This was a good indication of the depth of the crisis. Gurakuqi's agenda had remained unfulfilled; he had pinned his hopes on the opposition, not out of a commitment to radical social change, but instead to give Catholics and Shkodrans a position in Albania that he felt their culture, history, and economic importance warranted, and to put himself to work on the crippling financial crisis. Equally important, the Catholic minority had long considered Zogu's government an enemy of Catholicism.[105]

If the opposition was to seriously challenge the government, it required military support. While Gurakuqi was rallying the north and Noli was keeping the pressure on the government from Vlorë, the all-important and in the long run decisively important army started to join the opposition. The concerns of the military were threefold: firstly, it felt that without an end to the chaos the situation would invite foreign intervention from either Italy, Greece, or Serbia; secondly, the notion that Zogu was a tool of Belgrade had not fallen on deaf ears, especially in northern Albania, where hostility to the Serbs was highest; and thirdly, and possibly the most important factor, was the pathetic state of the army, for its members increasingly believed that by joining the opposition their position could be better secured under a new government. In addition, as noted by Grant-Smith, the army could not be counted on indefinitely to defend the government. The younger officers might 'become persuaded that by throwing in their lot with one side or the other the dead weight of the undue number of senior officers might be got rid of and promotion proportionately accelerated.'[106] Unsure of the dependability of the Tirana army garrison, the government undertook to distribute arms to whomever was willing to defend the government, and thus destroyed the gains of two years of disarmament programs.[107] Lastly, there had been some speculation that Zogu was prepared to follow the advice of League financial advisor Hunger to disband the army and create a reorganized gendarmerie under his direct control.[108] Thus, simple self-interest, and not any concern for the plight of the Albanian peasant, brought important divisions of the army to the side of the opposition.

Throughout mid to late May, the opposition gradually gained momentum from what had become three centres of resistance: Shkodër, Krumë, and Vlorë. On May 16, the commander of the army's Shkodër regiment and a close colleague of Gurakuqi's, Rexhep Shala, denounced Zogu and demanded his removal from the country. On the same day, Noli and the Vlorë-based opposition called for armed insurrection. As Noli remarked in his autobiography, he pondered the choices before him:

> I wonder, what would Napoleon do in this case? Of course, he would join with the people against the feudal landowners … And Skanderbeg, what would he do in this case? Of course, he would also join the people in the struggle against their tyrants. And Jesus, what would he do? Naturally, he would not fight. He was not a general. Nevertheless, for certain he would take the side of the poor, as he had always done.[109]

Not surprisingly, Noli chose to fight, and he was fortunate enough to have allies who had considerable experience battling Zogu. Bajram Curri, based in Krumë, was always ready for any excuse to engage Zogu in conflict, and the southern opposition found military support from Kasem Qafëzezi, a vice-colonel in the Permet garrison, and Shefket Korçë,[110] a military commander in the Berat area. When the Tirana military garrison refused to move on Shkodër for fear of precipitating a civil war,[111] Myfid Libohova, a member of Vërlaci's cabinet and a staunch ally of Zogu, went to Shkodër to try to convince that part of the opposition to return to Tirana. The government understood that the weakest link in the opposition was to be found in Shkodër and hoped to appeal to

Gurakuqi's sense of moderation in hopes of preventing an insurrection. Libohova, who had travelled there with the British minister Harry Eyres, met with no success.

A general call for revolution from Vlorë, where Noli was directing an administrative commission to oversee events, went out on May 23, and the opposition, allegedly with some 12,000, mostly peasant soldiers and a battalion of 400 from Bashkimi, began the long march to Tirana. On May 25 the fight began when Bajram Curri's forces took Krumë and then marched on Zogu's stronghold in Dibra and Mati in the northeast. The forces of Shala in Shkodër (which fell to rebels on May 31) and Qafëzezi joined the fight in a pincer-like movement on the capital. Vërlaci's cabinet resigned at the end of May, and a somewhat less confrontational one, with Illias Vrioni as both prime minister and foreign minister, replaced it. While there was an attempt to entice both the Vlorë and Shkodër opposition back to Tirana, the government rejected an opposition demand that Zogu quit Albania and that they be allowed to place their members in the War, Finance, and Interior ministries.[112] The new cabinet, however, came too late, and despite some hasty attempts to pass legislation in hopes of enticing the opposition back to Tirana, the opposition remained determined to push on.[113] By June 2, with limited fighting, the central towns of Berat, Fier, and Permet had fallen, and the rebels pushed toward Durrës and Tirana.

The government, despite all the warning signs, was totally unprepared to fight the insurrection, further testimony to Zogu's lack of influence. Throughout May, note after note had arrived at the War and Interior ministries advising them of the disastrous and pathetic condition of the Albanian armed forces. The Berat prefect advised the Interior Ministry on May 19 that the weapons depot had nearly 4,000 guns, of which over 2,000 were not working.[114] Surrounded by outdated and broken weapons, the underpaid and underfed troops were, not surprisingly, swayed by opposition propaganda. Zogu, who tried to repeat his March 1922 defence of Tirana, took to the field with only marginal support from his own Mati tribesmen and mercenary elements. Communist sources claim he could only count on 4,000 men, while the opposition had almost three times that number. When general mobilization was declared on June 1st, the majority of the armed forces had already changed sides, and Zogu could do little other than fight his way out of the country and seek exile in Yugoslavia. As had been so often the case in the past, Zogu was the most committed fighter for his cause.[115] The Vrioni government was doomed from the start, owing to a legacy of financial collapse and general ineptitude. Even three of the four Regency Council members fled, leaving only the Orthodox member, Sotir Peci.[116]

The months that preceded and followed the 1923 elections to the constituent assembly were indeed chaotic. They not only revealed the extreme difficulties of governing the state, but also made clear that much remained to be done in terms of eliminating the disintegrative trends in the country. In this period, Zogu saw his own power diminish, while Noli's stature grew to the point where it temporarily eclipsed that of Zogu. By the time of his resignation in February 1924, Zogu had, with only a brief lapse, held onto one form of power or another since the Lushnjë Congress, and he had won some important allies outside Albania because of his apparent ability to maintain internal stability. At the same time, he had earned himself many enemies, primarily in the country's northern and southern fringes. The country's fledgling progressive forces wanted radical change in Albanian society, while Catholic and Orthodox elements looked upon Zogu's dominance as a legacy of Ottoman rule and sought to improve their own situation. The army suffered immensely as a result of the country's financial crisis, leaving it wide open to penetration by the opposition. The famine in the north had not won the government any friends either, and more people than ever looked at the Tirana government as the root of all their problems. Lastly, the notion that Zogu was possibly working in conjunction with the Yugoslavs, if not to make the country a Serb province then at least to undercut the influence of Kosovar irredentists, was widely held by many in the opposition.

Elections, which were intended to usher in a period of state building, only worsened the situation since the country's main political groups were hopelessly divided. The murders of Coleman, De Long, and Rustemi made cooperation even more unlikely. Rustemi's murder, in particular, acted as a catalyst for a seizure of power and temporarily united the opposition in their determination to overthrow Zogu. Unity, however, was superficial, but the opposition was at least capable of capitalizing on the nationwide revulsion that accompanied the murder. The constituent assembly accomplished virtually nothing, a fact which strengthened the opposition. The key question – what type of state would Albania become? – remained a dead letter. The government in Tirana became increasingly cut off from the main economic, social, and political developments in the country. While the opposition placed the blame for this altogether pathetic state of affairs squarely on Zogu's shoulders, he in fact had little to do with it. By far the shrewdest politician in Albania, his resignation in February was for reasons other than to simply recuperate from his wounds. Possibly owing to the country's financial crisis and the growing strength of the opposition, he opted out of power to avoid being associated with an increasingly intractable situation, hoping to step in at the last moment to champion himself as the country's saviour. However, his plan backfired, and in a rare fit of incompetence, Zogu allowed his opponents to get the better of him.

Fan Noli's career changed fundamentally. After resigning from politics in March 1922, he turned to his preferred vocation: the Albanian Orthodox Church. Events thrust him to centre stage, although he was ill prepared for his new responsibilities. Armed with a belief that he could alter the main pillars of Albanian society, Noli faced daunting challenges. The very same problems that had contributed to political instability in the years after the Lushnjë Congress remained, and in many ways were intensified. While on the surface it appeared that a new era had begun, events proved that the forces that had catapulted Noli to centre stage were the very same ones that would provide fertile ground for continued instability and his eventual downfall. It took the combined disagreement of five key centres of resistance (progressives like Noli, Kosovar irredentists, the military, disgruntled beys, and Shkodrans) to force Zogu's temporary eclipse. That said, the political standings of Zogu and Noli in June 1924 are deceptive. Although temporarily in the political wilderness, Zogu, according to forces inside and outside Albania, was the victim of radical terrorism, and he was still the ally of powerful neighbours who had not been placated. Moreover, Zogu could boast over ten years of 'presence' inside Albania, whereas Noli's main experience was gained abroad and he only became a key figure in Albania's domestic political scene in the fall of 1923. His elevation came quickly, and a permanent defeat of Ahmed Zogu required more domestic unity, foreign support, and skill than Noli could manage.

3

Fan Noli in Power

By the beginning of June 1924 it appeared that Albania had made a fundamental break with the past, that substantial reform was a real possibility, and a new epoch was on the horizon. This was certainly how some leaders, especially Noli, viewed the situation. Fundamental questions, however, had not been answered, and Noli's seizure of power was shaky, to say the least. The implementation of a new order required a far more cohesive group than that which Noli led; it also required vital political and financial support from abroad, and skilled legislators willing to make the necessary sacrifices and compromises. Noli thus required considerable breathing space if he was to succeed in creating the type of Albania he envisioned. As the situation evolved, it became all too apparent that he had not dealt a final blow to the landowning class, that his neighbours greeted his victory with dismay, and that the Great Powers were unwilling to support him.

The defeat of the government was surprisingly easy and involved almost no bloodshed since few were prepared to risk their lives in its defence. U.S. estimates on casualties were 20 killed and 35 wounded in the northern theatre, and 6 killed and 15 wounded in the southern theatre.[1] In fact, only Zogu and his meagre group put up any resistance at all, the vast majority of people adopting an indifferent attitude and leaving the fighting to a few zealots. Even Mehmet Konica in London remarked that 'a revolution in Albania affects trade no more seriously than a General Election in England, and, in fact, involves a very much smaller proportion of the population.'[2] U. Grant-Smith's assessment of the success of Noli's faction is probably the most accurate; he argued that it was a product of the determination of the officers to prevent the abolition of the army, a general revolt against the influence of Zogu, and the disinclination of the Albanian tribesmen to participate in hand-to-hand conflict.[3]

The ease with which Zogu and his supporters fell was not the result of any mass movement of peasants and workers. Anton Logoreci's suggestion that Zogu allowed the government to fall in a 'fit of uncharacteristic political absent mindedness and military ineptitude' and that the insurrection was 'a feeble military coup staged by two army regiments'[4] is considerably more accurate, if not altogether fair. It was the army, tired of chaos and the failure to pay salaries, which decided who would run the country. By throwing their lot in with the revolutionaries, they shifted the balance of power, albeit temporarily, in Noli's favour. Even Luigi Gurakuqi, in a later interview with *Popolo d'Italia*, declared that the events of June 1924 were 'not a true revolution' but a 'coup d'état.'[5] As he saw it, the biggest single problem confronting the state was imminent financial collapse. According to Gurakuqi, who understood Albania's economic dilemma better than anyone, in the years prior to the June seizure of power, the governments dominated by Ahmed Zogu had plundered the public finances, plagued the country with corruption, and created massive budget deficits.[6] An officer who participated in the seizure of power confirmed Gurakuqi's gloomy assessment and noted that the Albanian treasury contained only sixteen paper lire.[7] That said, it was for some a coup and others a revolution.

When they liberated Tirana on June 10, the opposition was altogether unprepared to take control of the government. Press reports, which referred to Noli's group as nationalist insurgents, noted that 'news from almost every part of Albania describes the rejoicing of the population at the success of the Nationalist movement.'[8] However, the reality was somewhat different. Since there was little ideological unity among essentially three opposition centres – Vlorë, Shkodër, and Krumë – and each faction more or less possessed its own agenda, it was difficult to form a cabinet that could even marginally satisfy so many diverse interests. Despite considerable planning for a seizure of power since the funeral of Rustemi, important questions had obviously been left unsolved, and it was all too apparent that the forces which had overthrown Zogu were diverse and often at odds with each other. Hostility to Zogu appeared to be the only unifying force.

Early in June, the Vlorë-based forces had called for willing assembly members to leave Tirana for Vlorë, and had already established a provisional government with the liberal bey Sami Vrioni as leader, Noli as commissar for external affairs, and Sulejman Delvina as interior minister.

However, it seems that owing to the military importance of Bajram Curri, who, after all, had fired the first shot, the insurgents decided that the country should temporarily be under the joint dictatorship of Noli and Curri. This idea, however, was dropped out of fear of Belgrade's response to Curri's presence. Members of the Kosovo Committee, which had offered such vital military assistance to the insurrection, were not represented in the new cabinet.[9] Even the Kosovar leader Zia Dibra, who had returned from exile and had been promised a post in Noli's government, was excluded. In a conversation on June 11 with U.S. minister U. Grant-Smith, Ali Bey Kelcyra, Albania's one-time representative in Rome, confused matters even more by stating that decisions still needed to be taken on whether to form a provisional government under a military regime or issue a recall of the regents and the willing assembly members.[10] The confusion over just who should govern is an indication of three factors: Noli did not want to anger Yugoslavia and thus preferred to keep Curri, Prishtina, and Dibra behind the scenes; support for Kosovo was not something that unified Noli's movement; and, finally, cohesion among the various centres of resistance was lacking from the outset.

Only after considerable discussion and compromise did a permanent cabinet emerge on June 16 that was a coalition of four of the five pillars of the insurrection: the army, liberal beys, the progressives, and the Shkodrans. The Kosovo Committee was excluded. The cabinet was as follows: prime minister, Fan S. Noli; foreign minister, Sulejman Delvina; finance minister, Luigi Gurakuqi; education minister, Stavro Vinjau; war minister, Kasem Qafëzezi; interior minister, Rexhep Shala; agriculture minister, Qazim Koculi; without portfolio, Xhemal Bushati.[11] The cabinet thus represented diverse interests. Gurakuqi was a moderate, who had his own agenda and was by no means an advocate of the radical solutions proposed by Noli. Noli and Vinjau were undoubtedly the most radical, Koculi less so, and the army representatives, Shala and Qafëzezi, were simple careerists who had their own agendas, which cannot be classified as either moderate, conservative, or radical. While Shala and Qafëzezi had joined in the fight against the dominance of the landowners, it was not out of any opposition to the old system but because the large landowners held power. Qafëzezi was a well-established careerist who sought only to improve his prospects within Noli's new regime and had no use for radical change. Sotir Peci, the only remaining member of the Regency Council, had his own problems with Noli. While both he and Noli were honest patriots, they had a long history of conflict, and Peci, ten years older than Noli, had little faith in revolutionary methods.[12]

Peci's decision to remain in Albania, when the other three regents had resigned and fled, is not an indication of support for Noli, but rather demonstrates that he believed he could best serve the interests of the country by providing at least a semblance of legitimacy to Noli's government. For patriots like Peci and Konica, the gravest danger for Albania was not the internal one represented by the landlords, but the external threat which emanated from Albania's neighbours, especially Yugoslavia. Abandoning the country at such a critical moment would have deprived Noli of even the slightest thread of legitimacy, and Peci remained in Tirana solely in the hope of convincing Noli to legitimize the new government through elections or a recall of the assembly elected in December 1923.

In the insurrection, hostility toward the landlords had been a major factor, but so, too, had been the struggle of the northern and southern fringes against the Moslem dominance of Albania.[13] The *Times* of London made reference to Zogu's mid-May speech, which in 'effect called on the Moslems of central Albania to rally around him against the Christians of the North and South.'[14] Early speculation in press reports suggested it was doubtful that the north (Gegs) and south (Tosks) would be able to cooperate, and that owing to disagreements between the two regions, there might be two governments.[15]

What had been going on in the country during the months that followed the January 1920 Lushnjë Congress was a multi-sided battle. Noli was determined to uproot the landowning class through radical measures. For this agenda, he had the support of both the Bashkimi organization and Vatra, which now trumpeted Noli's success as the beginning of a new epoch. Gurakuqi and Shala, on behalf of the Shkodër Catholics, sought to address the imbalance that had so plagued Tirana governments since 1920: the continued dominance of Moslem beys at the expense of Shkodër. Their main hope was to secure a role for Shkodër they felt was in keeping with the city's cultural, historic, and commercial advantages over the rest of the country. The battle that raged throughout 1923 and early 1924 over the location of the capital continued unabated throughout Noli's tenure. The *Politika* newspaper continued to champion the cause of Vlorë as the capital, putting forth what were by then well-known arguments against the selection of Shkodër. Stating that Albania's 'main problem' was to protect the state from external dangers, *Politika* argued that Shkodër would not make a suitable capital.[16] *Politika* also attacked the organ of the Shkodër Catholics, *Ora e Maleve,* for resurrecting the Geg-Tosk split, which had opened up a regional antagonism at a time when the country needed national unity.[17]

The liberal-minded beys who joined Noli's group were less convinced of the need for radical reforms but instead hoped to break the power of Ahmed Zogu. While the liberal-bey component had no doubt offered support for radical changes at the outset of the revolution, it was primarily a cynical choice based more on a quest for power than desire for social reform. The Kosovo Committee, like the beys, was also not convinced of the need to substantially alter the domestic agenda of the state. Their support for Noli had little to do with his ideological appeal; they hoped only that Noli would adopt a more aggressive stance on the Kosovo question. Attached to the new government, albeit informally, the Kosovo Committee obtained at least moderate access to the corridors of power, which had been denied to them under Zogu, giving them long-sought legitimacy in the battle against Serbian policy in Kosovo. While Kosovo irredentists were not represented in the government, Noli pledged to try to internationalize the problem. In fact, only during Noli's brief tenure did Tirana attempt to articulate a policy for the troubled region.

As to the peasantry, whom Noli claimed to represent, events between 1920 and June 1924 had not given the impression that they were desperate for reform. Moreover, Noli had not made serious inroads in convincing the peasantry of the need to alter the system. Instead, the peasantry remained either indifferent or conservative in outlook and still tended to look on the beys as their natural protectors. Also, the final form of the state had not yet been decided, and this was another divisive factor. Noli was a staunch republican, while some members of his coalition, including Gurakuqi and Sami Vrioni, were still monarchists at heart bound by an oath of loyalty to Wied.[18]

The defeat of the Albania's Moslem aristocracy, which was the key component of Noli's agenda, was not universally accepted as the goal of the insurrection. Just as large a group in the coalition had no vested interest in the destruction of the social and political status quo. While Noli certainly wanted a wholesale social revolution, there was no indication, especially after Rustemi's funeral and the ultimatums to the government, that opposition to the landlords was a unifying factor. As U.S. minister Grant-Smith noted, the main problem at the time was less a struggle for a new Albania than a contest between the 'ins' and the 'outs.'[19]

Diversity of aims aside, Noli's assumption of the post of prime minister, although couched in terms of legality, contradicted the Lushnjë statutes and was entirely illegal. While stating that the Regency Council had authorized him to form a new government, the official announcement delivered to foreign representatives paid little attention to the fact that since there was only one member of the Regency Council in Albania (Sotir Peci), the council, according to Article 49, could not function.[20] Making matters worse, on July 1 the government announced that Peci, citing health reasons, had resigned. Noli announced that new regents would be elected in fresh balloting in later elections. A government decree stated that Noli was thus assuming the post as regent pursuant to Article 51.[21] Peci, however, returned to his duties in August and continued to pressure Noli to legalize his rule through a popular mandate. For the purposes of legitimacy, the fiction of a Regency Council was maintained throughout Noli's rule, although few inside or outside the country were fooled by the attempt to remain within the confines of the Lushnjë statutes. As Grant-Smith noted in a November situation report, it was 'a provisional government sitting at a provisional capital acting illegally under a provisional constitution.'[22]

On June 19, Noli's coalition government announced a twenty-point reform agenda, which, had it been implemented, would have led to a revolutionary transformation of the country. In his opening paragraph, Noli lashed out at the previous government:

> The destructive policy of the last Governments had created such despair in the country that insurrection and fratricide were at last the outcome. The result of the late Ministers Administration are a ruined budget with a large deficit, disorganization of the State in all its departments, insecurity throughout the country, anarchy among the organs of the State, the creation of personal powers outside and above those of the state together with assassination and attempted assassination of citizens and foreigners. These uncontested facts had endangered the foundation of the country, discredited us at home and abroad and cast a doubt in the mind of both Albanians and foreigners as to the capacity of our State to live.[23]

The twenty-point agenda was indeed ambitious and is worth quoting in full:

1 The general disarmament of the people without exception.
2 The denunciation of the inciters of fratricide and their main agents with expulsion and confiscation of their wealth or other punishments.
3 The reestablishment of tranquillity, order and the Sovereignty of the law.

 4 To exalt the authority of the State over any personal or extralegal
    power.
 5 To eliminate feudalism, free the people and establish democracy in
    Albania.
 6 Radical reforms in all departments, both civil and military.
 7 To simplify the bureaucracy and cleanse the administration. Besides
    ability and morality, the patriotism of workers will be taken into
    consideration.
 8 The security and rights of the employees and the determination of their
    responsibilities shall be established by a special law.
 9 To organize the communes so as to improve the conditions of villages
    and villagers and to extend powers at the village level.
10 Balance the budget by radical economies.
11 Change the tax system in a manner favourable to the people.
12 Improve conditions for the farmers and their economic
    independence.
13 Ease entry for foreign capital into the country while defending and
    organizing the economic independence of the country.
14 Raise the credit and prestige of the State in the outside world.
15 True independence of the judiciary.
16 Radical reform of the outdated tribunals.
17 To construct new roads and bridges and to take special care of the
    means of communication in the country.
18 Organization of the Department of Health to combat the diseases that
    are ravaging the people.
19 Organization of the Department of Education on a modern and practi-
    cal basis so that the schools should produce capable citizens, patriotic
    and able workers.
20 Friendly relations with all states, especially neighbouring
    countries.[24]

Noli went on to state that with the return of normal conditions, a general
election would be held by secret and direct voting to determine the support of the people.[25] At the outset, convinced that the country's previous
elections did not represent the wishes of the Albanian people, Noli prepared to govern by decree for ten to twelve months.

The program of the new cabinet represented the temporary triumph of
the progressive agenda over that of the more conservative or careerist elements. How Noli managed to convince the rag-tag group around him to
support the agenda is unclear. Noli later remarked that his group 'had the

majority when we put on our programme the agrarian reforms. We were in the minority when it came to implement them.'[26] He was prepared to use dictatorial methods to eliminate the vestiges of the landowners, while he also attached great hope to securing financial support from abroad. The program was a statement of Noli's vision for the country, and it is entirely possible either that Noli had never put the program to the cabinet or that some of his 'fair weather' supporters were willing temporarily to acquiesce and await a more opportune time to challenge the program.

Noli appears to have recognized that adequate support for the type of transformation he advocated was simply not there. Astute enough to realize that there was no real unity in Albania and having made few inroads outside of the Orthodox south, Noli needed time to eliminate the obstacles to the success of his program; these were the same disintegrative trends that had brought him to power in the first place. The suggestion by some historians that one of the keys to Noli's failure was his unwillingness to recognize that support for radical reform was lacking is mistaken.[27] Noli understood that the implementation of his reform agenda meant that over a period of months he would have to convince an indifferent, fearful, and conservative peasantry, whom he considered to be the most effective unifying force in the country, of the necessity of change. Noli, it appears, was prepared to implement a twofold plan: a period of authoritarianism lasting up to òne year, which would have enabled him to sway the mass of peasants and rid the country of potential enemies; and a prolonged period of external tranquillity that would allow him to concentrate on domestic concerns. Neither would be easy, and from the very beginning Noli seemed unsure as to where to direct the country's limited resources.

The need for substantial land reform, which had already been identified by the League of Nations and other observers, was obvious; the plight of the Albanian peasantry was disastrous. One of the fundamental conflicts at the time was between the peasants and large landowners, as over 50 per cent of the peasantry continued to work the large estates, on a sharecrop basis, for the Moslem landowners. As noted earlier, Noli had identified the system of landownership as one of the key sicknesses of the state and firmly believed that land reform needed to be implemented if he was to win over the peasantry. In this agenda, he had the full support of the country's progressive forces and the liberal papers *Dielli, Drita, Politika, Shqiptari i Amerikës,* and *Bashkimi.*

In the implementation of the twenty-point program, Noli could depend almost solely on the Bashkimi organization; it was this group and its newspaper that waged the most aggressive struggle against Albanian 'feudalism' and sought to ensure that the government stuck to its program.[28] Bashkimi had little use for the politics of compromise and remained an organization that appointed itself as an official check on Noli's government. Its membership pushed by far the most radical agenda in the country, which in effect amounted to a call for class warfare. Point two of Noli's reform plan, which called for an aggressive attack on the remnants of the old regime, was no doubt put there at the insistence of Bashkimi. As the heirs of Rustemi's legacy, and convinced that Zogu was responsible for his murder, Bashkimi was determined to eliminate Zogu and the conservative beys who supported him.

In keeping with its outlook, only Bashkimi declared the triumph of the 'Bourgeois-Democratic Revolution.' In its call for reform, Bashkimi declared its own five-point agenda, which mirrored Noli's program in calling for the implementation of real democracy, the denouncing of those guilty of fratricide and the confiscation of their wealth, the wholesale clearing of the country of 'spies, bootlickers and traitors,' general disarmament, and the insurance of economic independence for the peasantry through agrarian reform.[29] Bashkimi argued that Albania, as a farming nation, could only be taken out of its perpetual economic crisis by agrarian reform.[30] More importantly, Bashkimi echoed Noli's position, arguing that agrarian reform had to be implemented first. Only then should the government move to legalize itself through secret and direct balloting. Bashkimi remained the only political force in the country that never wavered from its program.

While land reform was necessary to emancipate the peasantry and destroy the landowning class, it was difficult to convince the entire cabinet of the viability of the plan, and from the very beginning this created dissension. Some elements, especially Shala and Qafëzezi, were opposed to the confiscation of land and did their utmost to defend the interests of the propertied classes. Nevertheless, the government tried to move on the question of land reform, although it was not until the fall of 1924 that they accomplished anything substantial. In a September interview with *Bashkimi,* agriculture minister Q. Koculi outlined the government's agenda: a commission had been formed which was charged with drafting a decree on agrarian reform. The main source of new land for the peasants would come from the appropriation of the property of the large owners, especially in central Albania. Each farmer with a family of up to ten people was to receive 4-6 hectares of land. Families of more than ten people would receive 8 hectares.[31] As for financing this project, the country hoped to float a loan abroad, possibly with the assistance of Vatra or the League of Nations, and establish an Agricultural Bank with 6 million gold francs in capital.[32] Finding foreign financial support, however, was dependent on Noli's ability to introduce internal stability and legitimize his seizure of power. As had been the case in the past, securing a loan was no easy task.

Not only was the proposed land-seizure plan illegal, in that Noli lacked a mandate from the assembly, it also angered the conservative elements in Noli's coalition. Outside powers, especially Great Britain, were equally dismayed, viewing the program as a Bolshevik-style initiative from a government that had seized power illegally. The main source of land would come from the country's seven large landowning families, who, as noted, owned land in excess of 2,000 hectares. For the most part, these families had fled either to Greece, Yugoslavia, or Italy. It is important to note that the proposed confiscation of property was to be a selective process. Those beys who supported Noli, who had returned to Albania with Zogu's departure, or who had suffered under Zogu's regime were not to lose their land, but would pay higher taxes. The confiscation of land, directed solely against political opponents and without any suggestion of compensation, was bound to raise questions at home and abroad, particularly because there were other alternatives, such as expanding the supply of arable land. The mere mention of another agenda might have bought off some of his critics. As Noli later remarked to journalist Joseph Swire,

> By insisting on the agrarian reforms I aroused the wrath of the landed aristocracy; by failing to carry them out I lost the support of the peasant masses. My government colleagues, and the majority of the army officers, were either hostile or at best indifferent to these reforms, although they had declared themselves in favour previously. Mr. Sotir Petsi (Peci), the Regent, opposed them violently and openly. Mr. Eyres (Great Britain's representative in Albania) succeeded in persuading everybody around me that agrarian reforms were a dangerous Bolshevik innovation.[33]

While Noli had little hope of rallying his previous supporters to the cause of land reform, his decision to confiscate land illegally did little to win him the outside support that might have placated internal opponents. It was possible that land reform per se did not anger the outside world, but rather the methods by which he chose to obtain an end that many observers, especially from the League, had already been on record as supporting.

In the aftermath of the seizure of power, rather than personally trying to garner support for the proposed changes and turning his attention toward the creation of a mass movement, Noli left that task primarily to Bashkimi and attempted to use force to implement the agenda. Trying to fashion his own version of the Zogist police state, he focused his main efforts on discrediting, trying, and later sentencing the members of the previous government for a multitude of crimes so that he could have them permanently out of the way. This was once again a reflection of Bashkimi's quest for radical class warfare and an aggressive attempt to root out real and perceived enemies of the revolution. Noli never doubted the validity of Bashkimi's agenda and was prepared to use any means to eliminate the large landowners. By the end of June, the government had extended martial law (originally imposed following the murder of the two Americans) for another two months in the prefecture of Durrës, to rid the country of political opponents. In early July, the government had already established a political court to deal with the question of *fratricide* – the charge made against those high-level officials who had militarily opposed the June revolution. The court was permitted to use a variety of sentences, including death, life imprisonment, expulsion, and confiscation of wealth.[34] Some 107 people were charged, including former regents Xh. Ypi and R. Toptani, parliamentary chairman Eshref Frashëri, former prime ministers A. Zogu, Sh. Vërlaci, and I. Vrioni, and former ministers M. Libohova, A. Dibra, M. Aranitasi, and K. Kota, along with a host of other former deputies and army and gendarmerie commanders.[35]

Encouraging even greater suspicion of his motives, the court claimed jurisdiction over foreign nationals, like Ceno Bey Kryeziu, 'and confiscated property of all persons arraigned before the court without regard to its eventual findings.'[36] For the enemies of Noli's regime who were unfortunate enough to have remained in Albania, the political court ordered their immediate incarceration. One author even noted that Noli also 'ordered several of his political opponents to be paraded continuously around Tirana's central square, whilst being force-fed cod-liver oil, until they defecated in front of the crowd.'[37] Trojan Kodding at the U.S. legation noted that 'the impoverishment of the landed classes has been accompanied by actions so hurtful to the pride of the beys that any liberal cause has probably been permanently maimed so far as they are concerned.'[38] Two prominent beys, who were brought for trial in Tirana, were made to walk from Vlorë to Fier (roughly 50 kilometres) even though they could pay their own transportation.[39]

The main agenda of the court was less the desire to see justice being done than to appropriate the wealth of landowners like the Berat-based Vrioni and the Elbasan-based Vërlaci families and the many other former leaders then in exile. Focusing efforts on Zogu, who remained in exile in Yugoslavia, charges of fratricide were also supplemented by an attempt to convict Zogu of the murder of the two Americans, Coleman and De Long. Eager to placate the United States and secure its support, near the end of June the court demanded that Zogu and others return to Tirana within fifteen days to answer questions regarding the murders of the Americans.[40] This agenda in itself was a reflection more of the need to satisfy the complaints of the United States and to further discredit Zogu than to ensure that justice was being served.

Having worked with Zogu in the Popular Party and even having served in the same government, Noli understood that he was not inclined to give up easily, and he recognized that Zogu was not about to accept the life of a permanent exile. The attempt to link him with the murders of the two Americans was designed to gain at least some support from the United States for keeping Zogu permanently out of Albania. Zogu did not consider Noli's seizure of power as anything more than a temporary setback. After all, his battle for influence in Albania had begun in 1912. He appeared to wait patiently in Belgrade for the inevitable fragmentation of the coalition, while fomenting disorder in the border regions where he maintained influence. Furthermore, Zogu was also not without allies abroad; his policy toward Kosovo had won the support of Belgrade, and other powers had lauded him for the apparent stability he had achieved as premier from December 1922 until February 1924. Championing himself as a guarantor of peace and stability, Zogu used his time in exile to convince Yugoslavia and Italy that his return would be in their interests.

While the determination to remove Zogu permanently from the political scene was essential to Noli's success, the government's agenda went deeper. In keeping with the general atmosphere of fear and paranoia, Noli also undertook a campaign to root out suspected enemies of the government in the army, gendarmerie, and state administration. This purge focused primarily on the army, which Noli hoped to de-politicize completely, along with the removal from the state bureaucracy of elements trained in 'old-style methods' or unsympathetic to the government. Scores of prefects, vice-prefects, mayors, and other local officials were ejected, as were some Albanian representatives in New York and Vienna. The purging of the state administration and the work of the political court were both pursued with great zeal by Bashkimi, which played an important role at the local level. Owing to its newfound purpose, Bashkimi witnessed a profound growth in the size and importance of its organization, finding support from the country's youth. It experienced growth from a mere three regional departments to over forty, including substantial expansion at the village level.[41] Bashkimi members became the shock troops of the 'revolution,' scouring the villages for both supporters and potential enemies. Membership in Bashkimi thus became the certificate of political dependability, as it was largely its members that filled the many vacant spots in the bureaucracy.

Both the Ministry of War and the Ministry of Interior advised the country's prefectures that harsh measures would be imposed on those who 'worked against the freedom and peace of the people' and that any violators should be sent to the military court in Tirana for trial.[42] All too aware of the regionalisms that plagued the country, the Ministry of Interior also warned that those people who tried to split the unity of the people with words like 'Geg' and 'Tosk,' 'Christian' and 'Moslem,' would be brought before the courts.[43] Finally, in late July, Noli's government also promulgated an ambitious program to deal with its suspected enemies: permits for arms were removed; those possessing long-arms that were not hunting rifles were obliged to turn them in to a military depot; secret and open meetings were cancelled; correspondence with those guilty of fratricide had to end; newspapers were to be brought before the censor before being printed; and a curfew was imposed in Tirana and Durrës.[44]

Noli's dictatorial style, which has been treated by communist historiography as necessary and justified,[45] did little to win him allies at home or abroad, or to encourage foreign financial assistance. As head of a government that pledged itself to the democratization and modernization of Albanian society, Noli would have been better served by proclaiming a general amnesty. After all, he and his supporters had been the most vocal critics of the previous government's refusal to proclaim a pardon for the participants of the March 1922 rebellion; and it is worth recalling that Noli had proclaimed in August 1923 that a general amnesty for those guilty of political crimes was vital if Albania was to move forward. As it stood, such harsh measures against members of the old regime only served to strengthen their resolve to restore the status quo and ensured that many observers would judge Noli's government as even more autocratic than its predecessors.[46] While Zogu had often acted harshly against his opponents, there was virtually no precedent for the scale of these measures, which amounted to an attempt to eliminate the government's opponents by force. The periodical *Near East* chastised Noli for his reversion to censorship and harsh measures, and declared that the Western powers 'had every right to look for something better from the head of a Ministry who was also a high dignitary of the Church, and who had spent years of his life in the civilised West.'[47] Noli's agenda, the paper argued prophetically, would 'fan the flame of vendetta and inevitably prepare for a further swing of the political pendulum.'[48] The only area where the government appears to have succeeded is the attempt to fill Albanian prisons.

Harsh retaliatory measures also went against the stated objectives of the government. Ali Bey Kelcyra, who like many other members of the opposition rejected Noli's methods, reported to Grant-Smith in early June that 'the victors would be moderate and just in their dealings with their opponents but they did expect to make the large landowners pay the costs of the revolution.'[49] Even Noli himself, in a later interview with a correspondent of the *Chicago Daily News*, contradicted the reality:

> The total absence of excesses, which usually accompany a revolution everywhere and especially in the Balkans, while speaking highly for the moderation and self-control of the members of the new cabinet, is at the same time the clearest evidence that they are in full control of the internal situation of Albania. Terrorism is of no use since the authority of the new government was from the outset and is now undisputed and unchallenged.[50]

The purge/counter-purge atmosphere which, unabated, had plagued Albanian politics since 1920 was not in keeping with the best traditions of democracy and tolerance to which Noli claimed so profound an attachment. Noli had already gone on record condemning the notion of 'patriot one day – traitor the next.' Noli's program did little to alleviate this predicament and laid the foundations for a whole set of counter-charges as well as a number of politically inspired murders after the collapse of his government.

The political court aside, Noli's government was failing to satisfy its main supporters. Impatient for the immediate implementation of the twenty-point agenda, *Bashkimi, Politika,* and *Shqiptari i Amerikës* all lamented the slow pace of change. By early July, *Shqiptari i Amerikës* was already complaining that the problem was having so many officials trained in old mentalities still at their posts.[51] Bashkimi, which, as already noted, was not a political party per se, maintained its position as outside and above Albania's political quarrels and kept a constant watch on what it identified as a massive gap between the government's stated program and concrete achievements. By September, Bashkimi was voicing criticism of the slowness of the political court and demanding speedy retribution against the former government.[52] The re-trial of Beqir Walter, who had made an attempt on Zogu's life in February 1924, initiated largely as a result of foreign pressure, was also condemned by Bashkimi. In its opinion, Walter was one of the first fighters in the revolution against the landowners.[53] *Politika,* in early August, noted that the momentum of June 1924 had dissipated, that the program being implemented was not that originally propounded by Noli, and that the government had failed to adopt an 'iron fist' against the 'defeatists, hypocrites and parasites.'[54] Even the Korçë paper *Gazeta e Korçës,* traditionally a supporter of Noli, suggested that the original aims of June had been abandoned and that 'elections should be called immediately.'[55]

If progressive supporters like Bashkimi were angered by the absence of serious reform and the continued presence of so-called enemies of the revolution, the moderates and careerists that took part in Noli's revolution were trying to pull the direction of the revolution the other way. Resistance to the confiscation of property occurred within two months of Noli's seizure of power.[56] Shala, Delvina, Kelcyra, and Qafëzezi eventually balked at agrarian reform and called instead for the protection of the propertied classes, declaring that private property would be respected by the government. This is not to say that there was no support in the country for agrarian reform, but that it was limited to Noli and Bashkimi, with the peasantry lacking a political organization that represented their needs. In keeping with its newfound prominence in Albanian politics, Bashkimi also undertook to organize a number of demonstrations, primarily in the heart of Albanian feudalism in central Albania in the towns of Berat, Fier, and Lushnjë, to push the government toward a resolution ·of the problem. At this time, Noli was preoccupied with his planned trip to the League of Nations, and while there were peasants who openly supported land reform, they had no organization outside of Bashkimi to press their case.

July and August witnessed three Bashkimi-sponsored rallies demanding that the government move toward a more vigorous confiscation of property. It was during this period that the real fault lines in the cabinet came to the surface. By far the most significant outpouring of support for the redistribution of land came on August 24 in Berat. The Berat demonstration has become central to communist historiography's assertion about the truly grassroots nature of the movement for agrarian reform, although this appears to be a distortion of the facts.[57] The Berat demonstration was the culmination of the failure of Noli's government to take concrete steps toward land redistribution, which angered Bashkimi's loyal supporters. The meeting, the largest of the time, included the leading lights of Bashkimi's departments in Vlorë and Fier, along with university students and Bashkimi members from Italy, who had come to Albania ostensibly for their summer holidays.[58] The meeting resulted in a strongly worded telegram to the government calling for the confiscation of the wealth and property of the Vrioni, Toptani, Libohova, Vlorë, Vërlaci, and Zogu families.[59] In response to the demonstrations, Interior Minister Shala and War Minister Qafëzezi dealt the near final blow to questions of agrarian reform by issuing a decree stating that private property would be respected.[60] The Interior Ministry further advised that any more disturbances of the Berat type would result in trials before the military court.[61] By the end of August, it was obvious that agrarian reform, as envisioned in the June program, was not something upon which a majority of cabinet members could agree. This lack of legitimacy, which was hampering both internal and external consolidation, had become a significant obstacle in the fulfilment of the program and a weapon which Noli's foes used to further weaken his position.

As with all points in the program, even the timing of fresh elections was a major source of friction. In the view of external observers, that Noli's government remained revolutionary was a major cause for supporting the exiled leaders of the previous government; most powers accepted that Vrioni's government had been illegally overthrown. Internally, the battle for new elections reflected the very same divisions evident in the debate over agrarian reform. The most extreme progressives, Bashkimi and Noli, maintained that new elections, which were an integral component of the twenty-point agenda, could only be held in the aftermath of the implementation of the entire program. Furthermore, Noli consistently maintained, at least until the end of October, that elections would not be held until the spring of 1925. According to Noli, the two most vital parts of the program, agrarian reform and the elimination of the old ruling class, had to be achieved prior to a general election.

As already noted, while the conservatives and careerists challenged that agenda, even some of Noli's more vocal supporters, such as Vatra and Faik Konica, also insisted that the government must legitimize itself in order to ward off the threat of external intervention. Sotir Peci, the on-again-off-again remaining member of the Regency Council, also believed that the government's best course of action would have been legitimization first, reform later. *Politika,* in an editorial of September 25, stated that new elections would bring both legality and normality.[62] Noli's inflexibility on this point, which earned him even more enemies, is difficult to explain. With an overall unwillingness to put his reform program to a test of popular support, Noli thus needed to work quickly if he were to survive. Agrarian reform, at least the type he envisioned, would take more than the simple confiscation of property and its redistribution among the peasantry. Lack of land was only part of the problem. The need for capital, as outlined in Koculi's plan, required a substantial loan. Capital could only come from abroad, and few international organizations or countries were willing to help a government that had not won any international recognition.

With the coalition fragmented and in need of direction, Noli and Gurakuqi embarked on a trip to the League of Nations at the end of August 1924 to plead for a loan, to deal with remaining border issues, and to defend the case of the Kosovars suffering under a variety of Serb policies. By this time, his government had achieved almost nothing substantial. Land reform, by far the most important component in Noli's program, remained on paper. No attempt had been made to mobilize the peasantry. Rather than remain at home and plod away at reform, Noli placed paramount importance on finding international support, and he gambled that if he could find financial support or even some international recognition abroad, he could then move forward on the key components of his program and mollify his domestic critics. Any foreign support would also undercut claims from members of the previous regime that Noli's government was illegitimate. Noli thus decided to put external questions above internal ones. This was a blunder, but not the first or last time an Albanian leader would make such a decision.

His near two-month absence (September and October) was neither astute nor well-timed; the forces that opposed his agenda began plotting behind his back. The liberal bey component continued to issue decrees from the Interior Ministry to the effect that private property would be respected, and tried to undercut, by force, the influence of Bashkimi. The government essentially split into four factions: Bashkimi, the National Democrats, the Radical Democratic Party, and a few loyalists surrounding Noli. Bashkimi continued to remain outside what it called petty politics and considered new elections a fatal mistake that would only deliver the country from 'one chaos to another.'[63] It decried the slowness of the political court and stated on September 16 that the government was in possession of a list of Zogu's spies that should be published.[64] More conservative elements in the coalition were grouped in the National Democratic Party, and more liberal forces in the Radical Democratic Party. By the end of August, these two parties had thrown themselves headlong into an anticipated electoral battle with open campaigning. *Bashkimi* and *Shqiptari i Amerikës* lamented this trend, denouncing it as a fragmentation of the revolution and calling the war between the two parties a war of personalities since both parties possessed identical programs.[65] *Politika* echoed concern about developments, which included the formation of cliques and the resurgence of regional antagonisms.[66] Declaring that the last election had been regional in outcome, *Politika* hoped that new elections would be based on other criteria.

Bashkimi's assessment of the situation was accurate as the two main parties did put forth identical programs, indicating that little had changed since the 1923 elections, when personalities, not policies, decided the outcome. The National Democrats, formed in Gjirokastër in October, included primarily members of the military and conservative beys like Sulejman Delvina and Regent Sotir Peci.[67] As the 'party of stability,' it called for, among other things, a war against regional tendencies, reduction and simplification of the bureaucracy, a progressive tax system, indirect voting, good relations with neighbours, and a more aggressive defence of Albanians living outside the state.[68] Delvina, whom Grant-Smith had described as 'a thorough-going Turk,'[69] had never hidden his desire to see the beys retain power, as long as they were his beys. The Radicals were in essence oppositionists prior to the Noli revolution and by and large the party of the June program. They supported land distribution and virtually the same program called for by the National Democrats, although they maintained the commitment to secret and direct voting.

By the middle of September, foreign diplomats from all quarters were predicting the collapse of the government. Trojan Kodding reported from the U.S. legation that Noli had put too much emphasis on agrarian reform, which eliminated the possibility of legalizing his government and allowed politicians to engage in what he called 'weak local policy.'[70] The removal of previous officials had made public safety less secure than 'it was at the time of the murder of the two Americans.' Kodding argued that the peasants and mountain tribesmen could see no benefits from the present regime, and trusted it no more than its predecessors; neither was either group capable 'of the mental effort required to comprehend the most elementary addition and the idea of gradual reform [was] beyond their understanding.'[71] Regional antagonisms, carefully glossed over in June, had also reappeared. The Shkodrans were still demanding prominence for their city and interests. Kodding also correctly predicted that upon his return from Geneva, Noli would be forced to resign or call new elections, and that the only way even superficial unity could be maintained was dependent on whether or not Noli and Gurakuqi were successful in securing a substantial loan.[72]

Since the government lacked international and domestic confidence, the military again began shaping the agenda. While Noli had hoped to de-politicize both the army and gendarmerie, the army found that it continued to have a considerable stake in the country's political course. The external threat seemed real enough to challenge Albania's independence. With Ahmed Zogu safely ensconced in Belgrade and Ceno Bey Kryeziu working the frontier villages for potential support, it appeared to individuals in the army and government that Zogu's exile forces, coupled with Yugoslav support, were preparing to re-enter the country.[73] Much of the army, which essentially had deserted Zogu in his hour of need, did not welcome the possibility of his return since they had done so much to force his ouster. Moreover, the military was concerned about the vicious budget cuts that Finance Minister Gurakuqi envisioned to put the country on a solid footing. Financial concerns aside, it was the fear that Noli's government could not defend Albania's independence that played the most pivotal role in shaping the attitude of the military. Throughout the fall, the country was rife with rumours of an imminent coup. By late September, American and other observers had already noted that an army-inspired coup or popular revolt was possible.[74]

Noli returned from Geneva in mid-October to find that his two-month absence had witnessed a considerable deterioration of his domestic position. This confirmed the suspicions of foreign observers that he was merely a transitional figure who could be ignored in the long run.[75] Unable to secure a loan, badgered by foreign powers to legitimize his government, and facing an imminent threat from Zogu, he had little choice but to acquiesce in the face of domestic pressure to put his program to a popular vote. Noli was unable to withstand the internal assault from those who sought his outright resignation – especially Sotir Peci, other members of the National Democrats, and the military.[76] Of the original four factions in the cabinet, Noli could only count on the support of diehard progressives like S. Vinjau and, on occasion, L. Gurakuqi. The conservative members of the coalition, who had used Noli's absence to stall any progressive legislation, now had the upper hand and were able to essentially dictate policy to Noli, who by then remained little more than a figurehead. The Shkodrans were disappointed by the fact that virtually nothing was done vis-à-vis their regionalist agenda. They were further disheartened when the government attempted to establish a unified public education system and to abolish separate religious schools.[77] As for the Kosovars, Noli's pledge to place greater emphasis on the plight of Albanians living outside the state had worsened his relations with Yugoslavia. Nevertheless, their best hopes still lay with Noli.[78] On November 13 the Regency Council signed a decree for new elections to be held beginning December 20 and ending on 20 January 1925.[79] Noli took the step unwillingly and Bashkimi denounced the move, but he was confronted with a simple choice between resignation and elections. Noli could not even muster support for direct voting, which had been a cornerstone of opposition policy for well over a year. Thus, by November, the main pillars of the June program had already been discarded.

Noli's June seizure of power had complex origins. It was not merely an inevitable result of a struggle between landlords and liberal-minded reformers; nor was it a bourgeois-democratic revolution. There was a small bourgeois class, found in the Catholic and Orthodox minorities, but they formed only a fraction of the movement. There had been struggle between the status-quo advocates and progressives throughout the early 1920s. However, the seizure of power was also the result of a war of personalities, careerism, and severe regional antagonisms. Zogu's position of dominance in the early 1920s angered both beys and officers in the military, who feared for their privileges. Political change in Tirana also opened up opportunities for individuals who had sought to advance themselves. This fact determined the military's attitude and was a decisive factor in shifting the balance in favour of Noli. Finally, Noli's victory was also the result of the combined discontent of the Catholic and Orthodox population. This was little more than a marriage of convenience as these two populations had not agreed beforehand on a unified agenda. With five pillars of the revolution and essentially three regional centres of discontent, it was unlikely that unity could be maintained. The murder of Rustemi, which had hastened revolution, came at a time when the opposition forces had yet to secure a program that would have achieved something more than superficial unity. Only a tiny proportion of the participants in the June seizure of power were capable of articulating a systematic program.

Noli tried, however, to take what was essentially a coup d'état with very limited aims, and transform it into a social revolution. In this he failed, and the forces that had catapulted him into the premiership were set to

facilitate his downfall. His decision to travel to Geneva, when all indications made it obvious that he should remain in Tirana, was the result of
two factors that ensured his failure: he hoped the international community would provide him with aid and recognition that could be used to
buy off his critics and move forward on the twenty-point program; and,
as his entire career until then made clear, he was more at home in the
world of international diplomacy than in the bizarre world of Albania's
domestic politics. He left at the worse possible moment.

By the end of November, Noli's experiment was finished. Internally,
the coalition had fractured beyond repair. *Politika,* headlining an editorial of November 6 with a plea for solidarity, accurately assessed the situation. While wrongly suggesting that Noli's cabinet had had visible unity
in June, *Politika* called for adherence to the June program, lamented
the disappearance of tolerance among the forces that overthrew the
old order, called for the elimination of sycophants and defeatists, and
implored the country's politicians to leave aside secondary problems and
concentrate on implementing the original revolutionary declaration of
June.[80] Despite such impassioned pleas from the country's progressive
press, politicians resumed the quarrelling that had so dominated political life since 1920. Noli succeeded in satisfying no one and in fact laid
the very foundations for the internal quagmire.

Externally, things did not look much better. Relations with neighbouring countries remained strained, and Noli was unable to effect much
change at either the regional or wider level. By the fall of 1924, the revolution had met with widespread failure as the internal failure was exacerbated by trends outside Albania. It was, however, the lack of external
support that proved to be Noli's greatest undoing, and his stubbornness
on internal questions was even more apparent when he sought to obtain
outside assistance. As had been the case prior to Noli's seizure of power,
Albania needed to facilitate the entry of foreign capital and secure a
loan. Gurakuqi had sought to bring some order to the disastrous legacy
of budget deficits and embarked on severe austerity measures, cutting
salaries at home and at foreign legations abroad.[81] Cuts in both salaries
and the size of government were made worse by the fact that, owing
to the failure to secure a loan abroad, salaries remained in arrears and
many lost faith in Noli's ability to govern. The steady stream of propaganda from exiles, who capitalized on Noli's mistakes, continued and
was successful in its attempt to accentuate differences both within Noli's
coalition and among the regions that had temporarily joined forces to
overthrow the old government.

4
Albania's Neighbours – Yugoslavia and Greece

While facing extraordinary obstacles inside Albania, Noli knew if the 'revolution' of June 1924 was to triumph, a tranquil external environment was needed. Point 20 of his reform agenda vowed to pursue that end. However, a peaceful external environment proved elusive, and Noli was forced to divert considerable time and effort from domestic questions to deal with meddlesome neighbours. Aware that he faced difficulty in consolidating his June victory internally, Noli instead chose to place paramount importance on solving external problems first. To be fair, the circumstances by which Noli came to power required that he give a high priority for foreign policy issues since his success depended on securing recognition and financial assistance. His main political experience was gained as an outside advocate of Albanian interests, and he knew that since Albanian independence in 1912, Albania's external predicament was a cause of perpetual problems. After all, the process of state and nation building, which began after the January 1920 Lushnjë Congress, could not succeed if Albania's immediate neighbours challenged not only borders, but the very existence of Albania as an independent state. Neither Greece nor Yugoslavia had been completely reconciled to the notion of an independent Albania, and both pursued policies that did little to encourage either Albanian democracy or the success of Noli's vision. Securing at least indifference from Albania's neighbours was vital to his survival since it would have given him much needed time to concentrate on domestic problems. Placation of both Greece and Yugoslavia, however, was no easy task.

It was unfortunate for Noli that at the time Yugoslavia and Greece were allied, thus eliminating the potential to play one country against the other. Both worked hand in hand to destabilize his government, often employing similar tactics. Belgrade's ability to destabilize Albania received added momentum with Zogu's arrival there as a political refugee in June 1924. The Greeks also had important leverage on Albania because of the Greek minority living in the south. While Noli, owing to his experience at the League and later in fighting border issues, had come to expect hostile behaviour from the Yugoslav government, Greece's hostile attitude was far more disappointing for him. In this difficult atmosphere, Noli's choices were limited: he could appease Greece and Yugoslavia through concessions; or he could try to consolidate his hold on power so as to make the destabilization of his government more difficult. Neither option was easy; each entailed sacrifices Noli was reluctant to make.

Yugoslavia

Noli understood that Albania needed good relations, especially with Belgrade, if his democratic experiment was to survive. In the years preceding Noli's seizure of power, relations between the two states were poor but not disastrous. Despite the fact that Noli hoped to open a new and better chapter, the situation worsened considerably.

[1]In early June, as the revolution progressed, Italy, Greece, and Yugoslavia watched carefully, hoping to profit from the chaos. By June 7, the Italians and Yugoslavs had issued a statement declaring a non-intervention policy in Albania,[2] yet Belgrade remained distrustful of Italian intentions and sought a government in Albania which was beholden to them. To recall, the main problem was Yugoslavia's insistence on border revision. Noli's early experience at the League, where he battled one Yugoslav accusation after another, had a profound impact on him. While he called for a new beginning, he remained deeply distrustful of Yugoslav motives. Immediately upon assuming power, Noli had sent Yugoslav prime minister Nikola Pašić a congenial telegram expressing the wish for good relations.[3] Pašić replied rather coldly, noting little more than that he was pleased to know that Albania was intending to pursue good relations with Yugoslavia.[4] Pašić's reply was so vague that it was not clear whether Yugoslavia would even recognize the new government.[5]

Belgrade's response to Noli's seizure of power was in fact decidedly negative. Belgrade wrongly identified Noli's victory as the product of Italian influence, and when it became clear that Noli was not a tool of Rome, the Yugoslavs were still unwilling to embrace him.[6] Most important was the question of Kosovo. Yugoslav leaders were pleased that the preceding regimes, especially the ones headed or controlled by Ahmed Zogu, had no heart either for pushing radical change in borders or pressing Belgrade to improve its treatment of the Albanian minority. Noli, who did not seek border revisions, did hope that the Kosovars would get a better deal within the Yugoslav state.

Zogu's presence in Belgrade as an exiled head of state also was a key determinant of policy. Since Zogu was called before a tribunal to answer for various crimes, Noli considered Yugoslavia's decision to allow him to remain within its borders, and continue essentially hostile political activity, to be an unfriendly act. The question of unresolved territorial issues was also at the forefront. In April 1923 the Yugoslav government had asked the Conference of Ambassadors to re-examine the decision regarding the monastery of Saint Naum in the southeast of Albania on the shore of Lake Ohrid, which had been awarded to Albania. Also, Albania's northern border had yet to be delimited, and the Yugoslavs were pressing for control of Vermosh (Vermoš) in the extreme north of Albania on the border with Montenegro. This process angered Noli considerably. It also required his government to dedicate both time and money to the solution of these problems through the often cumbersome League of Nations bureaucracy and the International Court of Justice at The Hague. Lastly, the Yugoslavs interpreted Noli's revolution as little more than a temporary triumph of Christians over Moslems, and they believed that it would bring little more than chaos. In the long run, Yugoslav statecraft feared that Italian intervention would spell the end of Yugoslav influence in the country.[7]

Zogu's neglect of the Kosovo question was not surprising. Given Albania's overall military weakness, this was a shrewd policy based on considerable realpolitik, which was more the norm than the exception in twentieth-century Albania. Zogu also understood better than Noli that stable relations with Yugoslavia were important in obtaining overall stability in Albania. Noli did not have the opportunity for such indifference, as vital military support for his government from the Kosovo Committee forced him to take a more aggressive stance on this issue.[8] As noted, Kosovar irredentists had already established a poor working relationship with Zogu, whom much of their leadership considered to be the next Esad Pasha Toptani, that is, a leader willing to achieve a compromise with the Serbs in return for political support.[9]

While Noli was by no means prepared to call for border revision, some of his supporters certainly were, and no doubt the Yugoslavs looked back

with nostalgia on the days when Ahmed Zogu was in power. Noli's decision to reopen the Kosovo question after four years of relative neglect was
not merely because the circumstances of his June victory dictated it. As
a firm believer in the League of Nations and the minority rights treaties,
he also felt that the Kosovars were not accorded full rights. Through the
League of Nations, he hoped to improve his brethren's plight, and this
was the first time that Albania's position on Kosovo moved beyond simple rhetoric. That the Kosovars lived as second-class citizens in Yugoslavia
is clear, but the circumstances were by no means ideal for Noli's agenda.
To abandon the Kosovars to their fate, as Zogu had, was anathema to
Noli. He felt strongly that while Albania was meeting its obligations to its
tiny minorities, Belgrade (and Athens as well) were violating accepted
standards. It was a difficult choice: to pursue much-needed good relations with the Yugoslavs or to defend the interests of the Albanian community in Kosovo. To have both was impossible, and it was not surprising
that Noli chose the latter.

Even though Noli kept the Kosovo Committee out of the government, which was a concession of sorts to Yugoslavia, Belgrade was not
satisfied. Noli, who did little more than take the Kosovar appeal to the
League in September and thereby try to internationalize the problem,
was subjected to an onslaught of criticism from the Belgrade press.[10] The
Belgrade *Politika* incorrectly noted that Kosovo Committee leader Bajram
Curri held a position in Noli's government and that he was also the head
of outlaw bands of criminals working against Yugoslavia. The Yugoslavs
were especially angry that Curri, whom they claimed was wanted by their
authorities, was to take part in Albania's delegation to the League in the
fall of 1924; this, they felt, displayed the Tirana government's disloyal
attitude.[11] Noli, according to the press report, not only worked openly
with Curri but, in agreement with the latter, sent organized bands of
criminals into Yugoslav territory.[12] As for Hasan Prishtina, another
Kosovo Committee leader, the Yugoslavs claimed he was a renegade
Yugoslav subject who had organized attacks on the Serb Army in 1915
and had been sentenced to twenty years penal servitude before fleeing to
Albania.[13] The Yugoslavs also hoped to take their accusations further and
tried to link Noli with both Bolshevism and revolutionary Macedonian
organizations. As to claims that Noli was in fact working with Prishtina at
the League in order to dismember Yugoslavia, the Albanians responded
that such accusations were groundless and that the head of the Kosovo
Committee had merely gone to the League to insure that minority rights
were applied to the Kosovars.[14] If it was not enough that the likes of

Prishtina were stirring up trouble in Kosovo, the Yugoslavs also considered him, and Finance Minister Luigi Gurakuqi, to be Italophiles.[15]

While Noli certainly did his best to assure the Yugoslavs that he was not seeking anything more than the respect of minority rights from Belgrade, his association with the Kosovars in his seizure of power and later at the League ensured that his room to manoeuvre with the Yugoslavs was limited. In order to appease the Yugoslavs, certain conditions (territorial and political) needed to be met before any progress could be made, and in each case it was difficult for Noli to acquiesce. His policies, which on paper sought to create a unified Albania, were not well received by the government in Belgrade as it had much to gain from Albanian disunity. Until June 1924, the Yugoslav government had always had 'a man in Albania' on whom it could count to represent their interests; Esad Pasha Toptani had been just such a man, as had the Mirdita chieftain Marka Gjoni. Zogu had fast assumed a similar role. With Noli in power, they had no such person. Given this predicament, it is not surprising the Yugoslavs eventually placed their hopes on the return of Zogu.[16]

Yugoslavia's stated neutrality in the events of May and June was farcical, and Albania's new leadership identified Yugoslav policy as seeking to increase instability in the country. In June 1924 the Albanian legation in Belgrade suggested that the Yugoslavs were in fact disappointed with the speed with which Noli's revolution succeeded and would have preferred a much more protracted conflict which could have been used to further the idea, stated repeatedly since 1920, that the Albanians were not ready for self-government.[17] When the fighting inside Albania ended quickly, the Yugoslavs instead attempted to prove that Noli's revolution was an illegal seizure of the legitimate power of Ahmed Zogu. Zogu's selection of Belgrade as his place of refuge was not surprising. Good relations with Ceno Bey Kryeziu, coupled with the simple fact that Zogu was willing to make some concessions to Belgrade in exchange for support of his return to power, ensured that as events unfolded in Albania, Zogu's stature and influence in Belgrade increased.

Zogu, who arrived on June 27 in Belgrade with Ceno Kryeziu and ten other officers, was eventually received as an honoured guest.[18] While it appears that the Yugoslav government was not immediately willing to welcome him with open arms and there was some suggestion that Zogu hoped to flee to Italy to lobby for support there, the Yugoslavs eventually decided that he should remain in Belgrade. It seems that both Zogu and the Yugoslav government needed to evaluate their positions before making any decisions. Zogu marketed himself well as a potential ally of the Yugoslav cause, while also playing on the fact that he had other options: Mussolini would also give him at least an audience. Yugoslav foreign minister Momćilo Ninčić was not oblivious to the fact that Zogu's presence in Serbia could be 'a useful arm for influencing the Albanian Government in future eventualities.'[19] The Yugoslavs immediately gave him accommodation at the Hotel Bristol, and a vehicle was put at his disposal. According to a report in the Albanian newspaper *Gazeta e Korçës,* the Yugoslav paper *Pravda* had declared Zogu a 'friend' of Yugoslavia and reported that he had had meetings with Prime Minister Pašić.[20] From the outset, Zogu clearly saw his departure from Albania as temporary while he prepared for his return. With so many issues outstanding, such as Saint Naum, Vermosh, and the Kosovo question, Zogu was well placed to appease the Serbs, and gaining support in Belgrade proved to be very easy.

Zogu's main tactic, one echoed by Belgrade, was to portray Noli's regime as unstable, lacking authority in the country, and threatening to regional stability. He did this through a carefully planned press campaign that gained support not only in Belgrade but elsewhere in Europe. As he later noted in his memoirs, 'The triumph of the revolutionaries had drowned the country in anarchy.' From across the frontier, Zogu 'watched the sad condition of his country and decided to try once more to save it from chaos.'[21] In an interview in the Belgrade *Politika,* Zogu declared that Noli's government 'did not represent the wishes of the people and that it would fall in a short time.'[22] Zogu also suggested that Noli's coalition contained far too many diverse elements to consolidate itself.[23] Zogu's argument was strengthened by the fact that Noli's government had received no outside recognition, especially from the Great Powers, who immediately adopted a reserved attitude toward it.[24] The Yugoslavs also played on the notion of chaos and inspired the rumours that Noli's seizure of power was solely the result of differences between Gegs and Tosks and Christians and Moslems. Zogu, who was the main source of these conclusions, was only too happy to encourage regional and religious cleavages.

Yugoslavia's attitude toward Zogu was simple realpolitik. First and foremost, since Prime Minister Pašić was a shrewd politician, he embraced Zogu as a man who was easily bought and was an important bargaining chip in the struggle to reduce Noli's impact on a broad number of issues. Thus, Zogu remained in Belgrade as long as he was useful. Had Noli been willing to satisfy some of Belgrade's key concerns, the Yugoslavs would have happily returned him to Albania to stand trial. What secured

Zogu's position was that unlike Noli, he was prepared to barter with Albanian sovereignty in order to gain Yugoslav assistance. That is not to say he was prepared to abandon his commitment to Albanian independence, only that he was willing to make certain tactical retreats to secure power. Noli was unwilling to bargain on any issue and hoped that support for his position would come from the international community, which would in turn pressure Belgrade.

Instead of trying to open a dialogue with Belgrade after his initial appeals failed, Noli decided it was completely futile to lobby for a change in Belgrade's policy as long as Pašić was at the helm. However, when Pašić was replaced by Ljuba Davidović as prime minister on July 27, he and his associates were elated and immediately began the process again of seeking some concessions on Zogu and his entourage. In his report of July 28 about the new government in Belgrade, Albania's minister in Belgrade, Ali Kolonja, reported that change was in the air, and that the new liberal government was willing to abandon the Serbian orientation in foreign policy in favour of opening a dialogue with the Albanians in Kosovo. The new coalition government of Davidović-Spaho-Korošec, Kolonja believed, would abandon the politics of Pašić and 'normalize external relations.'[25] Kolonja considered the new foreign minister, Vojislav Marinković, to be a 'loyal man' who was convinced of the necessity of good relations between Serbia and Albania.

The optimism, however, was misplaced, and no real change in Belgrade occurred, despite the best efforts of both Noli and Kolonja. With Davidović's assumption of power, Foreign Minister Delvina advised Kolonja that felicitations should be given on the formation of a new government and that he was to reiterate Albania's commitment to good relations. He hoped that the new government would move to recognize Albania and expel Zogu.[26] Apparently, Kolonja's appeal to the new prime minister took eleven days to reach the hands of Foreign Minister Marinković. Moreover, Marinković rejected a further request from Kolonja for a meeting with him to discuss recognition on the grounds that the new government did not have time to take up the question.[27]

When it became obvious that the change in Belgrade meant nothing, Albania again embarked on a fruitless battle to convince the Yugoslavs that Zogu's presence in Belgrade was the main obstacle to good relations. Throughout late June and July, Kolonja worked tirelessly to encourage a change in Yugoslav policy. Kolonja was also charged with the difficult task of keeping track of Zogu's movements and advising Tirana of his agenda. He sent a litany of protest notes regarding Zogu's undisguised attempts to use Yugoslavia as the base for his eventual operation against Albania. On August 19, Kolonja advised the Yugoslav foreign minister that Zogu was using the border zones as a means to provoke incidents inside Albania and that the continued presence of Zogu and his entourage in Belgrade was a menace to peace and good relations between Tirana and Belgrade.[28]

Kolonja's reports on Zogu's activities shed important light on his tactics. Zogu, along with Ceno bey Kryeziu, set out to create as much trouble as possible in the border regions, and they focused on trying to win over northern chieftains. Kryeziu, according to Kolonja, was extremely helpful in Belgrade because of his close relations with the Yugoslav government and his membership in Pašić's National Radical Democratic Party, and because he was a well-known 'friend of Prime Minister Davidović, whom he can visit any time of the day he wants, whereas other persons wait in queue.'[29] Zogu's agents were reported to be travelling around Albanian-populated regions of Yugoslavia paying out cash and making promises to potential participants in a seizure of power.[30]

However, it took time for Kolonja to finally accept that Davidović's government was not predisposed to breaking with Pašić's Albania policy. In his report of August 23, he stated that hopes based on a new policy under Davidović were unrealistic and the Yugoslav policy sought to prevent internal consolidation in Albania. Albania, according to official Belgrade, was an ally of Italy and the Kosovo Committee.[31] While the Yugoslavs had argued that recognition had been withheld pending a decision by England and France, Kolonja suggested that this was little more than pretext and that there were no sympathetic elements in the Yugoslav government.[32] Kolonja identified the roots of Yugoslav policy as highly personal in nature in that Belgrade had taken a strong dislike to Noli and his entourage. He noted that it would be very difficult to change this policy, and that the Serbs speculated that since some kind of civil war was inevitable, Serbophile elements (i.e., Ahmed Bey Zogu) would be victorious.[33]

Kolonja's report of September 30 had coincided with Noli's September visit to the League and his appeal, through an interview with *Vreme* and *Politika,* for good relations with Yugoslavia and other countries of the region.[34] Despite Noli's best intentions, he was condemned in Belgrade because he neglected to mention his commitment to good 'Serbian-Albanian' relations. Moreover, Belgrade interpreted Noli's request for a loan from the League as an aggressive act, arguing that the money would be used to arm the Kosovars for an armed struggle against Belgrade.

Border questions as well as Albania's alleged arming of Kosovo irre-dentists were the bulk of the problem, and Kolonja maintained that the Yugoslav press was trying to maintain an 'enemy spirit' against the Albanian state. The Belgrade government insisted that the activities of Kosovars, in using force to change Belgrade's policy of Serbianization, were the result of the 'inspiration and support of the Albanian govern-ment.'[35] Kolonja concluded that it was futile to hope for good relations, especially as long as Zogu remained in Belgrade. While he felt change in Belgrade might come in the long run, it would not come quickly, and even if the Croats participated in government, the foreign policy of Yugoslavia would still be guided by the Serbs.[36] As for Zogu, he was little more than a 'blind tool' for the development of 'Yugoslav expansion on Albanian soil.'[37] In the long run, as events later proved, Zogu was neither blind nor a mere tool of Yugoslav policy; when he later turned to Italy to undercut Yugoslav influence in Albania, Zogu actually held the upper hand in his dealings with Belgrade.

Kolonja's suspicions were confirmed by the attitude of Yugoslav foreign minister Marinković. While in Geneva, Noli called upon him, requested Yugoslav recognition, and 'professed the most friendly sentiments.'[38] Marinković replied that Yugoslavia would not recognize a government that was not recognized by its own parliament.[39] In a conversation with a U.S. diplomat, the foreign minister added that he felt Zogu's power was weakening and that regardless of what happened, Yugoslavia would remain neutral. Marinković also spoke at length about the Albanian issue, and his comments reveal little sympathy for the Albanian position. He argued that it was possible for Serbia to wield paramount influence in the country for three reasons: Albania adjoined Serbia; Yugoslav inter-ests coincided more closely with Albanian interests than those of any other foreigners; and, finally, since the Yugoslavs were, when compared to Albania, a rich people, Albania's proximity to Yugoslavia would allow them to benefit financially from strong ties.[40] Marinković concluded that, although a fine race 'and patriotic towards their tribe or village, the Albanians had as yet no real conception of an Albanian State.'[41] Given this assessment, neither a government headed by Pašić nor Davidović appeared ready to open conciliatory talks with Noli.

Noli's visit to the League witnessed by far the greatest downturn in relations between the two countries. Noli's continued association with Hasan Prishtina and Bajram Curri at the League only created tension. From an external perspective, it was damaging as Noli's prolonged absence allowed Zogu considerable opportunity to probe for weaknesses in the coalition and foment disorder in border regions while Noli was not there to defend himself. The most significant incursion took place on September 24 and allegedly included some 500 tribesmen from Montenegro. It also appeared to Albanian officials that Yugoslav intentions were not only designed to test Albania's military preparedness, but also to intimidate the border delimitation commission that was due to arrive in the disputed area.[42] More importantly, the Albanians interpreted the incursion as the first step of Zogu's plan to take power by force.[43]

The reaction of the Albanian government was vehement. In a letter of September 26 to Kolonja, Delvina did not hold back. Putting the country on a war footing, Delvina stated that the government had ordered general mobilization in the region of Shkodër, and as the result of a meeting there, arms would be taken up to repel the invading Montenegrins.[44] Delvina added that the 'premeditated attack' of the Montenegrins had produced an excited atmosphere and that 'it would be difficult to calm the population, when blood continues to flow,' and he warned that 'all the consequences of this arbitrary violation of our frontier would fall on Yugoslavia.'[45] On September 26, Kolonja, in a much less provocative manner, complained that Montenegrin tribes had crossed into Albanian territory on September 25, that the action was coordinated with the activities of political refugees in Yugoslavia, and finally that these incursions constituted a 'violent act against the integrity of the Albanian state.'[46] Albanian legations abroad were further advised that the 'attack' on Albania made it obvious that the Yugoslavs were determined to have Vermosh and if they could not have it legally, they would take it by force.[47]

Since Noli's government recognized that continued appeals to Belgrade were useless, its agenda turned to other parts of the outside world in hopes of finding support. The Foreign Ministry tried to enlist the support of Great Britain, a country that had been so helpful during the Mirdita crisis, appealing to British representatives in Albania on September 25 and noting that the invading Montenegrin tribes had engaged Albanian forces.[48] In Paris, the Albanian legation asked Eduard Herriot, president of the Conference of Ambassadors, to intervene with Yugoslav authorities in order to maintain peace in the border region.[49] It declared that, based on authentic information, the Yugoslav government was helping in the formation of bands under the orders of exiled Albanians with the goal of destabilizing the Albanian government.[50] The Yugoslav government repeatedly denied the accusations, pointing the

Fan Noli in 1908.

Fan Noli and the Albanian federation Vatra, Copley Plaza Hotel, Boston, 1920.

Albanian cabinet in January 1922. The individuals in the photograph from left to right are: Mehmet Konica, Albanian delegate to the League of Nations; Spiro J. Koleka, Minister of Public Works; Fan S. Noli, Minister of Foreign Affairs; Ismail H. Tatzati, Minister of War; Xhafer Ypi, Prime Minister; Ahmed Zogu, Minister of the Interior; Hysen Vrioni, Minister of Justice; Kole Thaci, Minister of Finance. Courtesy of the General Directorate of the Albanian Archives, Tirana, Albania.

Fan Noli and Avni Rustemi. From Nasho Jorgaqi, *Jeta e Fan S. Nolit* (Tirana: Ombra GVG, 2005), 605.

Fan Noli and Albanian students in Rome (1922). From Nasho Jorgaqi, *Jeta e Fan S. Nolit* (Tirana: Ombra GVG, 2005), 605.

Fan Noli at the opening assembly of the Albanian parliament (1920). From Nasho Jorgaqi, *Jeta e Fan S. Nolit* (Tirana: Ombra GVG, 2005), 607.

Fan Noli as bishop. From Nasho Jorgaqi, *Fan S. Noli: Antologji Fotografike* (Tirana: Aferdita, 2002), 61.

The Albanian parliament (1920). From Nasho Jorgaqi, *Fan S. Noli: Antologji Fotografike* (Tirana: Aferdita, 2002), 62.

Luigi Gurakuqi and Bajram Curri. From Nasho Jorgaqi, *Fan S. Noli: Antologji Fotografike* (Tirana: Aferdita, 2002), 65.

finger at Albanians and arguing that this was evidence of the Tirana government's inability to maintain order.[51] The Yugoslavs insisted that it was the Albanians that had crossed into Montenegro, stolen three hundred cattle, and abducted two young women.[52]

At the League, Noli attacked the Yugoslav government for its role in the incursion by Montenegrin tribes into Albania. Noli rebutted Belgrade's accusation that border incursions were instigated by the Albanians:

> Listening to the representative of the Serb-Croat-Slovene State makes one feel that this is all bucolic idyll, in the best taste. Sheep and oxen are grazing before the attentive eyes of two young ladies, when suddenly Albanian gallants arrive and carry them off with their sheep and oxen. The parents of these charming ladies and the owners of the sheep and oxen dash off in pursuit, but strangely enough the parents and proprietors choose the point of their invasion into Albanian territory just near the mountain of Vermosh, the controversial point of the frontier ... Is that not one more argument for the Council of the League of Nations to put an end to this state of affairs and settle once and for all the frontier questions between Albania and the Kingdom of Serbs, Croats and Slovenes.[53]

The Yugoslav representative, A. Koumanoudi, claimed that regular forces had no involvement and it was merely a battle between tribes. Moreover, he argued that incursions by Albanians were becoming all too frequent and that his government had routinely protested to the Albanian government. However, according to the Yugoslav representative, owing to the fact that there was 'no organized power in Albania,'[54] Yugoslavia has never been able to achieve satisfaction.

Despite Noli's well-put arguments and a demand by the League for both countries to do all in their power to maintain the peace, the work on border delimitation also soured relations. The work of the commission in the north dragged on and put even more strains on the Albanian government, which could ill afford the financial obligations.[55] Moreover, Albania's almost incessant appeals to the League failed to attract supporters. Great Britain did not agree that the border incursions were politically inspired. It felt that Albania's 'inconsidered appeals' to the League were becoming too frequent; Britain's representative in Geneva was instructed to remind the Albanian government 'that the time of the Council must not be wasted by such unnecessary representations.'[56] Moreover, Harry Eyres considered the affair little more than a feud over grazing ground with no political overtones and, based on his information, held the Albanians responsible for making the original foray into Yugoslav territory.[57]

With Noli's appeals abroad not having the desired effect, the Yugoslav incursions achieved some successes in Albania for Zogu. Both Belgrade and Zogu were hoping to sow dissension in Noli's camp, and with him out of the country, it turned out to be quite easy since the euphoria of Noli's June march into Tirana had faded. Pro-landowner elements in the country remained strong and needed only to be reminded that Noli's program called for the redistribution of land. While winning over elements that for the most part were outsiders in Noli's coalition, these periodic threats to Albanian sovereignty led to considerable dissension in the army, which began to wonder if Noli was capable of maintaining the country's independence. Even local government officials questioned what they deemed the government's weak policy toward both Zogu and his Yugoslav supporters, and called for resolute action.[58] The army began to agitate openly against Noli, hoping to install a military government to safeguard Albanian sovereignty.[59]

This type of activity weakened support for Noli both within Albania and outside the country. The Great Powers and the League increasingly viewed Noli and his government as little more than a nuisance, plaguing the Great Powers and League with complaints and memoranda, and appearing determined to undermine Balkan stability. Given these attitudes, the foot-dragging by the delimitation commission, which was trying to determine Albania's northern and southern boundaries on the ground, appears, in hindsight, almost intentional. Since it was gradually accepted by the vast majority of outside powers that Noli's grasp on power was tenuous at best, it began to make more sense to allow the Albanians and Yugoslavs to come to some agreement outside of the League bureaucracy, since any League decision would have disappointed one of the parties. It was all too obvious that the Yugoslavs were determined, especially vis-à-vis Saint Naum, to have the territory at all costs, and that a decision in Albania's favour would only create more instability in the region. While Noli hoped the international community would solve, once and for all, the outstanding border issues, the international community would have preferred that Yugoslavia and Albania find some common ground on their own. Noli stubbornly relied on the League for support, while Ahmed Zogu concluded that the fate of an Orthodox monastery was hardly worth the cost of perpetual hostility from Belgrade.

The question of Saint Naum, which in the long run assumed the most significance for both sides and was their most fiercely contested border region, was an extremely knotty issue that did much to damage Yugoslav-Albanian relations. Vermosh and Saint Naum had been awarded to the Albanian state in November 1921 and 1922 respectively.[60] The territorial battle was both technical and tedious and did little to enhance either Albania's or Yugoslavia's status in the outside world. Moreover, the Albanian government could again ill afford the costs involved in pursuing this issue, even when it came to choosing a lawyer. The Albanians selected Gilbert Godel, a professor of law at the University of Paris, ostensibly because he had the lowest fee. Both Yugoslavia and Albania attached tremendous significance to the monastery, making it highly unlikely that a solution acceptable to both sides was possible. Since many Albanian leaders already considered Albania's 1921 borders to be unjust, they were unwilling to cede away more territory, no matter how insignificant. For Noli's government, the situation was even more difficult; losing territory would not help maintain fragile domestic support. Delvina had told Albania's foreign representatives in Geneva and London that Saint Naum was important both from a strategic and political point of view as well as to the position of the new government.[61]

In the months prior to Noli's seizure of power, the government had received countless telegrams from cities throughout Albania demanding the maintenance of Albania's territorial integrity.[62] For the Serbs, the territory was also considered vital and worth fighting for. In a conversation on June 21, Yugoslav foreign minister Ninčić told Alban Young, a British representative in Belgrade that 'no Serbian Government could survive which consented to surrender territory which was already Serbian.'[63] As the summer wore on, tension between the two states became critical and reached a climax in the fall and winter. In addition to the question of Saint Naum, the delimitation commission had yet to solve the border dispute at Vermosh, and both Yugoslavia and Albania took the opportunity to accuse each other of violating the frontier.

In terms of the Monastery of Saint Naum, the Serbian case was far stronger, and most powers recognized that fact.[64] The Albanian government had based its argument primarily on the 1913 decision that Saint Naum was an integral part of Albania. The Albanians also had their own historical arguments, pointing out that Saint Naum was venerated by the Albanian people, that Saints Cyril and Methodius had taken Naum on as an interpreter of the Albanian language, and that after his death the monastery had been built and subsequently maintained by Albanians. As to strategic concerns, which comprised the third pillar of the Albanian case, the Albanians argued that the loss of Saint Naum would cut communication between Korçë and Elbasan.[65] But for the Yugoslavs, Saint Naum was part of the glory of Ohrid, the centre of medieval Slavic learning, which was part of Yugoslavia. They considered both locations as inextricably linked to Slavic culture and religion. The Serbs argued that the region was of no religious importance to the Albanians and that to award the monastery to the Albanians would prove that international justice did not seek the 'pacification' of Europe.[66]

The Serbs' historical argument was thus considerably stronger, and the Albanians would have improved their overall status had they simply abandoned claims to the monastery. There was virtually no chance that the Serbs would back down, given the monastery's ties to Slavic culture and Orthodoxy. It is obvious that the Great Powers hoped that Albania and Yugoslavia would find a solution that met the demands of both sides, and that was an opportunity for Noli to prove his ability to compromise. On September 4 the International Court of Justice had decided that the Conference of Ambassadors had exhausted its mission with regard to Saint Naum, leaving it incumbent on the League and the Conference of Ambassadors to enforce the decision. However, the idea that Yugoslavia would accept the decision of the Court seemed unlikely. According to Miles Lampson, head of the Central Department of the British Foreign Office, the Serbs

> would do all they can to evade carrying out the decision of the Hague Court. Indeed, if they are compelled to hand over the Monastery to the Albanians, it is perhaps not an exaggeration to say that they will concentrate all their energies on getting it back at the earliest possible moment and this will not make for peace between Serbia and Albania.[67]

Even the Albanians worried that if the Yugoslavs could not secure Saint Naum and Vermosh legally, they would be prepared to take it by force. Throughout the late summer and fall, Albania continually predicted that Yugoslavia would take some military action.[68]

With the Yugoslavs determined to have Saint Naum and Vermosh, and Noli unwilling to bargain, Zogu was well placed to satisfy Yugoslav demands. There is considerable debate among historians as to just what type of agreement Zogu and Pašić forged while he was in Belgrade. Scholars in and outside Albania have differed on this point, but there seems to be a general consensus that Zogu did come to a verbal arrangement with Pašić. That there was an accord seems natural, given that Yugoslavia had concrete goals in Albania and Zogu was willing to make sacrifices, at least temporarily, to facilitate his own return. Živko Avramovski has argued that Zogu and Pašić came to a kind of 'gentleman's agreement,' and that nothing was put in writing. In this interpretation, Zogu agreed to five broad points: abandonment of the claim to Saint Naum and Vermosh; abolition of the Kosovo Committee; a greater role for the Serbian Orthodox Church in the affairs of the Albanian Orthodox Church; the creation of schools for the Serb and Macedonian minorities; and improved trade and economic links in Yugoslavia's favour.[69] Other historians suggest the accord was much more encompassing and had been put in writing.[70] An Italian diplomat in Durrës claimed to have received on good information the terms of the Pašić-Zogu accord.[71] According to this account, the agreement, which had sixteen points, would have made Albania little more than a province of Yugoslavia. While it included the points outlined by Avramovski, it also suggested that Zogu's regime would eventually become part of the Karadjordjević dynasty, the Albanian Orthodox Church would be placed under the control of the Serbian Orthodox Church, the Albanian War Ministry would be abolished, and that Yugoslavia would play an active role in the Albanian armed forces and gendarmerie and have the right to recruit Albanian soldiers.[72] While this variant is interesting, it cannot be taken as legitimate, given the lack of confirmation from Albanian archival sources,.

It appears that while the question of Vermosh and Saint Naum was paramount, Belgrade also wanted an end to support for Kosovo from Albanian soil, and sought greater economic and political influence in the country. All this Zogu was prepared to provide in the short-run, until he returned to power. Zogu was too shrewd a politician to risk placating only one power, and he was extremely adept at taking advantage of the power struggle between Italy and Yugoslavia for influence in Albania. While Zogu was working to meet the demands of Pašić, his lieutenants were trying to undermine Noli's attempts to win Rome's favour and convince Mussolini that Italy would benefit from Zogu's return. With Zogu's willingness to make concessions in both Belgrade and Rome, Noli could compete only by outbidding Zogu. From Noli's perspective, although it might have made considerable sense to abandon the claim to Vermosh and Saint Naum and distance himself from the Kosovo cause in favour of dialogue with Yugoslavia, he could ill afford such a concession. Equally important, Noli's stubborn faith in the correctness of his program blinded him to the need for realpolitik closer to home.

In Yugoslavia, Noli found only one person willing to defend him: the Croat Peasant Party leader Stjepan Radić. Like Noli, Radić was a progressive thinker determined to solve the peasant question and supportive of a Balkan federation. Both men were willing to open a dialogue with

Soviet Russia. As part of Radić's wider attack on the Serbian political establishment in October 1924,[73] he issued an emotional plea on behalf of Noli, which the Albanians considered to be almost a watershed in their relations with Yugoslavia since he was the first Yugoslav politician to support the arguments Noli had been making all along. Radić stated that Albania's position in the Balkans was unfortunate since 'Italy, Serbia and Greece desire to occupy Albania. Italy from the sea, Serbia will take Shkoder and Greece will enter Epirus.'[74] Radić went on to state that the Albanian government was 'more progressive than the government of Belgrade' and that Albania maintains 'correct politics and has a wise man as Prime Minister.'[75] Radić's coup de grâce was his statement that 'the Croat people will not fight with Albania and that no Croats would pass Albania's border to seize its freedom.'[76]

In Belgrade, Radić's declaration was considered to be an act of 'betrayal' and widely condemned.[77] It was used to further arguments that Yugoslavia faced a danger from a Bolshevik plot and that there existed an alliance of Radić, Noli, and the Third International.[78] For the Albanians, Radić's declaration was above all proof of what Noli's government had been saying all along: Yugoslavia had hostile intentions toward Albania.[79] Delvina advised Kolonja that Radić's statements had created a 'profound impression,' and the Albanian Information Bureau advised all consulates and relevant press offices of the importance of Radić's position, especially in light of War Minister Hadžić's resignation. Hadžić, who resigned because of Radić's activities and rejected participation in a government that had Radić's support, dubbed Radić's actions 'defeatist.'[80] As well, Radić's declaration and the Albanian response was sent immediately to the League Secretariat as proof of what the Albanians had been arguing in the League throughout the summer and fall.[81] Noli was elated at finding a potential ally in what seemed a permanently hostile Yugoslavia. However, his hope that Radić's statements would somehow 'awaken' the Great Powers to Yugoslavia's position was not borne out. In the long run, however, Noli came to view Radić with considerable sympathy. In a letter to Radić, written at the end of 1926, Noli thanked Radić for the sympathy that he had 'always shown to the Albanian cause and to me personally.'[82]

Greece

If Belgrade's hostility to Albania intensified with Noli's seizure of power, Greek policy had maintained a degree of consistency since Albanian independence. The legacy of Albanian-Greek relations had not been favourable. As already noted, in the aftermath of Albanian independence in 1912, Greece had been steadfast in its demands that parts of southern Albania, or Northern Epirus, should become part of Greece. Added to this, when thwarted in its territorial ambitions, Greece often tried to use the Greek minority in southern Albania as a vehicle with which to destabilize Albania as well as to keep the territorial issue alive. From the Albanian viewpoint, Greece's position on the new state was embodied in two agreements: the 1915 Secret Treaty of London and the July 1919 Tittoni-Venizelos Agreement, both of which sought territorial gains in the southern provinces of Gjirokastër and Korçë. It was not the type of historical legacy that made for a spirit of cooperation.

The Greek position on Albania was also embodied in two additional agreements: the Protocol of Corfu of 17 May 1914 between Albania and Greece and the 1920 Treaty of Kapestitsa. In the former agreement, the Albanians had agreed to autonomy for the provinces of Korçë and Gjirokastër. According to Greek sources, the agreement met with 'the unreserved approval of the Prince of Wied.'[83] Wied, as noted, had arrived in Albania with virtually no idea what to expect, and one of his first orders of business was to deal with events in southern Albania. Under the leadership of George Zographos, the Greek Epirots had succeeded in establishing an independent Northern Epirus. Under pressure from all sides, including Greece, Zographos agreed to negotiate a settlement, and the end result was, in effect, full autonomy 'under the purely nominal hegemony of Prince Wied.'[84] Albanian historians argue, and not without foundation, not only that Wied did not know what he was doing, but also that the agreement was forced upon him by Greece and the Allied Control Commission.[85]

The Treaty of Kapestitsa of May 1920 also provided extensive guarantees to the Greek minority.[86] Fan Noli declared that it was agreed to only 'under the menace of Greek guns.'[87] The Greeks maintained that the Albanians only signed the agreement to assure Greek cooperation to counter growing Italian pressure for territory in Albania, and that with the removal of Italian troops in August 1920, the Albanians simply turned their backs on the agreement. According to the Greeks, the Albanians had violated both agreements. It was therefore not surprising that Greece greeted with considerable hostility the November 1921 decision by the Conference of Ambassadors to re-establish Albania's 1913 borders. Temporarily thwarted in its bid to secure territory, Greece continued to push for enforcement of the Corfu Protocol.

The Greek claim to Albanian territory is hard to define precisely, but would include the area south of a line drawn from near Korçë in the east to Vlorë on Albania's Adriatic coast, encompassing essentially the entire provinces of Gjirokastër and Korçë. Since the region was almost 25 per cent of Albanian territory and the most developed part of the country, from an economic standpoint, Albania could not survive without it. For the Greeks, however, its significance was less important economically than as an expression of the simple desire to expand and fulfill the Great Idea. The eventual post–First World War settlement of Albania's frontiers angered the Greeks considerably, and many felt that owing to Albania's territorial losses in the north to Serbia and Montenegro, the Great Powers were compensating Albania with territory in the south that was rightly Greek.[88] Greece challenged parts of the settlement, especially regarding some villages around the town of Korçë, and Greek troops remained there until 1924. The Greek position during Albania's early attempts at nation building was not a small factor in Albania's failure to consolidate a viable democracy in the early 1920s. Since Albania was overwhelmingly weak at the time, it laid the foundations for a later fear of Greek intentions that has plagued relations to this day.

Territorial claims to Albania's southern region were based on the false notion that it was primarily Greek, and that the Greek minority had not been accorded full rights in the Albanian state. In trying to prove the 'Greekness' of the region, Greek official circles used dubious statistical data to calculate the number of Greeks. While the number of Greeks in the inter-war Albanian state numbered roughly 50,000,[89] Greece put forth figures that were much higher. Greek claims were based on Ottoman census data of 1908, which suggested that the region in question had some 120,000 Greeks and 80,000 Albanians.[90] The Albanians countered with the argument that since the Ottoman Empire was a theocratic state, those Albanians who were Orthodox Christian were wrongly designated Greeks. By and large, however, the Greeks failed in their attempts to prove the region was more Greek than Albanian.[91]

While the Conference of Ambassadors had established a neutral zone around Korçë, pending the final delimitation of the Albanian-Greek border, a League commission of enquiry confirmed the validity of the Albanian claim. In December 1921 a three-person delegation arrived in Albania to observe firsthand the situation in Albania's southern perimeter.[92] The commission found, for the most part, that the majority of the citizens in the disputed region 'were in favour of the present regime,' and that a serious menace to Albanian independence was posed by the idea, primarily put forth by her neighbours, that Albanians were not inherently a nation.[93] In the much-disputed town of Korçë, League commissioner Sederholm noted that the population was 'entirely Albanian; the number of Greeks there is quite insignificant.'[94] In his May 1922 report, Sederholm also defended Albania's minority policy, stating that 'Greek schools for the Greek minority, which numbers about 16,000, are already established and are subsidized by the Albanian government in accordance with the rules laid down for the protection of minorities.'[95] Sederholm did add, however, that the Albanian government opposed the teaching of Greek in Albanian schools 'because it fears the influence of the teachers, the majority of whom have openly declared themselves in favour of the Pan-Epirot movement.'[96]

Joseph Emerson Haven, a U.S. diplomat based in Italy on special detail in Albania during the spring of 1919, had already come to a similar conclusion. In his detailed report on the political situation in the country, Haven suggested that the disputed province of Korçë had roughly 60,000 inhabitants, roughly 18 per cent of whom were in favour of Greek sovereignty.[97] Of those 18 per cent, he argued, half were seeking that end out of fear or had been promised material gain in the form of Moslem land and property.[98] Haven asserted that the Greek Church was engaged in a litany of activities designed to intimidate Albanians, including the burning to death of women and children, mutilation, and torture, as well as rape at the hands of Greek soldiers.[99] Haven found that the 'most intense hatred and loathing exists in Southern Albania for Greece, this hatred being shown by both Orthodox Christians and Musselmen. The cry is "We are Albanians first and religionists second." With the exception of comparatively few residents in the province of Coritsa [Korçë] and a few towns in the region of Chimara [Himarë], the country is absolutely Albanian in sentiment.'[100]

Even the British representative in Albania, Harry Eyres, who has been much maligned by Albania's communist and post-communist historians for anti-Albanian actions, defended the Albanian position on the disputed areas. In his May 1921 report to the Foreign Office, Eyres noted that the Greek government 'appears to make no distinction between Orthodox Albanians of the southern provinces and veritable Greek subjects.'[101] Eyres added that in Greece there was a 'set purpose to disseminate false news' and that Greek claims that the minority was being persecuted and schools were being closed had 'little or no basis in fact.'[102] Since at the time the Conference of Ambassadors had yet to confirm Albania's borders and Greece was lobbying heavily for a change in its favour, Eyres's attitude on the issue is important as Great Britain tended to support, at least partially, the Greek position. Eyres declared:

> ... it is in the hands of the Great Powers to create an independent Albania or the reverse but an independent Albania deprived of the provinces of North Epirus would not be a practical proposition from the economic point of view. It could not make headway against the financial difficulty.[103]

Eyres also joined in supporting the League commission's report that in both disputed provinces Moslems outnumbered Christians. In the long run, Greek claims of Albanian mistreatment fell on deaf ears, and Britain finally advised its representative to the Conference that further complaints not be heard and that matters be dealt with between the two countries on a diplomatic level.[104] In June 1922, Greece had appealed to the Conference of Ambassadors to enforce the Protocol of Corfu granting autonomy to the southern provinces. In a Foreign Office dispatch to Lord Hardinge, the British ambassador in Paris, Lord Balfour noted that the protocol was 'no longer a valid instrument. In the fist place the Epirots themselves violated it in July 1914, by occupying Koritza [Korçë]. In the second place it has been superseded by subsequent enactments ... It is also noticeable that the Greeks never mentioned the protocol during the time when they thought that Northern Epirus was going to fall to them.'[105] In July 1922, blocked in its attempts to internationalize the problem, Greece finally offered *de jure* recognition to the Albanian government but included a protest note on the southern frontier.

Underlying the question over territory was the question of religion. The use by Greece of religious identification to further its claims to the region goes a long way to explain why Albania's Orthodox community went to such great lengths in the inter-war period to secure its independence from the Ecumenical Patriarchate of Constantinople. Many church leaders, especially Noli, believed that the Patriarchate was little more than a tool of Greek influence. The quest for an independent Albanian Orthodox Church was initiated primarily by Orthodox Albanians who had emigrated to the United States; its success was achieved through the Herculean efforts of Noli, among others. One of Noli's key agendas had been to do away with Greek influence in Albanian Orthodoxy, and thus rid the country of what was clearly a negative influence since Greek clerics often worked as agitators for the Greek cause. Noli had made an important step early in his career when he translated the liturgy into Albanian, and the Berat Congress of September 1922 set forth the fundamental goals of the Albanian Orthodox Church. It declared that the metropolitans should be Albanian, and that the language of the divine liturgy should be in Albanian except in areas frequented by the Greek communities in and around Gjirokastër.[106] The decision to enforce Albanian nationality on church leaders was a direct blow to Greek influence in the country. Indeed, Greek clerics went to the greatest lengths to prevent the Orthodox Albanians from establishing an independent church.[107] A lack of qualified church personnel and hostility from the Patriarchate delayed the emergence of the autocephalous Albanian Orthodox Church.[108] However, the delays in officially recognizing the church were of little consequence, for the independence of the church was more or less a *fait accompli*. From the Albanian perspective, it was a monumental achievement and vital to the country's national unity.[109]

The suggestion that Greek Orthodox clergy were often using their position to further separatist causes was well documented by independent observers in the aftermath of the war. In 1919 American special representative Haven wrote that Greek teachers and priests in the provinces of Gjirokastër and Korçë were 'the chief offenders in the matter of propaganda as they can penetrate into a home without difficulty and once there, it takes courage indeed to defy them and thus become marked for certain persecution and possible torture and death.'[110] Sederholm later added that Greek church officials there were 'working openly for the detachment of Southern Albania and for its union with Greece.'[111] Sederholm also added that the Greek metropolitans had appealed to him 'in the hope that your feeling for what is right and just may result in ... the union of all the Northern Epirus with Greece.'[112] In the spring of 1921, Albania was forced to expel the bishop of Korçë, a Greek, because he had become, in the words of Sederholm, 'the mouthpiece of Hellenism in Albania.'[113] A cornerstone of Greek policy, an approach also employed by the Yugoslavs, was to encourage religious differences in Albania and stress that Albania was a 'little Turkey' hostile to Orthodox Greeks. To popularize the idea of two Albanian states, one Moslem, the other Christian, throughout the early 1920s Greece continually complained that Albania's majority Moslem population was actively persecuting the Orthodox minority. Albania denied this, stressed its well-documented legacy of religious tolerance, and added that while there was tension in the southern perimeter of the country, it was not between Moslems and Christians, but rather a rift had emerged because of the movement to create an autocephalous Albanian Orthodox Church and some citizens wished to remain under the Patriarchate.[114]

While Greek Orthodox clerics tried to further the Greek 'Great Idea,' other factors in the early 1920s had further created an atmosphere of mistrust between Albania and Greece. A key problem, deeply inter-twined with Greek territorial claims, was the murder on 27 August 1923 of General Tellini, the Italian representative on the international delimi-tation commission working in southern Albania. While the murder of Tellini and his staff may have been a product of mere brigandage and was not politically motivated,[115] the Greek government and press sought to implicate the Albanians. Yet the charge was scarcely credible as the Albanians had come to view Tellini as partial to their position in the disputed regions and in the aftermath of the collapse of the Tittoni-Venizelos agreement, saw Italy as an important source of support against Greek claims. In its response to the Greek accusations, the Albanian Foreign Ministry lauded Tellini's support and pointed out that Albania, which had been waiting a long time to obtain permanent borders at a cost the government could barely sustain, had little to gain by further delays.[116] The Greeks, on the other hand, realizing that Tellini was pro-Albanian, had much to gain by having him murdered and then trying to implicate the Albanians.[117] Whatever the reason, the Greek position and the virulent press campaign against Albania in the aftermath of the trag-edy were not the stuff of which friendly relations were built, and angered the Albanians considerably.

Population exchanges between Greece and Turkey, as a result of the 1923 Treaty of Lausanne, created another fault line in Albanian-Greek relations. In the spring of 1924, Albania accused Greece of including ethnic Albanians in the population exchanges in an effort to eliminate Albanians from the still disputed parts of southern Albania, especially some fourteen villages around Korçë, where Greek troops remained pending the announcement of a final decision by the Conference of Ambassadors. According to Albania's prefect in Korçë, on February 28 the Greeks were moving Albanian citizens, confiscating property, and acting in contravention of international law and counter to declarations made by Greece at the League of Nations.[118] Late in February 1924, the Albanian government asked the Greek government to end the exchange of Albanians of the Korçë district, as it was prejudging the decision of the Conference of Ambassadors and undermining good relations.[119] In the hope of gaining some international support, Albania's representative in London, Mehmet Konica, appealed on March 4 for British support, but was told to take his appeal to the Conference of Ambassadors.[120] From the Greek perspective, the Lausanne Treaty heightened the importance of the Greek community in Albania; having lost one important foothold in the Mediterranean, Greece was even more determined to preserve the last vestige of a Greek community in a region outside of Greece.

By mid-April 1924, the question of the fourteen villages around Korçë had been ostensibly solved when they were definitively awarded to Albania. Yet, despite the decision of the Conference of Ambassadors, Greece continued to press the issue and remained reluctant to comply with the decision. In early May, the prefect of Korçë again advised the Interior Ministry that Greece was continuing to force Albanians from their homes. Greece, which refused to accept the decision, sent a protest to the Conference of Ambassadors.[121] Moreover, in mid-May, it appeared to Albania that Greece was preparing some kind of armed action because of a large concentration of troops in the region of Florina and Jannina. An Albanian Interior Ministry report on May 15 advised the Foreign Ministry that Greece was preparing to occupy Korçë.[122] In response to the perceived threat, Albania prepared its own reaction but also undertook to advise the League and the Great Powers. While the movement of Greek troops came to nothing, it underlines the tension that plagued relations in the early stages of Noli's revolution. Greece, like Yugoslavia and Italy, adopted a policy of non-intervention in Albania's internal affairs, but nevertheless was willing to intervene if things deteriorated and threatened Greek interests.

When Noli came to power, he thus faced not only a serious territorial battle with Yugoslavia over Saint Naum and Vermosh, but Greek forces in the disputed area remained and refused to accept the decision to award it to Albania. Noli hoped that since he was an Orthodox Christian who spoke fluent Greek, he might establish an amicable relationship with Greece. Greece's alliance with Yugoslavia, which lasted until the fall of 1924, was one major obstacle. More importantly, as a nationalist who had been among the most vocal critics of Greek influence in the country's southern periphery and a founder of the Albanian Orthodox Church, Noli was considered anti-Greek. While he fought the dominance of large landowners in Tirana, he also sought to rid the south of Greek influence. The persistence of unresolved territorial claims, along with Greece's insistence that Albania was not doing all it could to meet the demands of the Greek minority, made Noli's situation extremely difficult.

But this became obvious only over time. At first, Noli hoped for amicable relations, and Greece appeared ready to reciprocate. On June 24 the Albanian Foreign Ministry advised the legations in Rome, Belgrade, Athens, and Paris that the 'Greek government had officially recognized the Albanian Government.'[123] Furthermore, according to the Albanian Press Bureau, on June 21 the Greek minister in Albania had declared his willingness to work for 'cordial and beneficial' relations.[124] Nevertheless, Greece chose to use the Noli interregnum to foster its own ends and never lived up to its official statements. At the same time, Albania's minister in Athens, Midhat Frashëri, advised the Foreign Ministry that Greece was preparing a new démarche before the Conference of Ambassadors to demand revision of the territorial settlement around Korçë.[125] Through its alliance with Yugoslavia and the blatant support of Yugoslav territorial demands, Greece hoped to force a new decision on the fourteen villages and possibly secure even greater concessions for the tiny Greek minority. Like Yugoslavia, Greece identified Noli's victory as a product of Italian influence and did not want to be left out of the potential spoils. But unlike Yugoslavia, Greece had limited means at its disposal to force change in its favour.

In order to achieve good relations with Greece, the outstanding territorial questions and issues relating to the Greek minority in Albania needed to be solved. Greece, through both governmental and nongovernmental groups like the Pan-Epirot Society, which promoted the unification of Northern and Southern Epirus, and the Greek Orthodox Church, attempted to force territorial changes in Greece's favour. Noli was thus forced to dedicate considerable time and effort to arguing Albania's case. Greece's refusal to accept the April 1924 decision led nowhere, and in August 1924 the Conference of Ambassadors handed down another decision, which confirmed the previous one. Greek troops were ordered to withdraw from the disputed area.[126] Yet Greece still refused to remove its troops. Worried that an already tense situation might become worse, Noli decided, in order to counter the Greek troop presence, to send a small number of Albanian reservists to the region in response to a War Ministry request.[127] Whether Noli anticipated an armed conflict is not clear, but by the summer of 1924 it seemed that the Albanian government interpreted the Greek position as preparing to secure the disputed territory by force. While Greek troops remained in the region until October 1924, three months after an evacuation order, Noli was forced to appeal even more often for League assistance, and during his visit to the League had to square off against the combined forces of Greece and Yugoslavia.

In the months prior to Noli's visit to Geneva, relations between Greece and Albania grew increasingly worse and were characterized by a stream of accusations and counter-accusations. Greece maintained that Noli's government had brought unparalleled anarchy to southern Albania, complete with violence against Greek churches and schools.[128] Since Greece had been thwarted in its territorial demands, it maintained pressure on Albania through the Greek minority. Tension was high as a result of complaints, especially from the Greek community in Himarë, a town just south of Vlorë on the Adriatic coast. On August 10 the Greek government made an official protest, accusing Noli's government of suppressing the rights of the minority in that region,[129] and the Pan-Epirot Society sent a vocal criticism to League general secretary Eric Drummond on August 22 claiming systematic persecution of the Greeks in Himarë.

Albania denied the accusations and instead suggested that the allegations were made merely because 'certain foreign elements [most certainly meant to denote the Greeks] had the goal of creating trouble in Albania,'[130] and that Albania actively complied with the League's minority rights treaties. Albania's response to Greek criticism of its minority policy was to raise again the issues of the forced removal of ethnic Moslem Albanians from the Korçë region and their transfer to Turkey, and the alleged mistreatment of the Albanian minority in northern Greece (Çameria). Greece insisted that a neutral commission had overseen the process and that there had been no irregularities. In a letter to the Albanian foreign minister on August 5, the Greek representative in Durrës, Nako Panourias, denied any wrongdoing in the population exchanges and suggested that those Moslem Albanians who did take part in the exchanges did so of their own free will.[131]

In the summer, the Albanian government, increasingly concerned about Greece's intentions, suspected that it was actively trying to foment trouble in southern Albania. Albanian police first arrested a Greek ship captain on charges of espionage. At the same time, the Albanian government grew worried that ethnic Greek teachers in the south were in the pay of Athens to make propaganda in Greece's favour.[132] While the latter suggestion remained within the confines of the Albanian bureaucracy, the arrest of the captain created considerable ill feeling. In August 1924 a Greek ship arrived in the southern port of Saranda with correspondence from Corfu. The captain of the ship was immediately arrested. The Greek government protested energetically, demanding his immediate release, an indemnity, and the punishment of the soldiers responsible.[133] The Albanian prefect in Gjirokastër was steadfast in his claim that the captain's purpose had been to 'gather information of a secret nature on the situation in southern Albania.'[134] While the Albanians eventually complied with the Greek government's request, it was only after three appeals and accusations that the captain had been tortured.

While incidents such as these seem rather insignificant, they are indicative of the general state of affairs that marked Greek-Albanian relations while Noli was prime minister. Greece remained unreconciled to Albania's borders and tried to keep the issue alive through the minority, while Albania began to see the minority as a kind of fifth column in the country. Matters worsened when Noli arrived at the League. In a letter of September 27, Noli appealed to the League for assistance in removing Greek troops from Albanian soil and reiterated the accusation that Greece was forcibly removing Moslem Albanians from the disputed area.[135] Greece denied the accusation and chastised Noli for calling for League assistance under Article II of the Covenant. The Greek representative at the League, M. Politis, noted that since the Albanian case against Greece was so weak, Noli had little choice but to fall back on Article II, 'which relates to the threat of war or serious circumstances which threaten to disturb international peace. Arguments of this kind are not put forward unless other arguments cannot be found.'[136]

The question of Greek troops on Albanian soil, which Noli considered to be a most serious problem, was also not solved to his satisfaction. While Greece welcomed League supervision of the population exchanges, its attitude on the evacuation of Albanian territory was marked by stalling tactics. Politis's explanation was feeble:

> The Greek government thought it its duty to exhaust all means at its disposal to cause the Conference of Ambassadors to change a decision which the Greek Government considered unjust. The Conference has, however, maintained its opinion, and its decision is final. This decision was taken on August 25, that is, at a time when our Parliament was not in session ... as soon as Parliament meets – that is, shortly – it will submit a draft authorizing us to accept this slight alienation from its territory. It is therefore clear that it is purely a constitutional point of order which has prevented my Government from carrying out the decision of the Conference of Ambassadors.[137]

Politis added that 'ceaseless clamours, however, reach us from this province which has now become Albanian; complaints of ill-treatment, of the closing of schools, of the suppression of every vestige of a civilisation centuries old.'[138] Noli did not think that Greece was compelled to submit the question to its parliament, and as to the suggestion that Albania was closing Greek schools, he added that there were '28 schools for the 32,000 citizens that speak Greek, whereas at Scutari [Shkodër] there are only 24 schools for a population of 110,000 which is exclusively Albanian. In Greece the Albanian minorities have no schools at their disposal.'[139]

While relations took a notable downturn during Noli's visit to the League, it was Greece's decision to support Yugoslavia's claim to Saint Naum that caused the most damage to relations. Both states had clearly agreed early on to support their respective claims, and each hoped to profit from the apparent weakness of Noli's government. During the July sessions at The Hague to decide the fate of Saint Naum, the Greeks had asked to present information on the issue, and the request was granted. In the long run, the Greeks furnished the Court with documents concerning the delimitation of the border around Saint Naum that suggested there was some difference in wording. Regardless, disappointment was the state of affairs in Albania. In a July telegram to Athens and Rome, Delvina noted that Greece had presented information supporting the Yugoslav position in The Hague, and that the move was a 'surprise to Albanian public opinion and in complete opposition with the formal assurances on an amicable policy toward Albania given by the Greeks.'[140]

However, with Greece's eventual abandonment of the Korçë district by the end of October, it appeared that Greece and Albania had an opportunity to improve the situation. Hoping to capitalize on the removal of Greek troops and the apparent end of border problems, which the Albanians wrongly identified as the main reason for Greek intransigence, Delvina advised the Interior Ministry on November 6 that with evacuation of the villages there existed the possibility of good relations.[141] Seeking to avoid any further complications, Delvina also advised that the Albanian army should not provide the Greeks with any pretexts that would undermine much-needed good relations.[142] Not only were Noli and his government extremely optimistic, but League observers had long assumed that once the boundary disputes were settled, relations between the two countries could move forward.

While doing battle with the Greek delegate in Geneva, Noli also took the time to speak out through several Greek newspapers on the need for good relations. In a September interview with *Politika,* Noli blamed poor relations on unresolved borders, but observed that a solution had been found. While noting that Greeks remained in Albania and vice versa, Noli defended his country's minority policy and declared that the minorities 'should not serve as an obstacle, but as bond and bridge of agreement between us.'[143] In several interviews while on a subsequent

trip to Rome, Noli declared a willingness to work for amicable and
beneficial relations and pointed to the need to develop stronger commercial ties. As well, Noli tried to dispel the myth that Albania was a
'little Turkey.' While acknowledging that Albania was a predominantly
Moslem country, he argued that it was a tolerant country, and proof of
that fact was that the head of all Albanians was an Orthodox bishop.[144]
In another interview with a Bulgarian newspaper, Noli added that in
Albania there was 'no official faith and religious fanaticism did not
exist.'[145] To the Greek newspaper *Nea Imera,* Noli stated that there was a
need 'to eradicate this little fight between us. We are a small state and
we have a need for peace.'[146]

The formal end of the Greek occupation of the fourteen villages and
Noli's call for a new beginning coincided with the end of the Yugoslav-
Greek alliance in October 1924. The rejection by the Conference of
Ambassadors of Greek territorial claims on Albania no doubt had something to do with the break (although there were other, more important
differences), as a common policy on Albania had been an element of the
alliance: not only in terms of supporting each other's territorial claims,
but also in hoping to foster and eventually capitalize on religious and
regional differences. In his report of November 19 from Athens, Mehdi
Frasheri advised Tirana that the Yugoslav government had denounced its
alliance with Greece. Frasheri identified two points relating to Albania
that forced a change in Belgrade: (1) the recognition of the Albanian
government by Greece without the agreement of the Yugoslav government; (2) the evacuation by Greece of the fourteen villages, which made
Belgrade's position on Saint Naum more difficult.[147]

However, this apparent breakthrough came to nothing, and Greece
and Albania were not able to begin a new chapter in their relations.
Firstly, the change came far too late for Noli to capitalize on it. The sched-
uled elections meant that most outside powers adopted a wait-and-see
policy. As well, forces opposed to Noli, both inside and outside the country, were gaining the upper hand. Secondly, Greece assumed that Noli
was a purely transitional figure and hoped to benefit from his departure.
Lastly, an abrupt change in Greek policy was inconceivable since Greece
refused to accept that southern Albania was rightly Albanian.

In the years between the Congress of Lushnjë in January 1920 and Noli's
seizure of power in June 1924, Albania's immediate neighbours did
nothing to encourage domestic stability. Both states had yet to reconcile
themselves to even the independence of Albania. A less hostile position

from Greece and Yugoslavia would have given Albania vital breathing space to begin state building and complete the task of nation building. However, Yugoslavia and Greece remained frustrated by the re-creation of an independent Albania and retained an interest in fomenting religious and regional discontent designed to call into question Albania's right to exist. Zogu's ability to avoid confrontation with both Greece and Yugoslavia had earned him allies in Athens and Belgrade. Both, for different reasons, would have preferred that he remain at the helm. For the Yugoslavs, Zogu was completely unwilling to interfere at any level in the Kosovo question – that was already proven. Moreover, Zogu seemed to understand that Albania needed some kind of *modus vivendi* with the Yugoslavs if any type of stability was to be maintained.

Noli's seizure of power worsened the situation considerably, and cooperation between Greece and Yugoslavia in furthering traditional policy goals received a new impetus. For the Yugoslav government, Noli's near activist stance on Kosovo was a considerable threat. Also, with Zogu in Belgrade, the Yugoslavs had an excellent opportunity to achieve some concrete concessions, especially in terms of border changes that they had sought since 1912. Noli, from the outset, was thus in a very difficult position in trying to secure good relations with the Yugoslav government. Judging from the type of arrangement Zogu made with Pašić, Noli's hands were tied and there was little that he could offer the Yugoslavs without doing irreparable damage to his domestic position. Breaking ties with the Kosovo Committee was out of the question since he would have lost their military support. Moreover, Noli's decision to carry the banner of the Kosovar struggle was not a cynical choice. Hopeful that the League would stand by him, he sincerely believed that his brethren to the north deserved a better deal. Any concessions on territory would have also met with derision, so that the question of Saint Naum and Vermosh was essentially closed as far as Noli was concerned. Zogu's eventual rectification of both concerns in Yugoslavia's favour came at a time when he was in complete control. Noli never exercised the type of control needed to entertain compromise with Belgrade.

Yugoslavia's policy of non-recognition, allegedly adopted because Noli's government was illegal, was an excellent tool for fostering internal instability in Albania. Noli therefore needed to legalize his rule in order to eliminate the means by which neighbouring countries could foster disorder and discontent. From a regional perspective, his first order of business should have been the legitimization of his own position. Armed with a mandate from the people, Zogu's position would have deteriorated considerably, especially since such a move might have appeased powers other than Yugoslavia. Yet, for reasons already discussed, Noli refused to go to the polls.

Greece, unable to achieve any substantive changes in Albania's borders, used its minority in Albania as a means to foster instability there. After finally offering recognition to Albania, Greece remained steadfast in its attempt to foster discontent among the Orthodox Greeks in southern Albania, by using the Greek Orthodox Church, Greek teachers, and other elements of the Greek population, and by keeping Greek troops in the disputed region until the fall of 1924. The continually hostile and provocative attitude toward Noli's government was no small factor in hampering the implementation of the reform agenda since dealing with external problems absorbed the bulk of Noli's time. Noli's assumption of power did little to assuage Greek concerns. His early battle against Greek religious influence was one factor, as was the fact that he was an Orthodox Christian. Greece's position on Albania, which was shaped primarily on the notion that Albania was a 'little Turkey,' lost much of its credibility with Noli in power. For official Greece, eager to convince the outside world that Orthodox Greeks were living under a state of siege because of governments dominated by Albania's traditional ruling class, a return of Zogu's clique was welcome if only to vindicate its position. While Noli had some distasteful avenues open to him to placate the Yugoslavs, Greek policy was carved in stone and he had no room to manoeuvre, barring a surrender of territory.

Facing poor relations with his neighbours, Noli put considerable emphasis on broadening Albania's ties with the outside world in hopes of finding an impartial supporter that could in turn pressure the Greeks and Yugoslavs. This agenda also faced serious obstacles, and Noli's policy decisions on an international level often served to worsen the relations with his neighbours. Armed with a fatal Albano-centrism, Noli seemed incapable of seeing the wider picture, and he unfortunately assumed that the Great Powers or the League would solve the regional dilemma for him. The Great Powers, while supporting the existence of an independent Albania, were unwilling to assume the role of perpetual mediator in regional problems. While Yugoslavia claimed that it was following the lead of the Great Powers in terms of recognition, it was the Great Powers that were following the lead of neighbouring powers. A peaceful Balkans, which meant that Albania had to find its own way to less hostile relations with Greece and Yugoslavia, was the cornerstone of Great Power policy.

5
Great Britain, Italy, and the United States[1]

Noli placed great hopes in Great Britain as his best possible ally. His experience at the League, where British support proved so vital on a number of issues, shaped his ideas. Moreover, as a firm supporter of the British parliamentary system, he hoped in the long run to establish a similar system in Albania. In an interview in Geneva with the *Times,* Noli declared that the Albanians would not soon forget that their country's admission to the League was due chiefly to Britain's and the Dominions' support.[2] Great Britain, he reasoned, was a disinterested power in a good position to help without undermining Albania's sovereignty. In the early 1920s, Noli's assessment of Britain was sustained and enhanced by British interest in Albania, which reached a peak in the early 1920s.[3] Britain had yet to 'hand over' Albania completely to the Italian sphere of influence, and sought the maintenance of Albanian independence in order to preserve both stability and the regional balance of power in the Balkans.

In the years that preceded Noli's revolution, Britain had not only helped to maintain Albanian sovereignty, but had also ensured itself a paramount role in the country. The British embassy recommended British military officers, such as Colonel W.F. Stirling, to aid in the reorganization of Albania's gendarmerie and Interior Ministry.[4] Stirling had tried to secure a position with the Albanian government in the spring of 1924 and, in a letter to Illias Vrioni, noted that because of the many friends and relatives who held 'high positions' in the British government and army, he hoped 'to influence English public opinion in favour of Albania.'[5] While the process of securing Stirling's assistance broke down with Noli's seizure of power, Noli's government was eager to maintain this connection. Interior Minister Shala wrote Stirling on July 17: 'If you have no serious family obligations I shall be very much obliged to have you come to Tirana, in order to take up with us the organization of our administration.'[6]

However, while Noli sought strong ties with Great Britain, he was continually frustrated by British intransigence on the question of recognition. Prior to Noli's seizure of power, Great Britain, through its minister in Durrës, Harry Eyres, had established a good working relationship with Zogu. Eyres, who played a key role in shaping British policy toward Noli, did not greet the new government with enthusiasm. According to Eyres, Zogu had brought much-needed stability, and Noli's group appeared poised to undermine this, especially vis-à-vis relations with neighbouring Yugoslavia. The quest for an oil concession, which Great Britain's Anglo-Persian Oil Company (APOC) pursued, also helped define London's attitude. Owing to entrenched policies and a crude assessment of Albania's potential to move beyond tribalism, Great Britain adopted a reserved attitude toward Noli, considering him merely a transitional figure.

In the days preceding Noli's seizure of power, Eyres had already worked in favour of the previous regime. Thus, when Noli assumed power, he had already developed a suspicious attitude toward Eyres, whom he identified as a partisan of Zogu. Neither could hide his dislike for the other. As an American diplomat noted, Eyres had said often that Noli 'ought to be hanged,' while Noli had adjured his friends to 'knock Mr. Eyres down for me when you see him.'[7] Early on, Eyres had been identified by American diplomats as a man who possessed profound influence with Zogu. Maxwell Blake, the U.S. commissioner to Albania, noted that Eyres was 'clean but slippery,'[8] and the American consul in Trieste added in April 1922 that Eyres was 'universally liked and has much influence in the councils of state. Undoubtedly the situation will result favourably to England in the matter of concessions for minerals and oil.'[9] It is true that Eyres had provided invaluable assistance to Zogu in March 1922; and in early 1924, he had helped Zogu win over dissident elements after the 1923 elections, while during the upheaval of June, Eyres had intervened and implored the rebel contingent to return to the government. Eyres even took the step of travelling to Shkodër to meet Luigi Gurakuqi in order to convince him to return to Tirana and cooperate with the government.[10] When that failed, Eyres adopted a hostile attitude toward the new government in Tirana. What seemed to concern Eyres the most was not the progressive character of Noli's domestic policy, but the prospects for both Albanian and overall Balkan stability with a government like Noli's in power.

Eyres had no faith in either Noli or his twenty-point program. Low expectations had long figured in Britain's Albania policy, as made clear as early as 1921 by Harold Nicolson in the Foreign Office:

> I submit that our general line should be to contribute towards Albania being given a fair start, while being very careful not to assume any responsibility for future developments. It is to be expected that once all external menace has been removed, the Albanians will revive their religious and tribal feuds to an extent which will render civilized government difficult if not impossible. On the other hand they do not themselves particularly care for civilized government and it is not for us to impose it upon them.[11]

Eyres held similar views. His early experiences in Albania revealed, not a struggle between liberalism and neo-feudalism, but a religious/tribal struggle. He thought what was needed was not reform, but a strong central government to enforce unity on a disunited populace. Eyres saw the authoritarian style of government that Zogu offered as consistent with Albania's level of development and contemporary needs. The notion that Albania had evolved little beyond the tribal stage shaped British attitudes, and Zogu, as both a 'bajraktar'[12] and politician, appeared as the most suitable ruler for Albania.

Eyres took up his post in January 1921. As this was his second visit to Albania, he had some experience with the country.[13] What Eyres saw in Albania was a deeply polarized society based on differences between the more educated and marginalized Christians and the dominant Moslem majority. In his first report, written in March 1921, Eyres noted the diverse interests of the Catholics, Moslems, and Orthodox communities. He added that 'as a rule' the Moslems were 'less intelligent and less educated than the Christians,' but their previous experience in the Ottoman government gave them control over the key government posts, and they had retained their Turkish methods.[14] For Eyres, the fact that former bureaucrats in the old Turkish structure continued to dominate Albanian politics was the crux of the problem. The marginalization of the Christian population was the result, and on all sides there were bad feelings.

However, while the Christian population had much to complain about, Eyres felt that Albania's demographics meant that the best the country could hope for was the dominance of one of the more enlightened beys or bajraktars who was willing to govern with a strong arm. As Eyres began to acquaint himself with the main figures in Albania, he came to identify

Ahmed Bey Zogu as the most suitable leader. Eyres was impressed by Zogu's attempts to disarm the northerners as well as his willingness, on several occasions, to defend his regime from the intrigues of other forces when all those around him fled, and he was not alone in his praise for Zogu. His colleague Robert Parr wrote in November 1922 that

> the only force that makes for coherence is the personal influence of Ahmed Bey [Zogu]. He alone enjoys the respect of the people and he alone of the men at present at the head of affairs can by birth and position be considered one of the real leaders of the country.[15]

Neither Eyres nor Parr, contrary to Albanian communist-era interpretations, supported Zogu because of his alleged commitment to the status quo in Albania – they simply felt he was the only person capable of governing. Eyres's intervention in the June 1924 upheaval was therefore not because he sought to defend the Moslem landlords, but because he felt that the continued 'coup counter coup era' plaguing Albania was not in anybody's best interest.

While Eyres worked against Noli's attempts to secure recognition, the Albanian government was just as steadfast in its attempt to secure British support. Immediately after assuming power, Noli telegraphed British prime minister Ramsay MacDonald, noting that the country's Regency Council had empowered him to form a new government. Since MacDonald was the prime minister of a Labour government and thus shared, as far as Noli was concerned, a progressive outlook, Noli assumed that recognition was a *fait accompli*. However, Noli did not receive an immediate response, and it appeared that Great Britain had formed a very 'negative opinion on the people that had taken part in the revolution against Zogu and his regime.'[16] It appears that the British government, because of Eyres, chose not to see Noli's revolution as anything more than an illegal coup d'état.

One way that Noli could have secured British recognition was through elections, as most powers maintained that Vrioni's government was legitimate. While Noli viewed his seizure of power as the natural culmination of a struggle between landlords and liberals, outside powers saw little more than the emergence of a highly unstable and illegal government based on the shakiest of foundations. It was up to Noli to convince them otherwise, and his failure to appreciate this was to cost him dearly. Because of his deep-seated progressivism, his faith in a new order based on the League covenant, Noli believed that the outside world would rejoice at his triumph and do everything possible to ensure his success. As had been the case in relations with Yugoslavia and Greece, Noli once again proved incapable of putting himself and his program within a wider context.

By the end of June, the attitude of the Great Powers toward Noli had already become solidified, as his first actions sent out the wrong message. From the very beginning, the British were extremely cautious. What concerned British representatives especially was the call for harsh measures against the members of the old regime. As well, the release of Beqir Walter, the young man who had made an attempt on Zogu's life in February 1924, deeply angered the British government, which interpreted the move as condoning assassination.[17] The release of Walter was even more ill-conceived when one considers that the attempt on Zogu was based on the custom of blood feud and thus had no political implications. Eyres, in a conversation on June 23 with Harold Nicolson, made these concerns clear and suggested that recognition be delayed pending a change in attitude toward the old government and a solution to the fact that Noli's government was unconstitutional.[18]

Mehmet Konica in London struggled to effect a change in British policy. Konica was optimistic that *de jure* recognition was forthcoming and that British public opinion supported Noli's government.[19] Konica, like Noli, was strongly pro-British in his sympathies.[20] Although Konica was no doubt a progressive and did serve Noli's government well, he found himself often at odds with Noli's agenda and more than once was left in the dark with regard to important decisions in Tirana. His 'pressure' on the British government, albeit well-intentioned, did not meet with success, and on one occasion actually succeeded in angering the British Foreign Office.

Konica desperately sought a meeting with Ramsay MacDonald in order to better outline the new government's agenda. On 3 July 1924 he wrote to MacDonald noting that in the past ten days he had made 'vain' efforts to secure a personal interview with him in order to make a verbal and personal communication on behalf of Noli.[21] The Foreign Office replied almost immediately and advised that, owing to the amount of work for the prime minister, any communication should be in writing.[22] Konica followed the instructions and communicated the new government's position to MacDonald. However, Konica was forced to follow the directives of Noli, who was often prone to histrionics, with often disastrous results for Albania. In his letter, Konica noted that a personal interview would have been better in order to avoid 'recording certain unpleasant facts.'[23]

The new Albanian government, he wrote, took issue with the British position that recognition would be withheld until the government had received a vote of confidence from the Constituent Assembly. Konica argued, although they are doubtless Noli's words, that this would mean that the government would have to reinstate 'the feudal cabinet, abolish law and order, sanction the state of slavery of the people and assist in the dismemberment of Albania.'[24] Konica also argued that immediate recognition from Great Britain 'would have great importance in the execution of social and economic reforms,' and that non-recognition 'would be a dangerous weapon in the hands of the expelled feudals and an indirect encouragement to them for endeavouring to return to power.'[25]

Konica, in the long run, should have ended his plea there. Instead, he went further and openly criticized Eyres. One Albanian historian notes that Eyres 'openly developed an enemy activity against the democratic regime as [did] no other diplomat in Albania, [and] the government of Noli tolerated that and did not take any action for his removal.'[26] The reality was somewhat different, as the government did attempt to remove Eyres. The secretary general of the Foreign Affairs Ministry, Xhafer Villa, had approached U. Grant-Smith and asked him if he would inform the British government of Eyres's activity.[27] Konica also informed MacDonald that based on information from a person of high integrity present during the events of June, Eyres had intervened in the struggle.[28] He argued that while the old government had been prepared to submit and put an end to the fighting, 'the British representative strongly advised them to continue their resistance and thereby has been the cause of further loss of lives and money.'[29] The accusations came directly from Noli, who felt that MacDonald, with his leftist sympathies, would certainly share his concerns and would recall Eyres immediately and replace him with a more sympathetic figure.[30] However, Noli's gamble failed. The accusations were not well received and did not serve to enhance the position of the Albanian government.

Konica received an immediate response from Prime Minister MacDonald on July 30. MacDonald noted that in the letter he had made 'serious allegations against His Majesty's Minister at Durazzo [Durrës].'[31] MacDonald went on to note that foreign representatives accredited to the Court of Saint James's are not 'at liberty to transmit statements regarding the conduct of His Majesty's Representatives abroad except on the instructions of their governments.'[32] The letter was returned to the Albanian legation in London. Realizing that his démarche had served no end, Konica appealed to Delvina for advice and undertook to defuse the situation. In late October, he wrote to MacDonald and tried to clarify his position. He noted that he regretted the fact that Great Britain had not offered recognition to the Albanian government and that he understood the British government's position. However, he felt that he had done his best to approach a difficult subject which involved interference in the internal affairs of his country. He had, however, made the allegations owing to an official request from his government, but had done so with 'reluctance.'[33] The Foreign Office advised Konica on November 5 that he was not in any way 'personally to blame for the procedure by which this matter was adopted.'[34]

Small blunders like this aside, there were fundamental differences between Great Britain and Albania, and the accusations against Eyres did little to improve an already bad situation. In response to Konica's pleas for recognition, the Foreign Office advised its legation in Durrës on July 28 that the British government's attitude had been shaped by the fact that Noli's government came to power by violence; recognition would be withheld until there was some 'clear expression of the national will that the Albanian government enjoys the confidence of the country.'[35] This point, which was later adopted by the majority of the Great Powers and Albania's neighbours, was to haunt Noli, and the failure to appreciate the link between elections and recognition was critical in his overall failure to appease the international community.

While Noli opted for a prolonged period of authoritarianism, other factors served to further undermine his credibility with Great Britain and other powers. Albanian communist historiography has long sought to exploit the link between Noli's so called anti-imperialist stance and the attitude of the Great Powers, especially Britain.[36] The basis of this interpretation has centred on the question of an oil concession for which Great Britain, Italy, France, and the United States all competed intensely. Albania's communist-era and contemporary historians maintain that Britain feared that Noli would overturn a concession offered to APOC and thus openly sought his downfall.[37]

The question of oil was significant, and while not the primary factor in shaping British policy, it was of great importance. Albania's occupation during the First World War had led to the discovery of what appeared to be rich oil reserves, and the struggle among the world's leading oil companies began in earnest after the war. It was the British who were the first to take seriously the exploration of prospective zones.[38] However, in the war's aftermath, since Albania lacked not only an organized government but also a formal policy on foreign investment and a concessionary system, the struggle for a government-approved oil concession was characterized by chaos as each of the concerns, backed by their respective governments, tried to secure an agreement from constantly changing Albanian governments. The result was that the Albanian government succeeded in promising something to everyone while ratifying no contracts.

While essentially four countries competed for the concession, it was APOC that emerged as the main contender and managed to outmanoeuvre the other competitors. By March 1921, when Illias Vrioni was in power, APOC and the Albanian government came to an agreement for a 200,000 hectare concession, which in effect amounted to a monopoly. With the decision to award the concession to APOC, several other companies entered the fray. In August 1922 an Italian concern, Compagnia Italiana di Petroli, and the U.S.-based Sinclair Oil called for a concession, and in October 1922, Standard Oil of the United States put forth its own bid. Owing to both governmental incompetence and the intrigues of the competing powers, the APOC contract never received ratification by the Albanian assembly, and the question was still on the books when Noli took power. Some pro-American elements hoped to promote U.S. interests, while others felt that the terms given to the British amounted to a monopoly. As well, there was a strong pro-Italian lobby in the Albanian government. Outside Albania, Italy, France, and the United States argued that APOC was getting both a monopoly and preferential treatment.

The debate on the oil concession reached its peak in the fall of 1923 when the Albanian assembly attempted to ratify the contract with APOC. Liberal forces in the assembly, especially Gurakuqi, opposed the agreement with APOC and were able to secure its rejection in the assembly. This defeat, according to communist-era historiography, was the result of pressure from the democratic opposition, fear of public opinion within the country, and pressure from other countries. The government's main argument in favour of the contract was that it was merely standing by agreements that had already been made by a previous government. However, some opposition members rejected the agreement as inconsistent with Albania's needs and called for the acceptance of the U.S. proposals as put forth by either Standard Oil or Sinclair. Not only was there pressure from within to block the APOC deal, but other interested parties, especially the United States, cried foul at the APOC concession as a clear violation of the open-door principle.

With the fate of the concession still undecided, throughout early 1924 the Albanian government was under pressure to make a decision.

The French legation, on behalf of Crédit Général des Pétroles, wrote the Albanian Foreign Ministry on 7 February 1924 advising it that the French government was displeased with the plans to award the concession to APOC. They argued that to award the concession to APOC would constitute a monopoly and would be a violation of 'open door' principle.[39] The Italian government, however, owing to what it determined to be its paramount interests in Albania, was by far the most hostile to the APOC contract. By the end of 1922, the Italian legation had already identified in Eyres a potential threat to its interests and complained that he had been encouraging nationalist elements in Albania 'in their opposition to Italian policy.'[40] Eyres, in response to these accusations, argued that the Italian minister at Durrës 'had used every effort to prevent any concessions being granted to British subjects' and that he had succeeded in blocking the oil concession.[41] That the Italian government attached great significance to the oil concession there is no doubt. In a November 1921 meeting in Rome between British and Italian representatives, the head of the Italian Ministry of Foreign Affairs' Albanian section noted that Italy 'must have the majority share in any oil concession granted by the Albanian Government.'[42]

British concern about the fate of this potentially lucrative concession is obvious. What probably concerned the British the most was that after the arrival of Noli, Luigi Gurakuqi was finance minister. Gurakuqi, who was considered by Eyres to be an 'Italophile,'[43] was already on record by September 1923 as being opposed to awarding of the concession to APOC. During the attack on the APOC contract in the fall of 1923, Gurakuqi was the main spokesman for abandoning the agreement. Through the Shkodër paper *Ora e Maleve*, Gurakuqi had attacked the terms of the contract with the British. While he did support an 'open door' policy on foreign investments, he hoped that Albania would get the best possible deal out of the concession. What this meant was that Albania would retain control over her vital oil reserves since oil was of 'great importance for the economic life of Albania.'[44] Gurakuqi also suggested that the refinement of the oil should take place on Albanian soil so as to aid in the creation of other industries in the country.[45]

Gurakuqi's assessment of the APOC contract was correct, as it offered little to Albania. Moreover, Gurakuqi argued that the contract would have guaranteed the British interests a monopoly, which, with insufficient returns for Albania, meant 'death for Albanian industry.'[46] An even more direct attack came when he drew attention to the fact that the U.S. concerns offered the Albanian state a higher percentage of the oil produced, and that the American companies were prepared to build a refinery and had asked for a shorter concessionary term.[47] It is possible that by the fall of 1923 the British had already taken exception to the country's progressives, such as Gurakuqi, who had opposed the ratification of the APOC contract in the Albanian assembly.[48]

For Noli, when the British government adopted its policy of non-recognition, he hoped to use the concession as a means to win over Britain. According to British sources, one of Noli's emissaries, Xhafer Villa,[49] attempted to use the oil concession as a means to encourage Britain to offer diplomatic recognition. In a June 1924 conversation with Robert Parr at the British legation,[50] Villa attempted just that, but he did not succeed. In a note to the Foreign Office on June 18, Parr noted that he 'ignored the proffered bribe and told him [Villa] that I had as yet received no instructions but that my personal opinion was that His Majesty's Government would be guided in this matter by considerations of the degree to which [the] revolutionary government was accepted by the Albanian people generally and of its intention to rule decently as manifested in its acts.'[51] It remains unclear whether Villa was acting on his own, or under the instructions of Noli. Regardless, the démarche failed to yield results, and Noli's government remained unrecognized. Throughout the rest of the summer and into the fall, the question of the oil concession remained unresolved, despite the best efforts of the interested parties. One of the main dilemmas, however, was that any concession of this magnitude needed the approval of the Albanian assembly, which had been disbanded pending new elections.

Although it seems that Noli continued to support the British bid, the Italians entered the debate with greater intensity in the fall of 1924. The Italian oil interest, like its U.S. counterparts, cried foul at the terms offered to the British and insisted that it had the better proposal. In October 1924, Albania's legation in Rome outlined the concerns of the Compagnia Italiana di Petroli, a joint U.S.-Italian venture based in Milan.[52] In the letter, Tefik Mborja, Albania's minister in Rome, advised the Foreign Ministry that during an October visit to Rome, Gurakuqi had met with representatives of the company and that the conditions proposed by this company were 'much better' than those offered by either Anglo-Persian or Standard Oil.[53] The Italian company sought greater details from the Albanian government as to the terms of the contract with the British and assured the Albanians that, unlike the British, they did not seek a monopoly on Albania's oil reserves.

Since confusion was the general state of affairs in the Albanian government, it is difficult to gauge just what Noli intended to do about the contract. By the fall of 1924, it appears that Noli was leaning toward the British, while Gurakuqi was prepared to defend the Italian bid. Progressive forces in the country, through the newspaper *Politika*, argued against the British bid. While Noli and others had pointed out that it was Britain that supported Albania's entry into the League and defended Albanian interests against Serbia, Kostandin Boshnjaku[54] wrote in *Politika* that the British government had also signed the Secret Treaty of London in 1915 and had insisted that parts of southern Albania should have been given to Greece.[55] In addition, the progressive press noted that it was Britain that seemed to be defending the interests of the old government and was flagrantly pursuing a colonialist policy toward Albania.[56]

Key support for the British bid, however, came from Konica in London. Early in his career he had already defended the British position on the basis that the Albanian government should stand by agreements made by previous governments. Konica had later argued that Great Britain was potentially the only true protector of Albanian interests. As to the U.S. concern, Konica was able to see the picture within a broader perspective, and he questioned whether the United States would come to the aid of Albania in the event of an invasion from the side of either Greece or Serbia.[57] Since the United States was at the time playing a limited role in Europe, especially because it was not a member of the League, Konica felt that Albania could be better protected by a more globally active power.

With so many trends inside the Albanian government and considerable pressure brought to bear on the government itself, it is not surprising that Noli's government was unable to find a solution that would satisfy so many divergent interests. Such an end required not only unity of purpose within the government but also an appreciation that the whole business just might have to be decided outside Albania's borders. By the fall of 1924, it seems that Noli had decided to reopen the whole question. In a telegram of August 1924, Konica had asked Noli whether the contract with APOC had been annulled because of opposition from Italy.[58] The Foreign Ministry responded immediately that the Albanian government was continuing the policy of the 'open door' and awarding concessions to the companies that made the best offer.[59] The British thus had considerable reason to fear that APOC would have been outdone by the U.S.-based Standard Oil, which did, as already noted, offer the better terms for the Albanian government.

While oil did have some effect on the British attitude, their position on Noli had taken shape long before Noli's government had formulated its stance on the oil concession. Moreover, Noli at no point articulated a position to the British representative. Hence, it is fair to say that the oil question did not determine the attitude of the Great Powers toward Noli. His failure, however, to stand by the previous agreement probably served to distance Noli from Great Britain. But the British had far greater concerns, and the bulk of the pressure on Noli had more to do with his failure to hold new elections, the potential threat he posed to overall Balkan stability, and his later flirtation with the Soviets. By far the key determinant of British policy was not some kind of ideological aversion to Noli, but instead that his often erratic behaviour threatened to undermine Balkan stability. In a December 1924 conversation between Britain's ambassador to Rome, Sir Eyre Crowe, and Yugoslav foreign minister Ninčić, the latter stated that he did not feel that Noli's government 'offered any prospect of stability.'[60] Crowe noted the British Foreign Office was in full agreement.[61] By the fall of 1924, it was even more clear to outside observers that Noli's days were numbered, and they were therefore prepared to shelve the concession dilemma until new elections were held or Noli was toppled – whichever came first.

Italy, which had concrete territorial and economic goals, sought to exploit Noli's weak position to extract concessions. While Noli had received a very positive telegram from Mussolini on June 20, which the Albanians interpreted as an act of recognition, the Italians later followed the British lead and instead opted to wait for Noli to legitimize his position through elections. Immediately following Noli's victory, Italian policy was less than clear, as both Zogu and Noli vied to obtain Italian support. However, Mussolini wavered and in the end chose to follow the British lead. The key determinant of Italian policy was just which Albanian politician – Noli or Zogu – would be easier to control. The Italian minister in Durrës identified Zogu as a patron of Yugoslavia, but Mussolini later decided that Zogu could be bought.[62] That Noli was prepared to go to great lengths to defend the political and economic independence of his country was clear to Mussolini from the outset, and the Italians were continually thwarted in their attempts to re-establish control over Albania. In addition to trying to secure predominance over Albanian oil reserves, Italy also tried to gain influence over the financial affairs of the country.

Since Noli had been given cause for optimism because of Mussolini's telegram, in mid-July the Albanian representative in Rome had an interview with the Duce to pass on a letter from Noli regarding the formation of the new government. Mborja met with Mussolini for a quarter of an hour and was extremely pleased with his reception.[63] Mborja, on Noli's behalf, explained that one of the country's key problems was the nagging question of borders, and that Albania desperately needed Italian support in the battle with the Yugoslavs over Vermosh and Saint Naum. Mussolini declared his support for the Albanian position, and added that it would be easier to offer support if Albania and Italy had a 'patto politico.'[64]

While it had been suggested, especially by the Yugoslavs, that Noli's revolution was the product of Italian influence, the Duce's attempt to gain a foothold in Albania flies in the face of that argument. Noli's unwillingness to enter into any alliance that might compromise Albanian sovereignty forced Italy to obtain leverage through loans to the government. Mussolini suggested that his government was prepared to float a loan of 100 million lire to Albania, but that the initiative had to come from Albania. Hoping to gain further control, Mussolini noted that he was confident that a guarantee for the money could be easily arranged.[65] Noli, however, remained wary of Italian intentions, but did not let the matter drop. In an attempt to better understand the Italian position, Mborja sought an interview with Baron Indelli, the chief of the Italian Foreign Ministry's section for Albania, Bulgaria, and Greece. Mborja tried to keep the discussion focused on three main points: new elections, a loan, and the problem posed by Kosovo irredentists in Noli's government. Indelli informed Mborja that he was speaking only academically and not in an official capacity. He stressed that Albania must move toward new elections, especially because Great Britain's attitude on this point was unwavering.[66] Indelli also noted that through the Italian minister in Durrës, Luigi Gurakuqi had made it clear that Albania desperately needed a loan. In an effort to move Albania closer to the Italian sphere, Indelli argued that Albania would face severe difficulties securing a loan from the League, owing to the huge demands placed on its resources by the reconstruction of Austria and Hungary. Indelli again stressed that it would be very difficult to get a loan when Noli's regime remained 'revolutionary.'[67] Elections, Indelli argued, would not only legitimize the government in the eyes of the rest of the world, but would also help to eliminate the impression that the government would not last long.[68]

Italy's overall position on Albania was not lost on Mborja, as he identified in Indelli's suggestions the Italian desire to give Albania a loan. Mborja felt that Italy did not want Albania to secure a loan from the

League but from Italy instead, so that Italy would have the 'main influence in the financial and economic life of the country.'[69] Aware of how
desperately Albania needed arms to thwart any attempt by Zogu to
return, Indelli added that there were ways that Italy could supply arms
to the Albanian army without causing suspicion among other interested
parties.[70] Mborja's assessment of Italian ambitions was confirmed by the
American consul in Florence, Joseph Emerson Haven, who met with
Mborja to discuss developments. According to Haven, Italy was fixated on
the idea of obtaining Albania as Italian territory, and its policy was to wait
until Albania begged for a loan and then demand concessions.[71] Haven
argued further that Italy relied on remittances from emigrants abroad,
and that Albania was ripe for Italian colonial penetration, especially
since the United States was 'practically closed.'[72] In Haven's opinion,
since Albania was six hundred years behind the times, Italy could supply everything from 'shovels to streetcars.'[73] Making matters more complicated, while Zogu was frantically trying to appease the Yugoslavs, his
lieutenants were busy in Rome trying to convince Mussolini that Zogu's
return would benefit Italy. Former finance minister Mufid Libohova did
much to discredit Noli's government through his own appeals to Italy
and his claims that Noli's government was illegal and terrorist, especially
since it had established the much-criticized political court.[74] Libohova,
through discussions and interviews in the Italian press, developed what
Mborja called 'massive propaganda' against Noli's government and tried
to portray it as anti-Italian, all the while promising the Italian government concessions when Zogu returned to power.[75]

The United States also opted for a similar position, although much of
its attitude was shaped by concerns about delays in solving the murders
of Coleman and De Long. While Albanian historians have also tried to
explain the American position in terms of the search for oil concessions,
the evidence does not bear out this conclusion.[76] Initial American interest in Albania in the aftermath of the First World War did come primarily as a result of pressure from American missionaries abroad and the
determination not to lose out in any potential concessions, especially
in oil. The first thrust to increase the American presence in Albania was
thus a direct result of economic ambitions. Prior to the dispatch of a
formal mission to the country, Charles Telford Erickson, a missionary
in Albania and a resident there for over fourteen years, visited the State
Department's Division of Near Eastern Affairs in June 1921. Erickson
advised the Americans that Great Britain was moving fast to secure an oil
concession and that a British consul was due to arrive shortly in Albania.

Erickson was at pains to point out that the United States stood to lose out if the policy of non-recognition was maintained. The State Department, according to an internal memo, was not prepared to recognize Albania since the government did 'not seem quite far enough advanced' and that the country lacked a constitution.[77]

As a result of Erickson's démarche, the Near Eastern Affairs Division suggested that, owing to potential resources in Albania, either the State Department or the Commerce Department should send an expert to investigate Albania's resources.[78] In another memo to Assistant Secretary of State F.M. Dearing, the Near Eastern Affairs Division advised that Erickson was again encouraging his government to 'wake up to the fact that there are some things in Albania worth going after.'[79] Erickson called for recognition and encouraged the United States to nominate a representative before any decision was taken on the oil concession. The fear that the British would secure what were assumed to be rich oil reserves also brought the U.S. Commerce Department on side early in the game, as well as the Department of State's Division of Near Eastern Affairs.

The road to recognition thus followed a bizarre path from one level of bureaucracy to the other, with Erickson providing the initiative. F.M. Dearing at the State Department in turn advised Commerce Secretary Herbert Hoover that owing to reports of rich oil wealth in Albania, it was advisable to 'inform the principal American oil companies, by means of a confidential communication, regarding the general aspects of the oil situation in Albania.'[80] Dearing was especially concerned that the Albanian parliament was on the verge of approving the contract with APOC. The main problem appeared to be the simple fact that the United States had not recognized the Albanian government, which was hampering its attempt to compete effectively with Great Britain. Once aware of the situation, Hoover intervened personally to help speed up the process for recognition. After receiving complaints from American oil interests, Hoover appealed to Secretary of State Charles Evans Hughes to deal with the question of recognition. In an April 1922 letter, he asked Hughes to give serious consideration to the recognition of Albania, or 'if actual recognition appears inadvisable, to the possibility of sending some American government agent into the country who can give a show of interest and support the claims of the Sinclair Oil Company.'[81] The situation, according to Hoover, appeared to be 'a clear case where a little assistance by the government can go far in support of legitimate American enterprise abroad.'[82]

While American business interests were one part of the picture, the United States had not altogether ignored other developments in Albania. In 1919, Joseph Emerson Haven had already been sent to Albania on special detail to help the United States shape a position on Albania at the Paris Peace Conference. As already noted, Haven was a pronounced Albanophile who tended to support the Albanian perspective without question. It was also Haven who suggested that the United States push for a mandate for Albania, owing to what Haven called the pro-American sympathies of the Albanian people. While Haven's reports never translated into official policy, his mission was followed by the lengthy visit of Maxwell Blake, who headed an American mission to the country. Blake, who arrived in June 1922, was no doubt sent to Albania as a direct result of the need to ensure a more level playing field for U.S. economic interests. The end result was that the United States finally offered de jure recognition on 28 July 1922.

Blake, not unlike his counterparts in the British legation, was also quite impressed with Ahmed Zogu. In his situation report of September 1922, Blake praised Zogu as the 'one outstanding personality in the country.'[83] Blake did not stop there and declared that Zogu had 'spirit and courage, qualities which amount for his present position as the popular hero of the day ... He is fearless, honest, uncompromising, and malevolent toward his enemies.'[84] However, despite Blake's upbeat reports and initially very positive meetings with Albanian officials, as well as pledges from the government to respect the 'open door' principle, the United States continued to play second fiddle to the British. As time passed, the United States was continually frustrated in its attempts to secure the oil concession, which over time soured considerably the initially good relations between the United States and Ahmed Bey Zogu.

As noted earlier, the United States argued that the British were receiving preferential treatment and that the 'open door' policy was being ignored. The State Department was, not surprisingly, under considerable pressure from Sinclair Oil, initially to aid in its bid to secure the concession. In September 1922, Sinclair Oil appealed to Secretary of State Hughes for assistance, stating that foreign interests, especially APOC, were hampering its attempt to secure a contract.[85] According to Sinclair Oil, in view of 'the importance of American control of foreign oil supplies,' it hoped that the State Department would instruct its minister in Tirana 'to give us the fullest support which it permits it representatives to give in such cases.'[86] Within two days of that appeal, the State Department advised the U.S. representative to 'render all appropriate assistance to American Oil Companies.'[87] In fact, judging from the origin of the majority of Sinclair Oil's telegrams, the U.S. legation fast became the headquarters for the company. Throughout 1922 and 1923, the U.S. government pressed to have the APOC contract rejected. The main problem appeared to be that the British simply had more people in their pay than the Americans, and the United States was unable to undermine Harry Eyres's profound influence on Ahmed Zogu.

The Albanians, not unmindful of their weak financial position, attempted to use the oil concession as a means to secure a loan, so that the question became even more complicated. Sinclair Oil was especially eager to help Albania secure the loan, and its U.S. office set about to find financial backing in the United States. So sincere was Sinclair's effort that Maxwell Blake advised the State Department that it seemed apparent that Sinclair would finally obtain the concession.[88] In October 1922, Sinclair's representative advised his home office (through the State Department) that hopes of securing the concession were improving, but it was necessary to guarantee a loan of one million dollars within six or eight months.[89] Despite optimism and agreement on the terms of a contract, Sinclair was stymied by the loan dilemma as the Albanian government, by playing the major interests against each other, altered its loan request to 2 million dollars.[90]

In the long run, Sinclair could not secure a loan on American financial markets and was thus, albeit temporarily, out of the picture. While the American government was disappointed with the setback, as well as the perception that APOC was manipulating Albanian politicians, the United States continued to press its case through legal means. Making matters more difficult for the United States, the entry of Standard Oil also weakened the position of Sinclair Oil. In an internal memo of November 16, Allen Dulles, chief of the State Department's Near Eastern Division, lamented that the entry of Standard Oil would make it possible for the Albanian government 'to start with the tactics of bargaining with two American companies which in Persia has been so successfully employed to the detriment of American interests.'[91] Dulles went further to state that while acknowledging it was a departure from State Department policy, he wished it were possible to 'call off the Standard until the Sinclair has had a fair chance to complete its negotiations.'[92]

Dulles's suggestion did not become reality, and the United States was confronted with a much better organized bid from APOC. By the spring of 1923, as noted, the Albanian government was maintaining that it was obligated to adhere to the original 1921 arrangement and award the

concession to APOC. The Department of State was outraged at possibly
losing out to the British and advised the American legation to inform
the Albanian government that the State Department 'would regret any
action which would tend to deny the principle of the Open Door as
applied to the development of the natural resources of Albania.'[93] State
Department officials suggested that in this case the United States cooperate with both France and Italy in blocking the APOC contract. However,
in the end the United States relied on independent representations,
which, so it was argued, would be 'more forceful.'[94]

The Department of Near Eastern Affairs, in an unsubmitted memo-
randum to the assistant secretary of state, argued the success of APOC
was based on two key factors: political pressure brought to bear on
Albania; and the cooperation of League representatives in furthering
British interests.[95] More concretely, American officials suspected that the
British 'were using threats bearing on Albanian territorial interests in
endeavouring to prevent the granting to an American concern.'[96] Grant-
Smith had made similar accusations in a telegram of 3 March 1923, stating that many Albanian officials felt that a failure to support the APOC
concession would bring about the annexation of the disputed provinces
of Korçë and Gjirokastër.[97]

The suggestion that League representatives were acting on behalf of
British interests had caused considerable consternation in Washington.
In a memorandum of 8 January 1923, the Division of Near Eastern
Affairs suggested that the United States lobby to have an American
appointed as financial advisor since the League sought someone who
could not be accused of partiality and the United States was 'the only
great power entirely neutral in the Albanian situation.'[98] The selection
of an American, it was argued, was not only in the best interests of the
United States, but also reflected the wishes of the Albanian government.[99] In light of the memo, the State Department's economic advisor
suggested that the United States should put forth some names because of
the fear that a British advisor would go a long way in supporting British
interests.[100]

Since an American did not obtain the post, the American legation
was left with only diplomacy as a means to undermine Britain's stronger position. As a result, Grant-Smith undertook an aggressive campaign
to draw attention to U.S. interests throughout the fall of 1923 and the
spring of 1924. On 4 September 1923, in response to U.S. complaints,
the Albanian government advised the American legation that under
international law the government was forced to honour the signature of

Vrioni on the contract with the Anglo-Persian Oil Company.[101] However, the U.S. authorities rejected this interpretation and, in a memo to Zogu, advised him that the U.S. government 'did not understand why the Albanian government should consider itself bound to give preference to the contract of the Anglo-Persian Company ... since this contract has been modified to such an extent that it can no longer be considered the same document that was signed by Illias Vrioni.'[102] Despite government intransigence, the United States was no doubt heartened by the stand taken by Gurakuqi and the opposition forces in the fall 1923 parliamentary debate. This helps to explain the initially positive attitude of the United States toward Noli's government. Noli also told the U.S. chargé d'affaires that the majority of the country was against the APOC contract and in favour of the American proposals.[103] Noting that he would oppose the APOC concession, Noli added that many feared that if 'the APOC proposals were accepted ... British influence would sooner or later become predominant in the country.'[104]

Throughout the spring of 1924, the United States was still unable to effect any change in policy. The U.S. legation was under pressure from both Sinclair and Standard Oil to have their respective proposal brought before the parliament.[105] On 17 April 1924, Grant-Smith wrote Vrioni to complain about the delays vis-à-vis the Standard Oil Company and noted that the delays were amounting to a contravention 'of the rights and treatment formally guaranteed to American citizens by the government of Albania.'[106] In a confidential report to the secretary of state, Grant-Smith explained that delays were attributable in part 'to a conviction that sooner or later someone will pay handsomely for the privilege of making first choice of the lands to be exploited.'[107] Despite these pleas, both American interests appeared to be sidelined, although the APOC contract remained unratified. The failure to give serious consideration to the U.S. proposals thus had the effect of further souring Grant-Smith's attitude toward Zogu. That, coupled with the murder of the two Americans, brought U.S.-Albanian relations to new lows. Noli's seizure of power, it was assumed, brought forth the prospect of positive changes.

There is little doubt that the United States initially greeted Noli's victory with enthusiasm. The legacy of U.S.-Albanian relations had hitherto not been good, as U.S. interests were clearly taking a back seat to the British. Noli's seizure of power thus presented the Americans with an ideal opportunity to cement stronger ties and secure the oil contract. For the United States, it appeared that Noli and his finance minister were partial to its interests and could solve the two outstanding problems: justice for the murderers of Coleman and De Long, and new opportunities for American economic interests. In a meeting with Noli in mid-June, Grant-Smith had impressed upon him the importance of both these points, but took no action that would imply recognition.[108] From the outset, the United States opted to wait and see just how Noli would deal with the outstanding problems in American-Albanian relations. Grant-Smith's distaste for Zogu was already well known, especially because of his attitude toward American oil interests and the foot dragging in the quest for justice. He was unwilling, however, to accept Noli's seizure of power without question.

In a report to Hughes on June 19, Grant-Smith made some of his reservations clear. He wrote that the authority of Peci to form a new cabinet was questionable; that the French had already expressed doubts about stability; the Greeks and Serbs could be counted on to covertly seek the government's overthrow; the British representative was strongly opposed; and it was a parliamentary minority that had established itself with the aid of the army.[109] But, Grant-Smith added, American interests would seem to lie 'on the side of continuance of the new regime which is at present favourably disposed towards us and committed against British pretensions.'[110] On several other occasions, Grant-Smith went to great lengths to convince the State Department that the United States could expect both a favourable resolution to the murders of Coleman and De Long and respect for the 'open door' principle.[111] If Grant-Smith argued that according to the Lushnjë constitution Noli's regime was wholly illegitimate, he was, nevertheless, a supporter of Noli's program. In a report of July 2 to Hughes, he noted that while doubting that Noli's ambitious program could be implemented in such a short space of time, should the government succeed 'in making a serious break in the wall of ancient privilege, the first real step on the path of political and social progress will have been achieved.'[112]

Despite obvious reasons for recognizing the new regime, Grant-Smith was extremely cautious. Hughes had already advised him on June 23 that the

> question of recognition would not appear to arise unless there has been a change in the head of state. If present government is in your opinion properly constituted and is in control of the country there would be no objection to your continuing to carry on with it relations which you had with its predecessor and the Department authorizes you in your discretion to do so.[113]

Hughes did add, in a later telegram, that Grant-Smith 'should impress upon the authorities at present in control the importance which this Government attaches to prompt and vigorous action to bring to justice those responsible for the killing of Coleman and De Long.'[114]

Thus, Grant-Smith had considerable latitude to shape the U.S. position on Noli's government. As Hughes made clear, the key point was the legality of Noli's seizure of power. As a stickler for details, Grant-Smith decided to leave Noli's government unrecognized pending some form of legalization. He had originally favoured a policy of recognition but interpreted Hughes's telegram quite literally and, despite the obvious benefits of recognition, chose instead to follow the lead of the other powers.[115] Had Noli opted to reconvene the parliament and managed to secure the backing of a majority of the deputies, it is clear that the United States would have offered recognition.[116]

The problem of the murders also remained a serious obstacle to recognition. While accepting that Zogu had shown no real interest in bringing to justice those responsible, Grant-Smith awaited concrete results from Noli. After seizing power, Noli's regime made immediate declarations that those responsible would be held accountable, and it did not hide its belief that it was Ahmed Bey who was responsible. However, the slowness of the investigation angered the United States, and the legation lodged a formal protest on September 24. The note stated that the legation 'has observed with growing concern the lengthening of weeks into months without any news of definite progress toward a satisfactory settlement of the issue raised by the murder of two American citizens ... any failure of the Albanian government to take vigorous action in the matter would be viewed with serious concern in Washington.'[117] Grant-Smith was not convinced that Zogu was responsible, and he noted that attributing the crime to Zogu suggested the political character of the trial and the nature of the 'evidence which will doubtless be produced.'[118] As the government moved toward formal charges in the Coleman–De Long murders, it became apparent to Grant-Smith that the decision to implicate Zogu was based on politics instead of law. It was doubtless this agenda that did more harm than anything else in undermining Noli's position with the United States.

Grant-Smith kept a vigilant watch throughout the summer and fall of 1924 on the proceedings against Zogu. As noted previously, Zogu, along with eight others, were tried in absentia, while seven other defendants were in jail., The months between Noli's seizure of power and the beginning of the trial in October were marked by a wait-and-see attitude

pending the evolution of Noli's regime, the status of the oil concession, and the results of the trial. While there was some confusion as to
whether or not the United States had moved to recognize Noli's regime,
no change in policy was undertaken.[119] Grant-Smith's assessment of
the trial was accurate: it was little more than a show trial against Zogu
and his minions designed to find at least one outside supporter for his
permanent exile.

The evidence presented against Zogu was of a limited character and
did little to create confidence in Noli's regime. The key defendant,
Veisel Lam Hidri, claimed he had received a letter from Zogu asking
him to assemble a group to ambush some foreigners at Mamuras. Grant-
Smith doubted this testimony and noted the following: Zogu was too
clever to write such an order down; no letter was produced at the trial;
and, finally, the letter's intended recipients were all illiterate.[120] The trial
concluded that Zogu had originally intended the murder of League representative Eugene Pittard in order to create 'disturbances' in the region
after his departure from the cabinet.[121] Zogu was denounced as the insti-
gator of the crime because, it was argued, he possessed great influence
over the authorities of the region, nothing could be done without his
knowledge, and he was actively supporting 'turbulent elements and fugi-
tive criminals before the elections for the purpose of using them as tools
of his personal and political ambitions.'[122] Responsibility for the murder
of Avni Rustemi was also laid on Zogu's shoulders, and the court pronounced a verdict of ten years hard labour.

For the unfortunate Hidri, who was hanged on December 22 in central Tirana, it appears that he became an unwilling pawn in a diplomatic
game that had little to do with a quest for real justice. Throughout the
trial, the underlying political motives became clear. The trial's president,
Major Rexhep Berati, paid an indiscreet and unexpected visit to the
U.S. legation on December 11.[123] Speaking with the legation's translator,
Kol Kuqali, Berati specifically asked if the United States would support
the sentence of death on Zogu should the court make it. According to
Berati, it would be sufficient 'if the United States insist that he at least
be expelled from Yugoslavia, the nest of Zogu's factions.'[124] Berati also
claimed that the British were supporting Zogu in order to gain the oil
concession. He added that in exchange for American assistance in ensur-
ing Zogu's removal from the Albanian political scene, U.S. oil companies
would obtain the concession.[125]

Placing even more doubt on the validity of the proceedings, the entire
transcript was sent to the State Department's Office of the Solicitor for

examination. The conclusions, which were delivered after Zogu's return to power in late December 1924, confirmed U.S. suspicions about Noli's real agenda. The solicitor concluded that 'the prosecution and conviction of Zogu appear to have been based more on political motives than upon any real desire to implicate him in the actual murder of Coleman and De Long.'[126] The report also concluded that the evidence produced against Zogu was primarily hearsay that would not be admissible in an American court.[127] The solicitor argued that while Zogu did have political supporters 'among the bandits infesting the region where Coleman and De Long were murdered, there appears to be no reliable evidence to the effect that Zogu had any direct connection with the murders.'[128]

It seems all too clear, given the nature of Noli's government and the dearth of recognition from foreign powers, that the move to condemn Zogu was designed to secure support from the United States for his permanent exile. Had Zogu been convicted, with reliable evidence, it is obvious that the United States would not have welcomed his return to power. Lacking support from all sides, Noli decided to use extra-legal means to secure an ally in his battle with Zogu. When the court reported its verdict, time was running out for Noli. It was already obvious that Zogu was preparing for a march on Tirana, so that the court needed to work quickly if the United States was to be brought on side.

As was the case in Greece, Yugoslavia, Britain, France, and Italy, Noli was unable to find any substantive allies within the United States. Nevertheless, as in Yugoslavia, where he found support from Stjepan Radić, Noli found one lone American supporter: Joseph Emerson Haven. Owing to his long experience in Albania, and his close friendship with Ali Kolonja, from his position as consul in Florence, Haven urged his government to adopt a new position on Albania. Haven offered a detailed analysis of the situation in Albania and declared that Noli's government was composed of liberal and democratic elements and was not a 'government of bolsheviks as some rumours have declared.'[129] Haven felt strongly that Yugoslav agents, with the complicity of Zogu, were responsible for the murder of Coleman and De Long, the motive being to create chaos to aid in Zogu's return to power.[130] As to Noli, whom he dubbed an enthusiastic admirer of America, Haven argued that his program deserved the support of other nations, 'which should contribute towards its success.'[131]

Haven also listed the already well known charges against Britain, France, Italy, Greece, and Yugoslavia. Great Britain was a determined supporter of Zogu because of the oil concession; France maintained a policy

which supported the political program of Yugoslavia; Italy was concen-
trating on economic penetration through offers of politicized loans.[132]
Haven felt it unnecessary to comment on the attitudes of Greece and
Yugoslavia, as 'their policies with respect to Albania are too well known.'
As to the oil concession, Haven considered Noli to be a full supporter
of the 'open door' principle who was prepared to support the bids of
Standard Oil and Sinclair Oil.

Albanian communist-era historiography suggested that an anti-imperialist
element in Noli's program led to his cool international reception.[133] This
viewpoint is inaccurate. Noli hoped to consolidate the political and economic independence of the country, but he was by no means an economic nationalist.[134] Noli realized that the transformation he envisioned
could not be obtained by self-reliance, but would require substantial assistance from abroad, especially from Great Britain, the United States, and
the League of Nations. Unlike Ahmed Zogu, he was not willing to compromise Albania's sovereignty to entice foreign capital. In the long run,
while economic concerns were not altogether absent, the attitude of the
Great Powers was shaped by other concerns, and winning over the Great
Powers did not entail the types of sacrifices that would have destroyed
Albania's independence. While there was no middle ground with Italy,
Great Britain and the United States might have been induced to support
Noli had he been willing to test his revolution at the polls, yet Noli real-
ized only too late the link between recognition and an election.[135]

In the aftermath of the First World War, for many patriots Great
Britain was potentially Albania's protector. After all, Britain did play a
fundamental role in Albania's entry into the League, and a small coterie
of British Albanophiles helped to promote Albanian interests. Britain
was also the first country to make concrete steps toward exploitation of
Albania's resources and from the aftermath of the Lushnjë Congress
played a prominent role in Albanian domestic affairs. Ahmed Zogu
gradually elevated Harry Eyres to the position of unofficial but influential advisor. British interests in Albania stemmed primarily from an
economic agenda and the desire to preserve overall Balkan stability.
It was the latter concern that eventually dictated British policy toward
Fan Noli and Ahmed Zogu. At no point in the four years of democracy
and chaos did Great Britain ever develop a policy that put any faith in
the Albanians' ability to establish a parliamentary democracy or carry
through on the type of reform Noli envisioned. Fan Noli, according to
Eyres, had no legal right to form a government, pushed a program that

was at odds with Albanian reality, waged a destructive war against his enemies, and was poised to undermine the fragile stability that characterized Zogu's leadership because of his inability to achieve a modus vivendi
with Albania's neighbours.

When Noli came to power, he was unwilling to accept that British policy
was the result of such cynical assessments. Owing to his own experiences
with Britain, he hoped for a warm welcome, a call for Zogu's arrest, and
assistance in implementing his twenty-point program. His decision to
seek the removal of Eyres is evidence of his naïveté and his belief that a
Labour government would support him. In the long run, it was both his
program and his actions that widened the gap between his government
and Great Britain. For Harry Eyres, who was the major player in deter-
mining London's attitude, Noli was a transitional figure who could do
little more than create instability in the region. While there is little doubt
that the British did fear for the oil concession, it was not the major factor
in shaping British policy. Above all, it seems clear that APOC could have
obtained the contract in exchange for recognition. Britain, which did
little to push the APOC bid during Noli's tenure, calculated that Noli's
position was so weak that it made no sense whatsoever to make any concrete agreements with his regime. That Noli's government lasted as long
as it did came as some surprise to Eyres.

Italy pursued traditional policy goals in Albania that only came to frui-
tion under Ahmed Zogu in the years following the collapse of Noli's
government. In the aftermath of the Lushnjë Congress, Italian influence in Albania waned considerably, and many Albanian patriots viewed
Italy with justified suspicion. Italy, like Greece, had concrete designs on
Albanian territory, and when the question of territorial gains was closed,
Italy sought willing collaborators in successive governments who would
help further its position. Since Albania had not yet been relegated to
the Italian sphere of influence, Italy faced stiff competition from Britain
and, to a lesser extent, the United States. When Noli obtained power,
many had judged his success to be a product of Italian influence. This
was not the case, and Noli worked hard at keeping Italian influence
in the country at manageable limits. Noli did expect recognition from
Mussolini, and he was disappointed that the Italian government did
not follow that route. Mussolini's decision to leave Noli's government
unrecognized was less the result of the desire to follow Great Britain's
policy, but more in keeping with the Yugoslav attitude, which opted to
avoid recognition. Italy hoped to use the question of recognition as a
means to influence Noli's attitude. This position was made abundantly

clear in the negotiations for a loan or for potential Italian support for Albania's territorial integrity. While Noli was certainly willing to barter for recognition with both Britain and the United States, Italy's histori-cal legacy in Albania frightened him. With Noli refusing to engage in a barter arrangement, and with Zogu's emissaries offering him everything, Mussolini preferred to wait for either Noli to come begging or Zogu to return.

The United States, which had yet to come completely to terms with the more cynical side of European diplomacy, was often left on the side-lines. While it is clear that the main motivation for initial U.S. interest in Albania was economic, the United States was never prepared to go the extra mile to become Albania's benefactor and protector. The legacy of Woodrow Wilson meant that Albanian patriots, especially the American-Albanian community, had argued since the First World War for the entry of U.S. influence and capital. Indeed, had the United States wished it, Albania could have emerged as a key U.S. dependency or protector-ate. However, the United States allowed itself to play second fiddle to British interests and was unable to effect any change in policy. At the time, the United States had at its disposal only moral arguments about the 'open door.' For Albania's cynical politicians, this was not enough, and U.S. economic interests, during the period of Zogu's dominance, were sidelined.

Noli's seizure of power brought new opportunities, and U.S. policy-makers recognized this, above all U. Grant-Smith, who loathed Ahmed Zogu and his British patrons. However, despite an initial willingness to embrace Noli, the United States backtracked. The reason for this was not economic, as Noli would have surely traded recognition for the oil con-cession, since many of his colleagues were already on record as support-ing the U.S. bids. The United States refused recognition because it stood by the policy adopted toward the Bolshevik regime: Noli's government had seized power illegally and was acting in contravention of the Lushnjë constitution. Noli's own actions served to worsen the situation, as he rarely inspired confidence in U.S. diplomats because of his poor grasp of the internal situation. Finally, the United States saw through Noli's attempt to use the trial against Zogu for political purposes. This act, more than anything, outraged U.S. decision-makers, who attached great significance to convictions in the murders of Coleman and De Long.

Facing an overall failure with the Great Powers, Noli had few options. Nothing he did seemed to satisfy any country, and his nemesis, Ahmed Zogu, seemed to be the preferred Albanian leader. While his stint in government made him cynical, as he was confronted with one failure after another, he always retained a faith in the Wilsonian promise of a new order, and there was always the League of Nations. It was the League, where Noli first earned his credentials as an orator and statesman, that was always his biggest hope. Even there, he was to find disappointment. His last chance, and one that represented the depth of his external and internal crisis, was the USSR.

6

The League of Nations and the Soviet Union

The League of Nations

In 1924, while Noli had hoped that Britain would assume the role, as it had in 1920, of a disinterested protector of Albanian interests, he also placed considerable faith in the League of Nations as a potential source of support. However, Noli's goal was frustrated by the intransigence of the League, which remained tied to the Great Powers and unable to move independently toward helping Albania. He also often served to make matters worse by adopting an arrogant tone with the organization, wrongly assuming that Albania was the centre of the world and that the success of his reform program was not only important for Albania, but also for Europe as well. Confronted with the League's attitude, Noli underwent a massive transformation, and by the time he fell from power, his view was considerably altered – no longer did he view the body as the culmination of a new age, but instead saw it as a vindictive and useless tool of the Great Powers bent on his destruction.

The League of Nations, like Great Britain, set relatively low expectations for the country's development, and this certainly did not work in Noli's favour. In an April 1923 report, the League's Commission of Enquiry noted that Albania should remain neutral and refrain 'as far as possible, from any active foreign policy.'[1] The report also noted, somewhat disparagingly, that the country 'was hardly ripe for universal suffrage or the more advanced forms of parliamentary government.'[2] In this analysis, the report argued, the Constituent Assembly's main challenge would be to create a strong central government and at the same time allow the various provinces to retain some control over local administration.[3] The notion of regional autonomy was important, as it confirmed other countries' suspicions that Albania lacked unity and that considerable differences existed between the north and south. While Albanian leaders were open to suggestions on the need for strong central government, any kind of regional autonomy was out of the question.[4]

Albania had been one of the first countries to appeal to the League for a financial advisor to help straighten out its disastrous financial situation, work toward the alleviation of the country's massive budget deficits, and pave the way to a much-needed loan. The League appointed J.D. Hunger, a Dutch citizen who had twenty-nine years experience in the Dutch colonial service. Hunger arrived in May 1923 and began a whirlwind tour of the peculiarities of Albanian financial life. Despite Albania's need for financial advice, Hunger's experience in the country was by no means positive, and he was often frustrated by the Albanian government, a fact which in the long run did little to improve Albania's relations with the League.

In his fourth report to the League, Hunger had already made known his concerns about the obstacles confronting him. He complained that he had attended only one cabinet meeting, that the Albanian government was ignoring the terms of his contract by drafting laws on financial and economic questions and presenting them to parliament without his advice, awarding concessions without consultation, and appointing foreigners to 'lucrative' government posts without his advice and approval.[5] Barely a year into his five-year contract with the Albanian government and just after the installation of the Vërlaci cabinet in March 1924, the Albanians decided that Hunger's contract should be terminated.[6] While the Albanian government attempted to hide behind the argument that it could not afford Hunger's services,[7] the primary reason behind the Albanian initiative was that the government simply did not want to follow Hunger's advice. Moreover, according to U.S. diplomats, Zogu was disappointed with Hunger since he had expected him to arrive with sacks of gold.[8] Conservative circles were also put off by Hunger's radical suggestions, which included the abolition of the army and the enhancement of a gendarmerie, a reduction in the size of the parliament and cutbacks in ministerial staff, and more days of free labour from the populace to aid in the construction of roads.[9] Equally important, since both Zogu's and Vërlaci's power was in large part based on the allegiance of the beys, Hunger's call for tax reform was anathema. In his second report, covering the period from July 24 to October 24, Hunger noted that Albania's wealthiest classes paid only 6 per cent tax, which was 'an extremely low percentage when compared with percentages paid by the same class of taxpayers in other European countries,'[10] and he called for a new income tax up to a maximum of 20 per cent.

Unwilling to listen to Hunger's astute advice, the Albanian authorities decided that Article 22 of the contract allowed them to terminate Hunger's employment.[11] The Albanian Council of Ministers, in turn, advised the Geneva legation to make this information known to the League. While this may have allowed the Albanians an easy way out, neither Hunger, nor the League, nor the government of the Netherlands was prepared to let the matter drop so easily. In fact, the struggle between Hunger and the Albanian government lasted nearly three months, and the bad feeling carried over into the Noli interregnum. Upon hearing the news that his contract was to be cancelled, both Hunger and the Netherlands government flew into action, claiming that in cancelling the contract the Albanians had offered no valid reason and that the 'prestige' of the League of Nations was involved.[12] In his own defence, Hunger pointed out that he had performed his duties as outlined in the agreement and that he did not accept the Albanian position that they could no longer afford his services since the improvements which he had proposed for the Albanian budget of 1924 would have justified his salary.[13] That the Albanians remained steadfast in their refusal to reinstate Hunger did little to help their image in Geneva; indeed, Benoit Blinishti noted in a late May dispatch to the Foreign Ministry that the manner in which the contract with Hunger had been cancelled had 'produced a very bad impression in the circles of the League of Nations.'[14]

Thus, when Noli came to power, he had inherited a particularly strained relationship with what he saw as a potential benefactor. Doubtless, League officials hoped that Noli would move to reinstate Hunger and thus open the way for League advice.[15] Even Great Britain intervened to help Albania extricate itself from its poor position. In a roundabout way, on June 11, the British delegation to the League had advised Albania's League representative to 'withdraw [the] letter to [the] League of Nations on the subject of the dismissal of the Financial Advisor and request the League Council in a private meeting to take such steps as they might think advisable to arrange [the] matter so as to save amour propre of Advisor.'[16] However, instead of following this course or reinstating Hunger, which would have been the proper decision in light of the League's disappointment with the dismissal, Noli postponed any immediate action. While being reluctant to bring Hunger back, Noli immediately advised Eric Drummond, League general secretary, that a new liberal government had been installed in Tirana that would require League assistance to get on its feet.[17]

As the summer progressed, Noli eventually decided that Hunger should not resume his duties in Albania. On 8 September 1924, Noli advised Drummond that he was sorry about the attitude adopted by the previous government and that

> my government has devoted the closest possible attention to the question, which it has considered in every aspect. The Government which I have the honour to head fully appreciates the great value of Mr. Hunger's advice to Albania. The best proof is that it is now engaged in affecting the economies recommended by Mr. Hunger ... In view, however, of the present financial situation, the Government regrets that it cannot ask Mr. Hunger to resume his duties.[18]

While the League did accept the Albanian government's position, it would have been far wiser to reinstate Hunger and bury the whole issue, in view of the fact that Noli desperately sought financial assistance from the League. Noli's decision to deal finally with Hunger's legacy in late September was a reflection of his growing concern with his failure to secure needed financial support. It should be recalled that by then Noli and Gurakuqi had decided to travel to Geneva to deal with border issues. However, Noli also hoped to interest the League in floating a loan to his government. This was Noli's first real opportunity to plead his case. His speech to the Fifth Assembly was a disaster and impressed few countries, with the exception of the USSR, which relished any attack on the Great Powers and the League.[19]

Noli's speech of September 10 to the Assembly chastised the League for its failure to give Albania a loan and condemned it for what he identified as a poor record in light of the high ideals that had given birth to the League in the first place. He said:

> But do tell me, Mr. Secretary General, why do you refuse to give Albania a loan to enable her to get on her feet. We need only 300,000,000 gold francs. Too much, you say. Well, I am going to climb down elegantly to the modest sum of 200,000,000 gold francs ... I beg your pardon, do you mean to say that you have never met me in your life and that you would not lend me a penny ...[20]

Noli managed to dig his grave just a little deeper when he went on to denounce parliamentary government:

> Perhaps the Secretary General meant to say that he is unwilling to negotiate a loan with a revolutionary government, without a parliament ... But do you

know what a parliament is? A parliament is a hall where heartless politicians meet to vivisect their own race, a hall full of poison gas, of tear-producing gas, of tango-producing gas, and of all the other gases with which the last war was fought to end all wars and establish peace ... But since you insist, we are willing to have new elections, and to convoke that pest, that calamity, that abominable superstition, the parliament after, say, two or rather three, years of paternal government.[21]

While Noli had good reason to be angry with the League, his speech, from all points of view, was an unmitigated disaster and even disturbed Luigi Gurakuqi, who would have preferred that Noli adopt a more conciliatory tone.[22] Gurakuqi chose a different approach. In a speech on September 3 to a League plenary meeting, he had praised the League for its assistance in alleviating the famine of the winter and spring of 1924, stating that 'but for the generous assistance of the League of Nations the fate of our poverty-stricken mountain people would have been appalling.'[23] That Noli, a representative of a small power with very little influence, chose to address the League in such an arrogant fashion cannot be considered to have been a wise policy. Such 'sweeping criticism would have caused resentment had it come from the representative of a major power; coming from the prime minister of Albania who had himself been at the birth of the League, it brought nothing but discredit to his government and to the country he represented.'[24] While Noli certainly did not see the need to be a sycophant, a more diplomatic appeal to the League might have better served his country's interests. Hindsight confirms that Noli's assessment of the League was correct, yet his attack was premature and only enhanced the notion that he was a dangerous figure bent on disturbing the peace in the Balkans. Needless to say, he left Geneva without the loan.

The Soviet Union

While Noli failed to appease his neighbours, the League, or any of the Great Powers, Albanian historians have long argued that a key reason for the hostile attitude toward Noli's government was his decision to normalize ties with the Soviets. The recognition of what was then still partially a pariah in world affairs was taken to be a clear indication of his progressive ideas, which served to anger the 'reactionary' powers. Moreover, many Albanian historians have considered Noli's recognition of the USSR to be a major, if not the most significant, reason for his downfall, since the Great Powers, bent on obtaining economic concessions in Albania, were wary of Noli's independent and anti-imperialist agenda.[25] Noli's courting of the USSR certainly did not go unnoticed; it aroused some suspicions of his intentions, and did do considerable harm, but much of the damage could have been undone had Noli's government possessed much-needed expertise and a defined agenda for the country's foreign policy. Noli's revolutionary government possessed neither. Lastly, while Noli's courting of the Soviets did serve to alienate outside powers, especially neighbouring countries, it did little more than enhance the already accepted notion that Noli was ill prepared to rule Albania and, more importantly, was a threat to overall Balkan stability.

Soviet-Albanian ties did not begin with Fan Noli, and in many respects he merely finished the work of his predecessor, Ahmed Zogu. The earliest indications of an emerging relationship began shortly after 1920. At the outset, the Albanian government had set up a quasi-mission in Odessa to oversee the repatriation of citizens of Albanian origin living in Ukraine. The Albanian representative there, Kosta Kollumbi, was the first individual to approach his government about the possibility of normalizing ties with the Soviets. The intentions were not political, as Kollumbi argued that by normalizing relations between the two countries, it would ensure the easy repatriation of Albanians living in Ukraine.[26]

Kollumbi, clearly acting on his own, obviously initiated the process, as made clear by a letter from Maxim Litvinov, deputy commissar for Foreign Affairs. In the letter addressed to President Ahsmed Zogu, Litvinov noted that the gentleman in charge of the repatriation of Albanians had raised the question of normalizing relations. Litvinov added that the government of the Russian republic desired 'normal and amicable relations with all peoples devoid of imperialist aspirations'[27] and that diplomatic relations would allow the two countries to solve any political problems.[28] Zogu, a more astute politician than Noli, and more keenly aware of Albania's position not only in the Balkans but also in the larger European sphere, was not one to make hasty decisions.

Before proceeding on the question of establishing relations with Moscow, the Albanian Foreign Ministry enlisted the opinion of its key legations in Paris, Rome, and London regarding the Soviet proposal. The Albanian legations responded quickly. None had a positive opinion about the proposal to establish diplomatic relations with Soviet Russia. On 30 January 1923, the Paris representative gave a curt reply and noted that as far as France was concerned, normal diplomatic relations were not a good idea.[29] The Rome legation also replied negatively and wrote that the members of Italy's fascist government were the 'mortal enemies' of the communists. Moreover, owing to the Soviets' good ties with Turkey and Bulgaria, the move would not be well received by the Kingdom of Serbs, Croats, and Slovenes or by Greece. Albania's London representative, Mehmet Konica, was equally hostile to the idea.[30]

Without any support from abroad, the Albanian Foreign Ministry wisely postponed the establishment of relations. Pandele Evangjeli, then Albanian foreign minister, wrote Litvinov on 17 April 1923 and advised him that the Albanian government was forced to view the question of establishing diplomatic relations with his country within the framework of the potential repercussions for Albania and within the context of the international situation. Evangjeli's final word was that Albania would not proceed in this matter in advance of the Great Powers, and that when those powers had fully resumed normal relations, Albania would be pleased to open the discussions again.[31] The first chapter of Albanian-Soviet relations ended there, and the government of Ahmed Zogu displayed remarkable political acumen and considerable skill in dealing with this issue.

It was little more than a year later that Noli's new government reopened the question of Albanian-Soviet relations. Once again, the initiative came from the Albanian side, not by an obscure representative in Odessa, but from Noli himself. One of Noli's first acts in terms of foreign policy was to reopen negotiations with Soviet Russia on recognition. On 4 July 1924 Albanian foreign minister Delvina wrote Soviet commissar for foreign affairs George Chicherin and noted that the new Albanian government was ready to establish normal and amicable relations between the Russian and Albanian peoples.[32] Noli's decision to recognize Soviet Russia was, officially at least, couched in vague terms. The official Council of Ministers' decision, signed by Noli himself, suggested that the main reason for the move had been 'to protect the Albanian citizens who happened to be in Russia and to defend the interests of the Albanian citizens whose property was confiscated by the Soviet Government.'[33] The task of fulfilling this agenda fell to Tefik Mborja at the Albanian embassy in Rome. Mborja immediately began a dialogue with the Soviet ambassador to Rome, Konstantin Juranev, and confidentially reported on August 1 that the Soviet representative had told him that the Soviet government would 'with great pleasure open diplomatic relations' and that little more was required than the naming of representatives.[34]

However, it was not long after the decision was taken that Noli's government began to backtrack. It appears that not only did Noli begin to appreciate the international implications of the decision, but that more conservative members of his government also questioned the viability of the move. On August 19, barely two months after the first steps had been taken, the foreign minister advised Mborja that, given the troubled situation in the Balkans, it was inopportune to open diplomatic relations with the Soviets. He was advised that in the event the Soviet embassy in Rome should seek some concrete information, he was to provide them with 'evasive' answers.[35] The note further advised Mborja that he should inform the press that Albania had taken action to stop Bolshevik propaganda in the country and that there were no Soviet agents on Albanian soil.[36] Despite the Albanian attempts to backtrack, the matter was by no means closed, at least as far as the Soviets were concerned. Foreign Commissar George Chicherin responded to Delvina's earlier letter on September 4, writing that his government was ready to formalize relations and that a simple exchange of letters would suffice.[37]

While efforts at damage control continued, Noli seemed to continue doing one thing while saying another. After chastising the League for its failure to provide Albania with a loan, in addition to meeting with Mussolini in Rome, Noli also paid a courtesy call at the Soviet embassy. According to a report in the *Journal de Geneve,* in a meeting with Juranev, both countries agreed to mutual recognition, and a delegation to Tirana was soon to be named.[38] Few other details of the meeting exist, but it served to raise more suspicions abroad about Noli's agenda. Since the meeting with Juranev came hot on the heels of two successive diplomatic failures, one in Geneva and the other in Rome, Noli was left with little choice but to turn to the Soviets. Once again, the stubborn and impetuous Noli acted on his own and took it upon himself to reopen the question of recognition without consulting with Albanian legations abroad, as had Zogu.

In the aftermath of Noli's meeting in Rome, the Western and Yugoslav press campaign against the move intensified and caused consternation in Albania's legations abroad, especially in Yugoslavia. The exiled Zogu made considerable capital out of Noli's alleged turn to Bolshevism and thereby enhanced his position with Belgrade. As early as December 2, the Yugoslav chargé d'affaires in London made the British Foreign Office aware of the imminent arrival of a Soviet representative named Arkadi Krakovetsky. He added that the Soviets were directing arms and money from their Vienna embassy and were encouraging Albanian tribesmen to make raids into Serbian territory.[39] Since Noli was identified as a sympathizer with the Kosovar cause, the Yugoslavs linked that policy with the decision to open a dialogue with the Soviets. The Belgrade journal *Vreme* noted that Noli worked with the head of the Kosovo Committee and that he was an agent of Moscow.[40] An article in the *Morning Post* on November 27 claimed that the Yugoslav government was in possession of documents proving that the Soviets had provided moral and material help to the Croat peasant leader Stjepan Radić, Fan Noli, the Kosovo Committee, and Macedonian revolutionary organizations.[41] The Belgrade press also insisted that the Tirana government was completely ineffective and that anarchy reigned in the country.

In Great Britain the press had also picked up on the impending recognition. A *Daily Telegraph* article on November 17 claimed that Albania was preparing to recognize the USSR and also hinted at the role of the Kosovo Committee in Noli's government. Konica, in an unpublished letter to the *Telegraph*'s editor, noted that such rumours 'were devoid of foundation' and that there were 'no Bolshevik agencies whatsoever in Albania nor have they indirectly made any propaganda whatsoever.'[42] However, even a diplomat as important as Konica was completely uninformed of Noli's agenda. This is best illustrated by the fact that with the publication of the *Daily Telegraph* article, Konica asked the Foreign Ministry whether the government was in fact about to recognize the USSR.[43] Britain also used its legation in Durrës as a means to probe Noli's intentions. In an early December meeting with Harry Eyres, Noli asked 'how Albania could not recognize the Soviet government when the Great Powers had done so, and there were many Albanians in Russia who complained of lack of protection.'[44] On this point, Noli was correct as Great Britain, France, Italy, Norway, Greece, Austria, and Denmark had offered recognition. Eyres, who felt that Noli was the only member of the government who was well disposed to the Soviets and sought some aid from them, did not believe that recognition would improve the plight of the Albanians in Ukraine. He further warned the Albanian government that it was 'highly desirable to suppress any Bolshevik activity which might exist in Albania.'[45]

As the situation worsened, the Albanian government was still attempting to undercut potential repercussions. Throughout the fall, the Foreign Ministry tried deferring the matter. The Foreign Ministry eventually advised Mborja in Rome on November 27 that, owing to the international situation and the tenuous position of the Albanian government, the exchange of representatives would have to be postponed pending the approval of a new parliament.[46] Mborja was asked to discreetly relay this information to the Soviet authorities and inform them that the whole matter was to be treated with confidentiality. However, it seems that the Soviets were not pleased with the decision to defer recognition, and Noli

tried to smooth over differences. On December 10, he advised the legation in Rome that while Albania had recognized Soviet Russia, because
of the electoral campaign, it was indispensable to adjourn the exchange
of representatives in order to avoid providing a weapon 'to reactionaries
and adversarial parties.'[47]

The Soviets, who wanted to push the issue and possibly create an incident, were unconcerned about the impact for Albania. Mborja did his best
to head off problems in Rome. He telegraphed Noli that after a meeting
with Juranev, the Russian ambassador stated that his government considered the adjournment of a Tirana representative an unfriendly act,
which would have repercussions for future relations.[48] However, while
the Albanian Foreign Ministry was doing its best to postpone the matter until after the elections, it was Vienna where the focus was shifted,
and in early December more chaos ensued. Virtually out of nowhere
the Albanian consul in Vienna advised the Albanian Foreign Ministry
about the impending arrival of a Soviet delegation.[49] The consul, Nush
Bushati, had received representatives of the Soviet embassy in Vienna,
and he subsequently issued visas for the new Tirana embassy staff.[50] The
Soviet minister at Tirana was to be Arkadi Krakovetsky, accompanied
by his wife, Elizabeth, P. Stoutschevsky, V. Leontieff and his wife, and T.
Barischnixoff. After issuing the visas, Bushati was invited along to the
Soviet embassy for tea, where the discussion turned to hard-core politics.
Both the Soviet ambassador at Vienna, V. Aousseme, and Krakovetsky
expressed their great sympathy for Noli and praised his speech at the
League as a masterpiece. He was also informed that Vienna was to
become the centre of Soviet political activity in the Balkans. Bushati was
elated at the royal treatment he was receiving and being privy to such
vital information on Soviet intentions for his country and the Balkans.[51]
The Soviets considered Noli a potential partisan willing to allow them a
foothold in an important region.[52]

Bushati's bombshell, which probably reached Tirana on December 14,
took the Foreign Ministry by surprise. The Foreign Ministry tried to head
off the Soviet legation by advising Rome that it was essential that the Soviets
not send their representative, otherwise Albania 'would be exposed to
a serious peril.'[53] Nevertheless, the Soviet delegation arrived in Tirana
on December 16 and was received by some members of the Albanian
Foreign Ministry and Konstandin Boshnjaku.[54] The Foreign Ministry,
seeking a viable scapegoat, advised Noli on December 17 that the consul
in Vienna had issued visas; that he had taken this action without direction
and should be relieved from his post; and that by taking harsh measures

against Bushati, Albania could show to the Great Powers its sincere disapproval of Bushati's action.[55] In a response on December 18 to Bushati's news, the Foreign Ministry reprimanded him for his actions, called the decision to issue visas a 'grave error,' and demanded that he, along with the consulate archive, return immediately to Tirana.[56] Once again, the Albanian government had to undertake damage control, but it was already too late. Legations were advised on December 18 that owing to the international situation, the seven-person Soviet delegation had been asked to leave and that the entire party had left for Italy that evening.[57] The Soviets later blamed the removal of the delegation on the 'universal pirate' Great Britain,[58] and George Chicherin, in a wider denunciation of British policy, stated that Eyres offered Noli British assistance in the battle against Zogu if he would expel the Soviet representative.[59]

Noli's decision to recognize the USSR, taken with a minimum of discussion, was both hasty and ill-conceived, but was consistent with his authoritarian style of governance and his poor grasp of Albania's role in the wider world. Noli lacked the support both inside and outside the country to pursue this course of action and, in the end, damaged his position from all sides. What prompted him to make this move has yet to be fully assessed. Albanian interpretations have laid emphasis on the dearth of international recognition and Noli's revolutionary ideas. The lack of recognition issue is clearly not viable since the initial decision came so quickly after coming to power that it is unlikely Noli had even contemplated the level of international isolation his country would come to endure.

The notion that the move was consistent with his own progressive ideas is probably more realistic, but not entirely adequate. Noli did have some sympathy for the Soviet Union and was prone to view it as the defender of small nations, especially after the publication of the wartime treaties. As well, many of Noli's supporters were even more inclined to be pro-Soviet than he was and probably put some pressure on him to make the move. The highly progressive Bashkimi organization, Education Minister Stavro Vinjau, and Kosovar leaders Bajram Curri and Hasan Prishtina no doubt supported the decision: Vinjau because of his leftist sympathies, and Curri and Prishtina because of potential support from the Soviets for the Kosovar cause. Curri, who has been called by one participant in the revolution a 'great friend of the Soviet Union,'[60] had been swayed by the Comintern position on Yugoslavia as outlined in 1922. Neither Curri nor Prishtina had any ideological sympathies with communism. As hardened warriors for the Kosovo cause, they chose their allies on the basis of realpolitik. Lastly, Konstandin Boshnjaku, an Albanian who had been in Russia at the time of the Bolshevik revolution and acted as a somewhat informal protector of Russian interests in Albania, might have also exerted some influence.[61] Boshnjaku seems to be responsible for orchestrating the initial presence of a correspondent from the Vienna office of the Russian News Agency, who arrived in Tirana in early 1924. As well, in the January discussion on the deaths of Wilson and Lenin, Boshnjaku was in the gallery acting as interpreter for the Soviet journalist.[62] However, pro-Soviet elements were the minority in his government, and Noli lacked the overall support to proceed with such a decision.[63]

Noli might have thought that the Soviets would be able to provide his government with a measure of financial aid, but again the timing of the recognition is not consistent with this argument. At the time, Noli still held considerable faith in the League of Nations. It was not until the fall, when Noli went to Geneva to address the League, that he probably lost his misplaced optimism, particularly after leaving Geneva empty-handed. That would certainly explain the meeting with the Soviet ambassador in Rome on his return from Geneva. When Noli failed to get money from the League, Italy, or virtually anywhere else, he turned to the Soviet Union. This step, which he took unilaterally, was designed more as a last-ditch attempt to get the West's attention than as an opening to unhindered Soviet penetration into the country.

What most likely shaped his decision at the outset was what he saw as the changing attitude of some powers, especially Great Britain, toward the Soviet Union. Recognition was thus intended to do just what the Council of Ministers' decision stated: to protect the interests of the Albanian minority in Soviet Russia. Owing to Great Britain's important role in defending Albania's interests after the First World War, Noli had considerable faith in Great Britain. Because the British had steadily been normalizing relations with the Soviets since de jure recognition in February 1924, Noli saw his move as consistent with trends in international affairs.

On a regional level, as noted, neither Greece nor Yugoslavia was well disposed toward his government; the courting of the Soviets did not help matters, but it was by no means the key to their policies. Noli, in his reform agenda, had declared his commitment to good relations with Albania's neighbours. However, the establishment of relations with the Soviets was inconsistent with his policy, especially vis-à-vis Yugoslavia. The Yugoslav government monitored the development of Albanian-Soviet ties with greater interest than any other country and, for the most part, kept Europe aware of developments. Even before Krakovetsky's arrival, a *London Times* correspondent had already noted great uneasiness in Belgrade.[64] However, the actual arrival of the Bolshevik legation pushed the Belgrade leadership over the brink and ensured that the exiled Zogu would gain their full support, as the Yugoslav government was convinced of a Bolshevik peril to the region, given the Communist Balkan Fedaration's call for self-determination for component parts of Yugoslavia, and the added fear that Albania would become a base for Comintern activity. In an interview with Eyres, the chargé d'affaires at the Yugoslav embassy in Durrës made it obvious that the principal cause of his government's hostility to the Noli regime was the proposal by the Soviets to establish a legation in Tirana.[65] Eyres had also been told by a diplomat from the Yugoslav legation that while in Rome, Noli had signed a secret agreement with the Soviets, although Eyres did not accept this assertion.[66] That the authorities in Belgrade were disturbed about the implications of a Soviet representative stationed in Tirana there is no doubt, but, as the evidence suggests, it was only one of several factors that shaped their attitude toward Noli's government.

The USSR and the League of Nations symbolized Noli´s difficult situation. The League was his first hope, the Soviet Union his last. Noli's initial enthusiasm about the League waned considerably, and by the time he left Geneva, most of his dreams were shattered. His cynical speech requesting a loan was a far cry from his statements in December 1920, when he presided over Albania's admission to the League. In four years of Albanian state-building, the League had accomplished little. Commissions of enquiry set off and reported back, and all recognized that the country desperately needed reform, financial assistance, and help in obtaining a loan. Despite a massive amount of paperwork, the League's activities in Albania never translated into concrete assistance. When the League finally named a permanent advisor to the country, the Albanian government sacked him, refused to implement his recommendations, and preferred to follow advice from Great Britain.

Noli, who mistakenly believed that the League was interested in solving Albania's problems, did not reinstate Hunger. Instead, he travelled to Geneva to seek financial assistance and chose to berate League members for not recognizing the Albanian problem as fundamental to European stability. His attitude toward the League, and Albania's position in the wider European arena, was also made clear in the struggle with Greece and Yugoslavia, in which he continually appealed to the League to solve regional conflicts. This help never materialized. In light of his own attitude and the League's inability to act independently of the Great Powers, it is not at all surprising that Noli left Geneva penniless. Without cash, he returned home to find that he no longer could command the unity required to implement his twenty-point reform agenda.

Faced with hostility from every quarter, Noli made a last bid to survive through the USSR. It was not a wise decision, but one that he thought might offer some concrete advantages. As to the impact of the episode on the eventual demise of Noli's government, one should not overestimate it. The recognition of the USSR was one of several external blunders that worsened Noli's predicament both inside and outside Albania, but it by no means sealed his fate. What the Great Powers, especially Great Britain, sought in Albania was stability. It was gradually assumed that Noli could not ensure this, and that had he permitted a Soviet presence in the country, he would not be able to control its influence. If such a course was allowed to continue unchecked, the implications for regional stability would be far-reaching.

7
Traitor One Day, Patriot the Next

By the beginning of December 1924, the Albanian experiment with reform was deeply troubled, and achievements after four years of flirtation with a compromised form of political pluralism were limited. The far from cohesive group that seized power in June had ruptured beyond repair, and the main camps were busy preparing for new elections that would, in theory, finally decide the main questions facing the state since 1920. By the time he returned from Geneva, Noli enjoyed little credibility in the country and was no longer capable of shaping events. As one Albanian historian noted, the 'democratic revolution' was surrounded.[1] On both fronts, external and internal, the government's position also gave little cause for optimism. Time, the very thing Noli needed so much, was short, and his hopes for a prolonged period of authoritarianism were dashed by forces both inside and outside Albania.

The move toward elections, which from all perspectives was entirely necessary, was especially propitious for Ahmed Zogu. During the intervening months in Belgrade, he worked tirelessly to gain support for his return. His willingness to offer concessions to the Yugoslavs and his disinterest in the Kosovo question had won their support, while Noli's brief flirtation with the Soviets enhanced Zogu's position even more. Greece, which believed there was much to gain from chaos in Albania, was following an 'anybody but Noli' approach to the situation. The Great Powers, especially Great Britain, tacitly supported Zogu because of his ability to keep order in Albania and to avoid confrontation with Yugoslavia and Greece. Italy also saw potential gains from prolonged instability, and had been offered lavish concessions for turning a blind eye to any seizure of power. Zogu and his supporters had also worked well in Albania's

northern periphery, fomenting disorder, distributing funds, and finding willing supporters. However, should elections go ahead, Zogu's claim
that the last government was the legal one would have rung hollow.

December was an especially hectic month as the government tried to
prepare for new elections and an attack from Zogu. In mid-November,
with Yugoslav support, rumours were circulated in the Belgrade press
that Zogu had left for Paris when in fact he was still in Serbia.[2] The
Albanian press temporarily fell for the ruse, but soon caught on; by
early December, Ali Kolonja possessed detailed information on Zogu's
agenda.[3] In a telegram of December 3 from Belgrade, he wrote that on
December 5 Zogu intended to depart for Prizren in Kosovo, and that he
would commence his attack from various frontier points on December
10.[4] Kolonja's report offered even greater detail, stating that the attack-
ing army would include refugee Albanians, Serb regulars, and former
White Russian soldiers of General Wrangel's army holed up in Belgrade
and looking for a war.[5] In another report, Kolonja added that the attack
was organized with Zogu leading from Prizren, Ceno Bey Kryeziu from
Gjakovë, Albanian/Montenegrin forces from Shkodër, and an attack
from Ohrid led by a Russian officer.[6] Kolonja estimated rebel troop
strength at 20,000 and predicted the offensive would begin with a revolt
staged in Zogu's traditional bastion in Mati.[7] The Foreign Ministry
added that Ceno Bey had departed for Gjakovë with a considerable sum
of money to organize troops and partisans there.[8] Even the Albanian
press anticipated an invasion in early December. *Bashkimi*, often referring to Zogu as Zogollivić or Esad Pasha Toptani II, wrote of the planned
attack and lamented that the Great Powers were ignoring Serb impe-
rial ambitions merely because Serbia was a good customer for arms and
ammunition.[9]

Kolonja was almost entirely correct in his assessment of the situation,
as Zogu's forces attacked from the north on December 14. According
to Joseph Swire, Zogu's invasion force included 1,000 volunteers from
the Yugoslav army and 1,000 reservists. In addition, Zogu had 500 of his
own tribesmen from Mati, 40 officers from Wrangel's exile army, and
16 Yugoslav army officers. Materiel included 2 batteries of mountain
artillery, 10 heavy machine guns, and 20 light machine guns.[10] On the
same day, Myfid Libohova launched an offensive from Greece toward the
frontier at Kakavia. The diplomatic effort intensified while the military
engaged the insurgents. In a memo to Albanian legations abroad, the
Foreign Ministry stated that bands organized by the Serbs, and armed
with canons and bombs, had attacked, and that a Greek-supported force

occupied Kakavia.[11] Because of the attack, the government announced
that elections would be delayed by one month. In the initial battles,
the government desperately tried to prove to the outside world that the
chaos was not the result of internal problems (as had always been the
case hitherto), but rather the result of Yugoslav meddling. The Albanians
possessed ample proof of outside interference, and the Foreign Ministry
advised foreign legations that some of the captured prisoners were
Serbs and that the weapons originated in Serbia.[12] In a communiqué of
December 19, the Foreign Ministry implored the Yugoslavs to cease assistance to the rebels, and added that continued support was not only a violation of the neutrality pledge, but a menace to good relations between
the two countries.[13] By all accounts, it appears that the Serb forces were
expected to aid Zogu only along the Yugoslav-Albanian frontier. Once
Zogu was again on Albanian territory, Yugoslavia withdrew and restated
its neutrality.[14] Zogu continued the march toward Tirana with his followers and the refugee Russians. Immediately after Libohova's forces
crossed into Albania from Greece, the Greek government also resumed
its policy of non-intervention and proclaimed that the troubles near
Kakavia were an isolated case that would not be repeated.[15]

Since the Albanian military was again ill prepared to fight the invaders,
and found itself in the same position as in May, Noli naïvely hoped that
diplomatic activity would force Yugoslavia to abandon its overt assistance
of Zogu. Noli assumed that without Yugoslav support, Zogu did not have
a realistic chance of success. It was clear to virtually any observer that
the Yugoslavs were prepared to offer concrete assistance to Zogu. This
was despite Belgrade's constant pledge of neutrality, as well as an early
December agreement with Italy, as in the case when Noli seized power,
that both countries would observe the strictest neutrality in the emerging crisis in Albania.[16] As one Albanian historian noted, Yugoslav diplomats were no doubt 'pleased with Italian passivity.'[17] The declaration of
neutrality from both Italy and Yugoslavia was, once again, farcical. At the
very least, Yugoslavia could count on territorial changes as outlined in
discussions with Zogu, and Italy might have been able to push for a mandate over Albania because of its right to protect Albanian sovereignty.

Fear of Italy's long-term intentions forced Noli to place his greatest hopes on the support of the United States and Great Britain. The
United States, as already outlined, was not a viable source of protection and remained reluctant to stand by Noli's government. Noli had
a better chance with Great Britain, where the task of finding support
fell once again to Mehmet Konica. It was not an easy assignment since

Noli's political capital, nearly bankrupt when he achieved power, had declined even further. In his initial reports, Konica appeared confident that Britain would urge Belgrade to maintain neutrality.[18] The British representative in Belgrade did make a démarche to Pašić, who gave assurances that Yugoslavia was neutral, that it was offering no assistance to any political refugees, and that nothing was known of Ahmed Bey.[19] Konica also advised the Foreign Ministry on December 16 that Pašić, who insisted that accusations against his government were merely the intrigues of Noli, had promised the British representative to give orders to the frontier authorities to prevent the organization of bands.[20] Britain was unwilling to push the Yugoslav government, and on December 19 Konica wrote that while there was some sympathy in the British government for Albania, it would not get involved.[21] In Italy, Mborja worked on any representative who was willing to listen. Britain and Italy did make démarches to the Yugoslav government, but without effect. In a telegram of December 15 from Rome, Mborja suggested that his discussions with the British ambassador in Rome and the foreign minister's cabinet chief were positive and would achieve concrete results in Belgrade.[22]

The role of Yugoslavia was well known, and despite some démarches no power seemed willing to bring Belgrade to task for the interference, primarily because Noli's cause looked so hopeless. In a memo of December 18 to the State Department, the U.S. minister in Belgrade, Percival Dodge, noted that it appeared 'highly probable' that the Yugoslav government was actively assisting Zogu.[23] In a telegram of December 23, Harry Eyres was even more precise, noting that it was 'perfectly clear that Serbia has actively supported Ahmed's invasion.'[24] Despite overwhelming evidence, the Yugoslav government maintained its innocence in the whole affair. In a note of December 20 from the legation of the Kingdom of Serbs, Croats and Slovenes in Washington, the Yugoslavs dispatched a lengthy reply to the Albanian suggestions that its government was behind the chaos in Albania:

> The truth is that the present revolutionary movement in Albania is only a reaction against the misrule and tyranny of the Government of Tirana of which the chief supporters and partisans are such people as Bairam Tzur (Curri) and Hassan Beg Prichtina (Prishtina), two well-known brigands, who have on their consciences the deaths of thousands of Serbs, many of them women and children.[25]

The Yugoslavs also added that while they would maintain the principle of non-intervention, they cited Tirana as a centre of Bolshevism and blamed

Noli for bringing on the problem by seizing land illegally. Maintaining to
the end the argument that Albania was a country that lacked unity, the
Yugoslav government insisted that chaos was the natural state of affairs in
Albania, that an Orthodox Christian could not effectively rule a Moslem
country, and that Albania should be placed under international supervision.[26] The Yugoslav government also noted that, owing to an election
campaign, it could not afford to 'indulge in foreign adventures at this
moment.'[27] However, Percival Dodge noted quite accurately that Pašić
'might well find such a diversion to be useful in provoking a nationalist
reaction in his favor.'[28]

Albanian requests for diplomatic support received a muted response.
The appeal to the League was especially futile since the whole question, which required considerable haste, languished in the League
bureaucracy. On December 18, Noli made his first appeal to the League
secretary, reiterating the accusation that the troubles originated in
Belgrade, and on December 20 Noli upped the ante and asked for intervention under Articles XII and XV of the League Covenant.[29] Secretary
General Drummond advised the League Council of Noli's appeal and
requested that representatives of both Yugoslavia and Albania provide
him with any information that might be of value for the investigation.[30]
Not exactly the hasty response that the situation dictated. In his note to
Drummond, Noli appealed to the League to save 'the Albanian people
from the horrors of a foreign invasion.'[31]

Despite the relative ease with which Noli's government was toppled,
the government did its best throughout the two-week battle to convince
the outside world that all was well. In a communiqué of December 18
from the Albanian Information Bureau, the government denied reports
that both Shkodër and Gjirokastër were occupied by Zogu's supporters,
and maintained that the military situation was favourable for the government.[32] On December 22, just two days before Zogu's march into
Tirana, the government reported that 200 were dead and wounded
in Mati, there was demoralization in enemy ranks, and that reservists
had responded with great enthusiasm to the appeal of the government.
The announcement added that all political parties and the people were
together with the government.[33]

Inside Albania, Noli made efforts to rally the people behind his government. In an impassioned plea, he called on Albanians to resist the
foreign invasion, and likened the situation to 1920 when Albanians had
rallied together to expel the Italian forces.[34] Noli went to great lengths to
stress that it was not a civil war but a foreign force challenging Albanian

sovereignty, and that the battle was a war for 'freedom and independence' against Serb soldiers and weapons.[35] For a brief moment, it even
appeared that the much sought-after unity was achieved, with a proclamation in mid-December from Bashkimi, the Radical Democrats, and
National Democrats that they 'would fight shoulder to shoulder against
the present danger that threatens the Fatherland from the traitors sold
to foreigners and endeavouring to crush Albania.'[36] Despite the fact that
these groups had little in common, Zogu's return boded equally poorly
for all of them.

The main problem was that Yugoslav assistance ensured that Zogu's
forces were simply better equipped than the Albanian forces, which were
desperate for equipment to counter their better-armed opponents. It is
worth recalling that the Albanian military was no different than in June
1924 – underpaid, under-equipped, and unprepared. In the last days of
his government, Noli finally decided that only Italy might be induced to
offer concrete military assistance. The Albanians were at pains to note
that Zogu's incursion had the support of both Greece and Yugoslavia,
hoping that Italy would act to preserve a semblance of influence in
Albania. While Italian diplomats had denied any suggestions that they
were seeking to profit from the chaos by seeking a League mandate for
Albania, the reality was somewhat different.[37] In Rome, Tefik Mborja was
probably closer to the mark when he informed the Foreign Ministry that
Italy's refusal to intervene with Belgrade was based on the fact there was
too much to gain by the prolongation of chaos in Albania because its case
for a League mandate would achieve added credibility.[38] Despite his best
efforts, Mborja found that while Italian public opinion supported Noli's
government, Mussolini was unwilling to push the Yugoslavs. Rather,
Mussolini tended to accept the Yugoslav position that support of Zogu
was justified by Noli's accord with the Soviets, which was interpreted as
a means to support the Kosovars in an attack against Yugoslavia.[39] In a
telegram of December 16, Kolonja added that it appeared the Italians
also did not want to displease the Serbs by taking a resolute position.[40]
More to the point, after a long discussion with the secretary of the Italian
Foreign Ministry, Contarini, Mborja was cynically informed that by expel-
ling Italian forces from Vlorë in 1920, Albania reduced Italy's 'possibility
to effectively aid you in the present circumstances.'[41]

Italy was willing, however, to circumvent its neutrality since it did
consider offering military supplies to Noli. This was more the result
of the potential benefits Italy could reap than any feelings of loyalty to
Noli. Beginning in mid-December, the Albanians authorized the Rome

legation to work toward a secret deal for arms.[42] The negotiations were long and arduous, but in the first days it appeared that the Italian government authorized the arms transfers. On December 18, Mborja wrote that every effort was underway to speed shipments and that all necessary formalities were near completion.[43] On December 19, Mborja informed the Foreign Ministry that the Italian Ministry of Foreign Affairs was not opposed to the arms sales, but they would not do it for free.[44] Mborja further noted that time was crucial and that 500,000 liras must be dispatched immediately.[45]

However, owing to what can only be judged as the speed of Zogu's success, the arms deal eventually collapsed. The Albanians made every effort to meet payment deadlines, and it appeared that arms were on the way. In an undated telegram, which was possibly Noli's last, he informed the Rome legation that Stamati had telegraphed there was no authorization to ship the arms.[46] In the harshest of terms, Noli ordered Mborja to inform the Italian Foreign Ministry that this was in contradiction to Albanian information and that without arms everything was lost. There was no reply from Rome. In a report from Belgrade on December 22, Ali Kolonja best described the attitude of all the Great Powers when he wrote that everything depended on the resistance of Noli's government.[47]

Resistance, however, was not the government's strong point, and no mass support for the government crystallized, confirming Mehmet Konica's suggestion in June 1924 that a revolution has no more effect in Albania than a general election has in Great Britain. Having failed to secure support from abroad, and with a poorly equipped army and a relatively disinterested populace, Noli was forced to flee Tirana on December 23. As he had done in May, he chose Vlorë as his base for resistance.[48] According to press reports, as had been the case in June, the population welcomed the insurgents when Zogu entered Tirana on December 24. According to witnesses, Fan Noli was seen departing Tirana 'loaded with valises,' while at the Ministry of Finance 'the state funds were being loaded into an automobile.'[49] Sadly for Albania, it was the second time in six months that it was cleaned out. Faced with disaster in Vlorë and with no reason to expect moderation from the insurgents, on December 25 Noli fled to Bari, where he called on Zogu to establish a 'composite and conciliatory cabinet' as a means to put an end to political unrest in the country.[50] A *Times* editorial mocked the suggestion, noting accurately that 'conciliation and compromise were not the hallmarks of Noli's government.'[51] Even Noli's long-time ally Faik Konica was critical of Noli's administration. In an editorial of 6 January 1925 in

Dielli, Konica wrote that Noli had some positive achievements, including the liberation of the contested villages in southern Albania, Greek assurance that no more Albanians would be forcibly removed from northern Greece, victory at the Hague on Saint Naum, and a balanced budget. Konica added, however, that Noli had contributed to a demoralization of the army that subsequently turned officers into rebels, had allowed criminals to go free, made poor choices in government appointments, promised reforms but forgot each one, and governed without a parliament.[52]

Still confident of some support from Great Britain, Noli stated that he hoped to travel to London to plead his case to the British government.[53] On December 27, as general commander of operations, Zogu advised all of Albania's foreign legations and consulates of his version of events. Owing to what he called a reign of terror, violent acts, deportations, and expulsions, a resistance group was formed in Mati to overthrow the revolutionary government.[54] Zogu added that tranquility now reigned in Albania, that the old government would return, and that in the meantime he would direct the affairs of state.[55]

U. Grant-Smith's assessment of the whole affair was little different from his reports on the June seizure of power. In a report of December 26 to the State Department, he described the atmosphere:

> ...wild rumors of wild men about to descend from the mountains; panic among those who remained, both men and women; further appeals for asylum to the American Minister who managed to avoid compliance (none were made to the Yugoslav, or Italian or German representatives in Tirana); be-flagged streets; the advance guard of the victors entered the town, took over the gendarmerie [*sic*] and opened the prison doors; tales of brigandage in the streets; general disquiet during the succeeding night; entry of the victorious commander amid the exclamations of the same populace which gave a similar reception to the victors after he had been driven out seven months ago; the band played in the public square and the merchants wondered when the first demand for gold would be made.[56]

Grant-Smith estimated that some 10 people were killed, 20 were wounded, and that some 97 Russian exiles took part.[57] He added that there was no indication of a Serb presence.

Zogu moved quickly to satisfy his supporters. One of the government's first acts was to officially withdraw the appeal to the League for assistance. As well, Myfid Libohova, as acting foreign minister, asked Drummond to inform the members of the League that the accusations brought by

Noli against the government of the Serbs, Croats, and Slovenes were 'unfounded and that we do not share them.'[58] In terms of outside supporters, Zogu, as outlined in his discussions with Pašić, almost immediately made border rectifications around Saint Naum and Vermosh in Yugoslavia's favour. More importantly, the members of the Kosovo Committee fled, and Hasan Prishtina was later assassinated in Salonika. The same fate befell Luigi Gurakuqi and Bajram Curri. As to the oil concession, APOC did receive its 200,000 hectare concession, although throughout 1925 Zogu and APOC were forced, because of pressure from the United States, France, and Italy, to permit a role for the other major players.

International recognition, which Noli could not obtain, trickled in because Zogu temporarily reconvened the disbanded assembly on January 15 and Vrioni was again prime minister, thus giving his seizure of power a hint of legality. Sixty-four members of the assembly returned. The very brief reincarnation of the Vrioni government was merely a temporary facade that confirmed Zogu's capacity for shrewd decision-making. Zogu knew better than to assume power himself, as he would then find himself little better off than Noli. Zogu waited until the end of January before seeking the assembly's approval for the creation of a presidential republic, establishing himself as the country's first president and doing away with the Regency Council, established in Lushnjë in 1920. The new constitutional framework looked, at least on paper, something like the one found in the United States. Zogu's key change, however, was to concentrate power in his hands – he controlled the army, the cabinet, the judiciary, and even the constitution. The presidential 'stage' was another temporary step on the road toward a monarchy, since he used the intervening years until 1928 to lay the foundations for his own personality cult. He subsequently bowed to the 'wishes' of his people and assumed the title of King of the Albanians. Proclaiming himself King of the Albanians, as opposed to King of Albania, was about all he was willing to do for the Albanians, who found themselves living outside the state.

Since the legal government was, albeit temporarily, back in place and the situation in the region appeared stabilized, there was little cause to withhold recognition. The British never even raised the question of recognition since 'constitutional forms' were observed in re-creating the Vrioni cabinet; the British treated the Noli interregnum as a mere 'interlude.'[59] The French and Italians also adhered to this policy. Eyres could not conceal his pleasure at Zogu's return, writing the Foreign Office that Zogu was determined to create a 'decent government' and that he was 're-establishing order and that the people welcome his strong hand.'[60] Albanian communist historians maintain speedy recognition was the result of the willingness of Zogu to satisfy the oil concession in Britain's favour, and that APOC had also offered financial assistance to Zogu.[61] Both Bernd Fischer and Jason Tomes suggest a clear link between APOC and Zogu. Fischer noted that in early January 1925, Zogu granted the concession to APOC, as APOC had already 'invested large sums in direct payments to Zogu.'[62] As a result of subsequent complaints from Mussolini, Zogu later gave the Italians a concession.[63] While he may have relied on Yugoslavia to return to power, Zogu chose Italy as the country's new benefactor, and a series of economic and political agreements eventually all but eliminated Albania's independence.

As to the United States, some historians suggested that Standard Oil also financed Zogu's return in collusion with APOC.[64] This accusation is, in fact, ridiculous since the two companies were vicious competitors. The American oil interests, as made clear by the events throughout the period, were almost constantly ignored, and U.S interests initially received nothing from Zogu. On 5 January 1925 Grant-Smith requested a position on Zogu's seizure of power, given the fact that he was sentenced by an Albanian court. Since the United States had rejected the court's findings and if Grant-Smith found the old/new government firmly established, Secretary of State Hughes wrote that the United States would 'not be disposed indefinitely to withhold recognition.'[65] On January 20, in light of U. Grant-Smith's suggestion that the government was stable and the fact that Italy, Great Britain, France, Greece, and Yugoslavia raised no objections, Hughes advised him that if he could obtain assurances from Zogu that prosecution against those responsible for the murders would be pressed, the State Department would accord recognition.[66] Not surprisingly, Zogu moved quickly to clear himself of any involvement in the Coleman / De Long murders, and the United States never really achieved a satisfactory conclusion to the tragic affair.[67]

Back in control, Zogu eliminated the vestiges of Noli's brief legacy, and many of the instigators of the revolution were assassinated.[68] Noli wandered around Europe looking for allies and even took part as a Balkan delegate to the 'Friends of the Soviet Union' Congress in Moscow in 1927. Eventually he returned to the United States to concentrate on his real passion: the Albanian Orthodox Church.[69] He also earned a bachelor of music degree in 1938, and subsequently a doctorate from Boston University in 1945 with a dissertation on the Albanian national hero Skanderbeg. Noli never returned to Albania.

Zogu, who some historians have credited with finally unifying the Albanian nation,[70] chose to concentrate on creating stability, while always holding out the potential for reform. Substantive land reform never materialized – that only came with the communist seizure of power in 1944. The need for a benefactor, which dogged Noli to the end, was solved as Zogu turned his back on his Yugoslav supporters and allowed Italy to gradually assume the very control Noli was so unwilling to permit. Unlike Noli, Zogu's interest was not in eliminating the disintegrative trends that plagued Albania and creating a unified and reformed country, but rather in using disunity to his advantage. It was that strategy, more than anything, that allowed him to govern Albania until his dependency on Italy culminated in an invasion in April 1939. Noli later argued that the June 1924 revolution marked an abrupt shift in the history of Albania and thus created an epoch.[71] This was true as, more than anything, Noli's fall marked the end of Albania's experiment with political pluralism, reform, and experimentation in foreign affairs. The period of democracy and chaos, which was the hallmark of the 1920-5 period, gave way to permanent authoritarianism and, ultimately, conquest by a foreign power, but also to the first significant efforts at state building that came with Albania's communist rulers.

8
Conclusion

In its broadest sense, the purpose of this study was to chronicle the vicissitudes of state and nation building efforts in Albania that culminated in Fan Noli's seizure of power in June 1924, his subsequent fall in December of the same year, and its implications for Albania in the interwar period. With very little time on his hands, Noli sought to fundamentally alter the main pillars of Albania's domestic and foreign policies. He thus confronted the main obstacles to stability and democratization, apparent throughout the early 1920s in the Balkans, and attempted to eliminate them through radical reforms. Albania's and Noli's experience in this period was not dissimilar from other Balkan states. Many patriots throughout the region sought to implement radical reforms and tie their country's destiny to Western Europe, but instead they saw the triumph of authoritarianism and intolerance. The Albanian case, in both its external and internal context, makes it clear how difficult this agenda was.

Much of what Noli sought to implement was difficult, and he lacked the political acumen to navigate the very difficult climate that shaped the Balkans in the First World War's aftermath. To be fair, the implementation of his vision for Albania would have been difficult even for the most experienced of politicians, given the nature of external and internal challenges. Throughout the Balkan region, the forces of the status quo retained the upper hand, and Noli was not the only politician to suffer defeat. Nor was he the only Balkan leader to meet indifference from the Great Powers and the League of Nations. Noli, however, did face obstacles that were specific to both him and Albania. He was a neophyte in the Albanian political milieu and only became a serious political figure in 1920-1 after his success at the League of Nations. Upon returning to

Albania, he gradually emerged as the major opposition to Ahmed Zogu and Albania's traditional ruling class of Islamic landowners. Even more gradually, he declared himself the spokesman of the oppressed peasant masses.

While Noli saw the battle between the forces of a new order and the old as a battle between good and evil, the political chaos that dominated the years following the Lushnjë Congress in January 1920 was more complex. It was thus only partly the result of a battle between Noli's version of liberalism and the old order's landlordism. The second attempt at statehood, which came with the Congress of Lushnjë, brought to the surface not only severe antagonisms that had not been solved in the preceding years but also new opportunities. These included the legacy of a national awakening that had yet to fully integrate the country. This ensured that both religious and regional differences also shaped the political battle. Ottoman rule had marginalized Orthodox and Catholic citizens, and the continued dominance of Moslem beys created deep rifts, which were not merely social in origin, but political, regional, and personal. Noli, as did Zogu, understood that the country remained fractured, and he felt that only through radical measures, which would include the destruction of the traditional ruling class, could the disintegrative trends be eliminated.

If Noli could count on the support of Bashkimi and Vatra in that agenda, for a vast number of political figures there were other problems. Just as large a group was only hostile to Zogu's continued dominance and sought to gratify themselves with the benefits of political office. It was precisely the vast array of viewpoints that made the period prior to Noli's seizure of power the zenith of Albanian political life in the interwar period, but also a period that was utterly devoid of substantive political achievements. Even the most basic questions were left untouched as Albania slid deeper and deeper into chaos. The Lushnjë Congress called for a constituent assembly as soon as possible, although elections were repeatedly postponed. Loans and foreign concessions, stated by League observers as urgently required, never came. The period after the 1923 elections highlighted the divisive trends in the country, and it was precisely this combination of factors that paved the way for Noli's seizure of power. His triumph presented for him (and a few others) the possibility of a social revolution. For the majority, however, it was a coup d'état that presented, not the opportunity for radical change, but a redistribution of political power.

Regional, religious, political, and personal antagonisms were intensified by the question of Kosovo. Not all patriots accepted Albania's borders as definitive, and those who did not were by far the greatest source of political instability. For Zogu, the most persistent thorn in his side was not the liberals surrounding Noli, but the Kosovar irredentists, who had twice nearly succeeded in ousting him in 1922 and 1923. More to the point, if Zogu's return to power in December 1924 was owed to Yugoslav assistance, Noli's seizure of power six months earlier was owed primarily to the military assistance of the Kosovo Committee and the Albanian army. The role of disgruntled Kosovars did much to shape the course of events. Their struggle had little to do with questions of reform and democracy, but instead sought the creation of an ethnic Albania, and they chose allies on the basis of that aim alone.

Thrust onto centre stage in June 1924 by the combined discontent of five groups (Kosovars, Shkodrans, the army, so-called liberal beys, and progressive-minded reformers), Noli had yet to articulate a carefully planned program or make himself the link between the peasants and Tirana. Making matters worse, he was not even a truly national figure: his impact was primarily limited to the Orthodox fringe in the south, and he never managed to transform his vision for a reformed and western-ized Albania into a mass movement. This ensured that when he assumed power, he was forced to share it with those who had little use for radical change. It is worth recalling that it was only in the months following the elections of the fall of 1923 that Noli tried to rally progressive forces in a battle against the ruling class. It took the tragic death of Avni Rustemi to temporarily unite the opposition to Zogu. In such a short time, it was unlikely that even the most skilled politician could have transformed the discontent of a small group into a mass movement that could have maintained power in the long run. Such a transformation would have been measured in years, not months. Noli, the self-proclaimed spokes-man of the peasants, spent little time combing the villages, as did his contemporaries Stjepan Radić in Croatia or Alexander Stamboliskii in Bulgaria. Noli's premature seizure of power thus did as much to scuttle the hopes of those calling for a reformed Albania as it did to provoke a premature conflict with the forces of the status quo when they still pos-sessed the upper hand. As had been so often the case in the past, Noli's impatience and stubbornness proved to be his undoing.

While in power, Noli seemed virtually unable to govern, and he was incapable of unifying the forces that overthrew the previous government. Convinced that only he had the best interests of the nation at heart and unwilling to compromise, Noli failed to see that he had no mandate for radical change. He fell back on methods that he had previously criticized as he laid the foundations for a form of authoritarianism that differed little from that of his predecessors. He imposed censorship, waged a vindictive struggle against his opponents that did nothing to end the cycle of vengeance, used extra-legal methods to permanently silence opposition, and, for the most part, did little to implement the twenty-point agenda. By the time he left for Geneva in August 1924, his committed base of supporters were lamenting the government's foot-dragging, and the cynical ones were calling for a slowdown and the retention of the status quo. His two-month departure for Geneva was badly timed, as it created a dangerous leadership vacuum. At a time when the forces of reform and westernization desperately needed unity, the pillar of the movement was in Geneva berating the League of Nations.

Noli's vision for a new Albania, however, did not collapse merely because of the internal contradictions. The outside world, while not destroying Noli, did much to hasten his fall. Noli certainly believed that this was the case:

> It was purely a case of foreign intervention. Zogu's restoration was supported from all Albania's neighbours and feudal landowners who were exploiting the country. They hoped that Ahmed Zogu, leader of the landowners, would help them realize their plans for the partition of Albania among them.[1]

This statement in Noli's autobiography is only partly true. Zogu did find support both at home and in exile for a restoration of the status quo. Moreover, Zogu would certainly not have been successful without assistance from the Yugoslavs (and General Wrangel's army) in the initial attack on Albania. However, Noli's diplomatic failures did much to create the conditions for Zogu's return. Faik Konica, as president of Vatra, was probably closer to the mark when he noted in *Dielli* that

> those who claim that Zogu is a traitor should look about, and they will discover that the majority of Albanians might be described as traitors. I put forward the following thesis: a man who has the backing of the majority of the people has a right to rule that people. The Albanian people do not want reforms and reformers, they do not want new things, nor people who strive for new things.[2]

The external atmosphere was equally bleak in the early 1920s and sheds important light on the nature of post–Paris Peace Conference

Balkan politics. Not only were Albanian patriots deciding on the very nature of the state, but Albania's place in the Balkans was still an open question between 1920 and the consolidation of Zogu's dictatorial rule in early 1925. As the smallest, poorest, and weakest of the Balkan states, Albania's destiny was influenced substantially by forces outside its borders. Albanians had continually battled for the right to independence: once in 1912, and on successive occasions after the First World War. The struggle for the right to exist as a nation-state, when Albania's neighbours sought to highlight the divisive factors, had important implications. It ensured that considerable resources were wasted fighting battles abroad, especially at the League and the International Court, to the detriment of a search for national consolidation at home. Border problems, made worse by the intransigent attitude of both Athens and Belgrade, drained the country's finances and helped to ensure that Albania always hovered on the edge of bankruptcy. A bankrupt state is hardly a breeding ground for stability.

Since a financial benefactor was vital for Noli's survival, the Great Powers were in a position of considerable influence. The attitude of the Great Powers, however, did little to help consolidate Noli's vision. Economic interests, especially the quest for a potentially lucrative oil concession, did play some role in shaping policy toward Albania and Noli, as all the interested parties considered the oil concession worth fighting for. Yet while oil was important, no Great Power was willing to accept that Albanians were capable of sustaining a democratic state along Western lines. Albania's political chaos in the early 1920s did little to encourage a reassessment of that policy. As a result, Great Power policy was based on the need to preserve stability in a region with vast potential for conflict. Zogu, who appeared to best suit Albania's political climate, became the main beneficiary of that position. Plagued by religious, regional, and tribal differences, Albania needed a government more concerned with stability than with upheaval, in order to prevent civil war and a wider war for the spoils by Albania's neighbours. Moreover, with so many Albanians living outside the state, the Great Powers, especially Great Britain, sought a leader who could be counted on to avoid provoking Albania's more powerful neighbours. Italy's policy was even more cynical: seeking only the conditions to secure a predominant influence in Albania. The United States, which stood to gain considerably with Noli's victory, never considered Albania a vital interest worth fighting for. The League, tied to the interests of the Great Powers, proved incapable of independently aiding Albania.

The policy of non-recognition, which became a cornerstone of Great Power policy, was more a result of Noli's actions than a determination of the outside world to crush his progressive movement. Legitimizing his government would have eliminated international concern, but it took Noli far too long to appreciate the link between elections and recognition. Moreover, delays in legalizing his government served only the interests of his enemies. Noli did little to alleviate the justified fears of the Great Powers. Internally, he embarked on widespread repression, which cast doubt on his position as a progressive, to say nothing of his role as a church leader. Both at home and abroad, he often appeared erratic and prone to histrionics, and thus seemed a dangerous threat to regional stability. At the League, he earned even more enemies, and his decision to initiate relations with the Soviet Union confirmed, not the notion that he was a communist, but that he simply had no idea what he was doing. His government was more than willing to barter concessions for recognition and was extremely flexible in its attitude toward legality on a broad number of issues.

Noli's cause with the Great Powers was further damaged by his failure to resolve problems with Albania's neighbours. Once again, Noli needed time. Unfortunately both Yugoslavia and Greece viewed Albania merely as an opportunity for territory. Yugoslavia, throughout the period, became the determined enemy of Albania and did everything possible to hinder the quest for consolidation and political stability. Yugoslavia's attitude toward Albania was shaped by two overlapping factors: borders and the Kosovo question. The question of borders was used as a key means to destabilize Albania financially and politically. However, it was the question of Kosovo that ensured Yugoslav hostility to Noli's seizure of power. With such a numerically vast and restive Albanian population in Kosovo and elsewhere, Yugoslav policy was best served by the maintenance of a compliant regime in Tirana. Only Zogu offered such a prospect. Moreover, Yugoslavia had little to gain with the emergence of a strong and politically stable Albania and did the utmost to foment disorder among a people still in the process of nation building.

Greece, allied with Yugoslavia for most of the period in question, tended to follow the Yugoslav lead and also did little to aid Albania's consolidation. Like Yugoslavia, the question of borders became a vital way to promote instability. Economic and political instability would therefore add greater credence to the notion that Orthodox Greeks could not live in safety within the Albanian state. Instability could also lead to Albania's partition and a renewed chance to recover Northern Epirus. Unlike

Yugoslavia's leaders, who developed a strong personal dislike of Noli, Greek leaders adhered to a policy that was in place since Albanian independence in 1912. Noli's seizure of power made matters worse, but it was difficult to envision a set of circumstances that could have improved the situation. Noli sincerely sought good relations with Greece, and the responsibility for failure to open a new chapter in this area lies primarily with Greece. As was so often the case in the history of Albanian-Greek relations, Greece chose nationalism over realpolitik and missed an historic opportunity to influence developments in Albania in a positive way.

In terms of stabilizing relations with Greece and Yugoslavia, which was a key to his survival, Noli faced difficult choices. In fact, there was little he could do that would have appeased either the Yugoslavs or the Greeks short of ceding important territory or making concessions that would have undermined his domestic support even more. Noli was left with little room to manoeuvre as he scrambled to find support. Noli sincerely hoped that the Great Powers or the League would solve the regional dilemma for him. The Great Powers (and thus the League), in turn, waited to see if *he* could solve the regional dilemma. He could not.

At the outset, Noli had known the magnitude of the task facing him. His five anarchies sermon and the twin dangers of imperialism and feudalism isolated what he saw as the barriers to the establishment of Albanian democracy. Unfortunately, this perspicacity in recognizing the forces of disintegration was not matched by a realistic program to eradicate them. Indeed, his policies served to exacerbate these tendencies in the short term. The commodity he needed most was time to consolidate a fragile central authority. Given his failure to reconcile internal divisions, time could only be bought by securing Great Power intervention and a foreign loan which could prop up the economy and potentially ensure the support of some of his more cynical supporters. Noli's greatest failure, then, was his inability to convince the Great Powers of his viability as a stable and reliable force in the Balkans. It was not a fledgling democracy deserving of support that they saw, but something closer to U. Grant-Smith's vision of 'wild rumors of wild men about to descend from the mountains.'

Notes

1. Internal and External Challenges

1 Albanians arrived in the region during the Byzantine Empire. According to Noli, Ibrik-Tepe was a military outpost for the Empire, chosen because it was close to Constantinople. Many Albanians travelled there to become soldiers and remained after the fall of Constantinople in 1453. See Fan S. Noli, *Autobiografia* (Prishtina, 1968), p. 3.

2 Arshi Pipa, 'Fan Noli as National and International Albanian Figure,' *Sudost Forschungen* 43 (1984): 242.

3 The consecration of Noli as a priest was apparently not accepted by the Patriarchate in Constantinople, 'reportedly on the grounds that Noli was not a fit and proper person for spiritual advancement.' See Bernd J. Fischer, 'Fan Noli and the Albanian Revolutions of 1924,' *East European Quarterly* 22 (June 1988): 147. Noli became a bishop in the Albanian Orthodox Church in July 1919, and in November 1923 he was elected Metropolitan of Durrës, making him spiritual head of the Albanian Orthodox Church.

4 Quoted in B. Kondis and E. Manda, eds, *The Greek Minority in Albania: A Documentary Record, 1921–1993* (Thessaloniki, 1994), p. 31.

5 Rexhep Qosja, 'Fan S. Noli (1882–1965),' *Gjurmime Albanologjike* 1 (1969): 198. The Great Idea evolved as an expression of Greek irredentism in the nineteenth century and as an ideal to unite all Greeks – including those on Albanian territory – in the Ottoman Empire. In the twentieth century, it can also be interpreted as calling for the recreation of a Byzantine Empire. See Yorgos A. Kourvetaris and Betty A. Dobratz, *A Profile of Modern Greece in Search of Identity* (Oxford, 1987).

6 See below for more details on Vatra.

7 Noli's membership in the Albanian parliaments of 1921 and 1922 came through his connection with Vatra, which was allocated one seat. In the 1923 elections for a constituent assembly, he won a seat in the district of Korçë in southern Albania. See Noli, *Autobiografia,* pp. 79–80.

8 Ibid.

9 Pipa, 'Fan Noli as National and International Albanian Figure,' p. 246.

10 Arkivi Qendror i Shtetit (State Central Archives of Albania, hereafter AQSH), Fan Noli – Fondi Personal, F. 14, D. 19, f. 7. It is interesting to note that Noli excluded Great Britain from this list.

11 *Ligjëron Fan Noli,* collected by Lefter L. Dilo (Tirana, 1944), pp. 64–5.

12 *Official Journal – League of Nations* 4 (1923): 498.

13 As noted earlier, Zogu was made minister of interior in the government established at the Lushnjë Congress. He subsequently held that post in two other cabinets. See Bernd J. Fischer, *King Zog and the Struggle for Stability in Albania* (Boulder, 1984), and Jason Tomes, *King Zog: Self Made Monarch of Albania* (Stroud, 2003). Fischer's study remains the best academic study of Zogu and his legacy, while the more recent monograph by Tomes is certainly more entertaining.

14 Fischer, *King Zog,* p. 15.

15 Ibid., p. 16.

16 Piro Tako, *Fan Noli në Fushën Politike dhe Publicistike* (Tirana, 1975), p. 100.

17 Qosja, 'Fan S. Noli (1882–1965),' p. 200.

18 Fischer, *King Zog,* p. 16.

19 Zogu established a presidential republic in January 1925 and in September 1928 converted the country to a hereditary monarchy.

20 Faik Konica, *Albania: The Rockgarden of Southeastern Europe* (Boston, 1957), p. 152.

21 Ahmed Zogu, 'King Zog Tells His Story' (unpublished manuscript, Tirana, 1932), p. 26 (available on-line at http://www.albanianhistory.net/texts20_1/AH1933.html).

22 Stefanaq Pollo and Arben Puto, *The History of Albania: From Its Origins to the Present Day* (London, 1981), p. 187.

23 Communist historiography has interpreted the period preceding Noli's seizure of power solely within the framework of this struggle. See Selim Shpuza, *Revolucioni Demokratiko-Borgjez i Qershorit 1924 në Shqipëri* (Tirana, 1959). In English, see Pollo and Puto, *The History of Albania,* pp. 176–96.

24 The elections were held in April 1921.

25 The districts and estimated populations were Tirana (55,000), Berat (140,000), Durrës (75,000), Dibër (100,000), Elbasan (95,000), Gjirokastër (150,000), Korçë (150,000), Kosova (currently known as Kukës, and not to

be confused with the Kosovo region of Serbia) (60,000), Shkodër (130,000), and Vlorë (55,000). See *Les Balkans* 6 (July 1934): 40.

26　Stavro Skendi, *The Political Evolution of Albania* (New York, 1954), p. 6.

27　Ibid., p. 7.

28　Ibid.

29　Pollo and Puto, *The History of Albania,* p. 186.

30　Hasan bey Prishtina was born in 1873 and graduated from the French Lyceum in Salonica. He later studied law at the University of Constantinople (Istanbul). He was a key organizer of the revolutionary movements in Kosovo, leader of the Committee for the Defence of Kosovo, and later a member of Noli's group. He was assassinated in 1935 in Salonica on the orders of Zogu. See Aleks Buda et al., *Fjalori Enciklopedik* (Tirana, 1985), pp. 867–8.

31　Neil Shehu, 'Formimi i Federates Atdheu dhe Programi i saj,' in Academy of Sciences of the People's Socialist Republic of Albania, *Çështje të Lëvizjes Demokratike dhe Revolucionare Shqiptare në Vitet 1921–1924* (Tirana, 1977), p. 63.

32　Aleks Buda et al, *Historia e Shqipërisë* (Tirana, 1965), p. 529.

33　See *Statuti i Shoqnis 'Bashkimi'* (Tirana, 1924).

34　Nicholas Pano, 'Konica and the Albanian Community in the United States,' conference paper delivered at the Vatra-sponsored symposium on Konica at Fordham University, New York, 22 April 1995.

35　Federal Writers' Project of the Works Progress Administration of Massachusetts, *The Albanian Struggle in the Old World and New* (Boston, 1939), p. 65. In 1920, only 6,000 people reported Albanian as their mother tongue in the United States. However, since many of the migrants arrived from what was the Ottoman Empire, there were difficulties in establishing who was an Albanian. Many probably reported Greek or Turkish as their mother tongue. See 'The Albanians' in Stephan Thernstrom, ed., *The Harvard Encyclopedia of American Ethnic Groups* (Cambridge, 1980), p. 24.

36　Noli was the head of Besa-Besen. While Noli and Konica had corresponded, the two men did not meet until 1909. See Jup Kastrati, *Faik Konica* (New York, 1995), p. 213.

37　Federal Writers' Project of the Works Progress Administration of Massachusetts, *The Albanian Struggle in the Old World and New,* p. 69.

38　Quoted in ibid.

39　While Konica later served Zogu as minister in Washington from 1926 until 1939, he always maintained that he did so out of a duty to serve his country and not because of loyalty to Zogu. Until the end, Konica remained hostile to Zogu, whom he characterized as an 'erratic and treacherous barbarian' (Konica, *Albania,* p. 147).

40 The figure for the 1921 census in Yugoslavia is 441,740. Ivo Banac sug-
    gested, however, that census takers deliberately falsified the statistics for
    both Albanians and Hungarians. See Ivo Banac, *The National Question in
    Yugoslavia: Origins, History, Politics* (Ithaca, 1984), p. 58. The figure for 1931
    was 505,000. See Paul Robert Magocsi, *Historical Atlas of East Central Europe*
    (Toronto, 1993), p. 141. His statistic is from 1931.
41 For an interesting discussion of the legality of the Serb takeover of Kosovo,
    see Noel Malcolm, *Kosovo: A Short History* (London, 1998), pp. 264–6.
42 Ibid., p. 268.
43 Joseph Swire, *Albania: The Rise of a Kingdom* (New York, 1971), p. 291.
44 Djordje Stefanovic, 'Seeing the Albanians through Serbian Eyes: The
    Inventors of the Tradition of Intolerance and Their Critics, 1804–1939,'
    European History Quarterly 35 (2005): 478.
45 In addition to Montenegro, Kosovo, and Macedonia, there were also
    Albanians in Northern Greece (Çameria). See chapter 4 for more details on
    Albanians in Greece and their impact on political developments.
46 Malcolm, *Kosovo*, p. 268.
47 Records of the Department of State Relating to the Internal Affairs of
    Albania, 1910–1944, Record Group 59, National Archives Microfilm
    Publication M1211, National Archives, Washington, DC (hereafter
    Department of State), U. Grant-Smith to the Secretary of State, no. 354, 19
    November 1924, 875.01/256. Grant-Smith, U.S. minister in Albania, had a
    brief conversation with Curri on November 18.
48 Alex N. Dragnich and Slavko Todorovich, *The Saga of Kosovo: Focus on
    Serbian-Albanian Relations* (Boulder, 1984), p. 125. Noel Malcolm suggests
    that the Kaçak movement had 10,000 active rebels (Malcolm, *Kosovo*,
    p. 273).
49 Quoted in Swire, *Albania*, p. 389.
50 Fischer, *King Zog*, p. 45.
51 AQSH, F. 251, V. 1920, D. 33. f. 28–29, 4 October 1920.
52 *League of Nations – Monthly Review* 2 (1–31 October 1922): 255–6.
53 Ibid.
54 For example, between 1920 and 1924 budget deficits ran between 5 and
    10 million gold francs. In 1921, Albania imported over 17,000,000 gold
    francs worth of goods and exported just over 2,000,000 gold francs worth
    (Fischer, *King Zog*, p. 48).
55 See *League of Nations – Official Journal* 5 (April 1924): 727.
56 Tomes, *King Zog*, p. 54.
57 In the years 1920–4, the Albanian army ranged in size from 5,300 to 5,500,
    with some 245 officers and 160 vice-officers.

58 *League of Nations – Official Journal* 5 (Jan. 1924): 166.

59 Swire, *Albania,* p. 50.

60 Northern Epirus includes the southern Albanian provinces of Korçë and Gjirokastër. For more details, see chapter 4.

61 Noli published a number of appeals in the Albanian emigré press and even met with U.S. president Woodrow Wilson, who apparently told him that he had 'a vote at the Peace Conference and I will use it in favour of Albania' (Noli, *Autobiografia,* p. 76). Noli's claim has never been substantiated by any other sources. It is doubtful Wilson ever made the assertion.

62 Cited in Pipa, 'Fan Noli as National and International Albanian Figure,' p. 245.

63 Noli, *Autobiografia,* p. 87.

64 For this point I am indebted to Professor Nasho Jorgaqi. See also Pipa, 'Fan Noli as National and International Albanian Figure,' p. 243.

65 AQSH, F. 251, V. 1920, D. 33, f. 5.

66 The first came in October 1913 when Ismail Qemal posed the question to him hypothetically in the period when Albania hoped to secure a 'Western' king. The second offer came in September 1920 from Mehmet Konica, and on that occasion Herbert took the offer very seriously. See Margaret Fitzherbert, *The Man Who Was Greenmantle: Biography of Aubrey Herbert* (London, 1983), pp. 122–3, 229.

67 AQSH, F. 251, V. 1920, D.33, f. 28–29, 4 October 1920. However, in a private letter to Herbert, Nicholson warned him that he was 'all for the Greeks recovering [territory] up to Voiussa and none of your arguments will move me from that attitude' (Fitzherbert, *Greenmantle,* p. 218).

68 *Journal of the First Assembly of the League of Nations,* no. 21, 8 December 1920, p. 174. Noli credits Cecil with organizing a bloc to push for Albania's acceptance in the League (Noli, *Autobiografia,* p. 78).

69 AQSH, Fondi Personal – Fan Noli, F. 14, V. 1921, D. 86, f. 7.

70 Tako, *Fan Noli në Fushën Politike dhe Publicistike,* p. 100.

71 Pipa, 'Fan Noli as National and International Albanian Figure,' p. 246.

72 Italy retained control of the island of Sazan, just off the coast of Vlorë. The expulsion of Italian troops and the liberation of Vlorë is considered the key victory of Albania's first cabinet. See Anton Logoreci, *The Albanians: Europe's Forgotten Survivors* (London, 1977), p. 53.

73 Swire, *Albania,* p. 348.

74 Publications of the Permanent Court of International Justice. Series C, No. 5-II, *Question of the Monastery of Saint Naoum,* p. 148.

75 Çameria, a coastal region in Greek Epirus, had a community of roughly 20,000 Albanians in 1923. See Dimitris Michalopoulos, 'The Moslems of

Chamuria and the Exchange of Populations between Greece and Turkey,'
Balkan Studies 27 (1986): 304. For more details see chapter 4.

76 *The Question of the Monastery of Saint Naoum*, p. 148.

77 Ibid., p. 147.

78 M.E. (Edith) Durham (1863–1944) was a well-known promoter of the
Albanian cause both before and after the First World War. She won the
hearts of many Albanians, especially in the north, for her pioneering studies
of Albanian tribal customs. She was also involved in relief work in Albania
prior to the war. In the war's aftermath, she made a final visit to Albania in
1921, and she was also secretary of the Anglo-Albanian Society. For brief
details on Durham's career, see the introduction by John Hodgson to
Durham's *High Albania* (London, 1985).

79 Harold Temperley, who had an active career in the British diplomatic service and subsequently became a famous historian, was well acquainted with
the Balkans and was the British representative on the Albanian boundary
commission. For details of Temperley's impressive career, see *Who Was Who*,
vol. 3 (London, 1941), p. 1332. Barnes also served on the boundary commission and later worked as an advisor for the Anglo-Persian Oil Company.

80 There was considerable disagreement over which body – the League, the
Allied Supreme Council, or the Conference of Ambassadors – had the right
to determine Albania's frontiers. Noli would have preferred to let the League
handle the matter, while both Greece and Yugoslavia argued that the League
was not competent in the matter since Albania was admitted into that body
without definitive borders and that the matter was in the realm of the Allied
Supreme Council. See Arben Puto, 'La Question du statut international de
l'Albanie devant la Société des Nations et la Conférence des Ambassadeurs,'
Studia Albanica 2 (1965): 19–44.

81 AQSH, Fondi Personal – Fan Noli, F.14, D. 112. f. 4.

82 Ibid., f. 4.

83 Ibid.

84 The reply was dated on 19 September 1921 (ibid., f. 7).

85 Ibid., f. 8.

86 Ibid., f. 5.

87 Ibid., f. 6.

88 For the full details of the affair, see Publications of the Permanent Court
of International Justice, Series C, No. 5-II, *Question of the Monastery of
Saint Naoum*.

89 Ibid., p. 228.

90 Ibid., p. 169.

91 Ibid., p. 176.

92 Ibid., p. 45.
93 Swire, *Albania*, p. 365.
94 Zogu, 'King Zog Tells His Story,' p. 17.
95 Both Albania's northern and southern borders still needed to be delimited, and this process dragged on considerably. Yugoslavia was pressing for
Vermosh in the north and also sought control of the Monastery of Saint
Naoum on Lake Ohrid. Greece maintained troops in fourteen disputed villages near Korçë. See chapter 4 for more details on frontier problems.
96 Recognizing that the territorial integrity of Albania was a 'question of
international importance,' the Conference of Ambassadors stated that in
the event of an attack on the independence or frontiers of Albania, their
re-establishment was entrusted to Italy. For full details on the technicalities
of the Albanian case at the League and the Conference of Ambassadors, see
Puto, 'La Question du statut international.'

2. Creating a Revolutionary Situation

1 Pipa, 'Fan Noli as National and International Albanian Figure,' pp. 246–7.
2 Between November 1920 and 5 December 1921 there were three cabinets. Illias bey Vrioni held office as prime minister in two cabinets until
16 October 1921. A temporary cabinet, called the Sacred Union, was established in October 1921 to deal with the threat posed by the establishment of
the Mirdita Republic. It resigned on December 6.
3 Hasan Prishtina formed an entirely Geg cabinet on 7 December 1921. He
invited Fan Noli to take part as foreign minister, although Noli declined.
Prishtina's resignation was the result of pressure from Zogu, who marched on
Tirana with a thousand of his followers from Mati. See Fischer, *King Zog,* p. 33.
4 Britain's representative in Albania, Harry Eyres, advised the Foreign Office
on March 7 that according to the Albanian government, the whole affair
'was an Italian plot to obtain a protectorate of Northern Albania,' and that
while he did not feel the evidence was conclusive, there was 'much cause for
suspicion' (*Documents on British Foreign Policy* [hereafter *DBFP*], series 1,
vol. 22, no. 780, p. 841).
5 Noli, *Autobiografia,* p. 89.
6 *DBFP,* series 1, vol. 22, no. 780, p. 841 (see footnote no. 3). In a dispatch
of March 13 to London, Eyres noted that the Albanian government unof-
ficially asked him to mediate the crisis and he persuaded Jusufi to retreat.
Bernd Fischer noted that Eyres's assistance was not soon forgotten by Zogu,
and he was subsequently elevated to the position of personal advisor. See
Fischer, *King Zog,* p. 32.

7 For further details, see chapter 4.

8 Curri was under sentence of death for his role in the rebellion, while Hasan Prishtina was banished from Albania. The Albanian Interior Ministry and legations abroad kept a vigilant watch on the activities of both these men. See Buda et al., *Historia e Shqipërisë,* pp. 510–11.

9 Ibid. Zogu became premier in a new cabinet formed on 2 December 1922.

10 Ibid. Curri and Prishtina again attempted to overthrow Zogu in January 1923.

11 Angered by Konica's ongoing and often satirical attacks in *Dielli,* Zogu even banned the paper's circulation, although the U.S. minister reported that the paper was still finding 'its way into Albania by means of first-class mail and is being read ostentatiously by the members of the opposition' (Department of State, Grant-Smith to the Secretary of State, 6 June 1923, 875.00/89).

12 Zogu never married Vërlaci's daughter. Upon becoming king in 1928 and as part of his alleged commitment to westernization, he set his sights on European nobility. In 1938 he married Countess Geraldine Apponyi from Hungary. See Fischer, *King Zog and the Struggle for Stability in Albania,* pp. 258–62.

13 Hilmi Verteniku, 'Problemi i Asamblesë Kushtetuese dhe Zgjedhjet e vitet 1923,' *Studime Historike* 4 (1968): 121.

14 Owing to a communist-inspired ban on even the mere mention of regionalism or religious differences, Albania's communist historians have ignored these trends. Albania's ruling Party of Labour, which governed Albania from 1944 until 1991, took considerable effort to eliminate what it called the obstacles to national unity and modernization. These included religious and regional differences embodied in the Geg/Tosk split. For more details on this component of Albanian communist rule, see Nicholas Pano, 'The Albanian Cultural Revolution,' *Problems of Communism* 23 (July–Aug. 1974): 44–57.

15 To recall, voting was based on a kind of electoral-college principle. For these elections, every 500 male Albanian citizens over the age of twenty, based on census data from the country's ten administrative districts, chose a delegate for the second round of voting, in which an assembly would be elected from a pre-determined list. There was one assembly member for every 10,000 citizens. The second round was notoriously corrupt.

16 Foreign representatives were especially concerned about the implications of Zogu's fall from power. Robert Parr, first consul at the British Embassy, tried to convince the U.S. representative that there should be agreement among foreign governments that recognition would be withheld from any group

that had 'arbitrarily forced the resignation of Ahmed Bey and his ministers.' Much to the chagrin of the U.S. legation, Parr in the end circulated a report stating that the U.S., Italian, British, Greek, and Yugoslav representatives had agreed on this policy. See Department of State, Merrit-Swift to the Secretary of State, 30 November 1923, 875.00/107.

17 So-called independents took this position merely as a tactical manoeuvre. They were primarily linked to the conservative beys. See Verteniku, 'Problemi i Asamblesë Kushtetuese dhe Zgjedhjet e vitet 1923,' p. 136.

18 See *Shqipëria e Re,* 21 October 1923.

19 AQSH, Ministria i Punëve te Brendshme (Ministry of the Interior, hereafter MPB), Periudha i Zogut, D. 1, f. 9, Report of the Prefecture of Shkodër, 1 January 1924.

20 AQSH, Fundi Personal – Luigi Gurakuqi, D. 29, f. 60–61.

21 Ibid.

22 Department of State, Merrit-Swift to the Secretary of State, no. 174, 31 October 1923, 875.00/102.

23 Ibid.

24 *Gazeta e Korçës,* 1 December 1923.

25 Masar Kodra, *Fan Noli: Në Rrjedhat Politike të Shoqërisë Shqiptare, 1905–1945* (Prishtina, 1989), p. 39.

26 Ibid., p. 40.

27 Dilo, *Ligjëron Fan Noli,* p. 57.

28 In a meeting in Permet on August 24, Noli had reiterated his call for direct voting and declared that the new assembly should be in Vlorë. See AQSH, MPB – Periudha i Zogut, V. 1923, D. 6, f. 157.

29 Ibid., f. 156, Report of the Interior Ministry on 25 August 1923.

30 *Shqipëria e Re,* 2 September 1923.

31 AQSH, MPB – Periudha i Zogut, V. 1923, D. 6, f. 156, Report from the Prefecture of Korçë on 14 August 1923.

32 Nicholas Pano, *The People's Socialist Republic of Albania* (Baltimore, 1968), p. 22.

33 Fischer, *King Zog,* p. 57.

34 According to *Shqiptari i Amerikës,* in the Catholic zones only 200 votes went to the government (*Shqiptari i Amerikës,* 8 December 1923).

35 See *Politika,* 2 October 1924.

36 Federal Writers' Project of the Works Progress Administration, *The Albanian Struggle in the Old World and New,* p. 71.

37 This argument is made in Verteniku, 'Problemi i Asamblesë Kushtetuese dhe Zgjedhjet e vitet 1923,' p. 136.

38 Pipa, 'Fan Noli as National and International Albanian Figure,' p. 248.

39 Buda et al., *Historia,* p. 533.

40 See chapters 3 and 4 for more details on Kryeziu. He was first appointed as Albanian ambassador to Yugoslavia in 1925 but apparently began plotting to remove Zogu and was then transferred to Czechoslovakia. He was finally assassinated on Zogu's orders in October 1927. For details on the bizarre events that surrounded Kryeziu's murder, see Cyrus Leo Sulzberger, *A Long Row of Candles* (Toronto, 1969), p. 47.

41 *DBFP,* series 1, vol. 26, no. 45, Durrës, 15 February 1924.

42 So politicized was the situation that the assembly could not even find agree-ment on how properly to deal with the deaths of Woodrow Wilson and Vladimir Lenin. Noli, who hoped to deliver the main eulogy in Wilson's hon-our, was thwarted by a motion which, according to Grant-Smith, was designed to prevent Noli 'winning fresh laurels as an orator and even in the British interest to avoid a recital of the benefits conferred on Albania through the intermediary of the late statesman and by the American people in general.' Avni Rustemi also proposed similar treatment for Vladimir Lenin, who had also died in January 1924. Rustemi argued that not only was Lenin 'the great-est champion of human rights,' but it was well known by many Albanians that he 'had defended high principles and that he denounced the 1915 treaty that would have partitioned Albania.' Apparently, a third of the assembly's mem-bers voiced approval of Rustemi's motion, while the conservative beys began banging their feet and thumping their desks. In a rare display of cooperation, the assembly observed five minutes silence for both Lenin and Wilson. See Department of State, Grant-Smith to the Secretary of State, no. 218, 6 February 1924, 875.032/6; and Selim Shpuza, *Revolucioni Demokratike-Borgjez i Qershorit 1924 në Shqipëri* (Tirana, 1959), p. 18.

43 Department of State, Grant-Smith to the Secretary of State, no. 223, 1 March 1924, 875.032/7.

44 Krumë was the centre of Kosovo irredentists.

45 AQSH, MPB – Periudha i Nolit, V. 1924, D. 910, f.1–2. Konica appealed to the new assembly on January 21 to reopen the Vatra office.

46 That the assassination was prepared by radical elements of Albania's oppo-sition forces has long been maintained by Albanian communist historiog-raphy. See Buda et al., *Historia,* p. 537. It was a blood-feud attack with no political implications.

47 Zogu, 'King Zog Tells His Story,' p. 19.

48 Noli, *Autobiografia,* p. 90.

49 Ibid.

50 Ibid., p. 91.

51 Ibid.

52 Zogu, 'King Zog Tells His Story,' p. 19.

53 AQSH, MPB – Periudha i Zogut, V. 1924, D. 67, f. 1.

54 Fischer, *King Zog*, p. 58.

55 Department of State, Grant-Smith to Secretary of State, 4 March 1924, 875.002/9.

56 On March 3 Vërlaci's government received a vote of confidence with 53 votes for and 26 against.

57 *Dielli*, 8 April 1924.

58 *Shqiptari i Amerikës*, 4 March 1924.

59 Department of State, Grant-Smith to the Secretary of State, no. 255, 10 May 1924, 875.00/128.

60 *Ora e Maleve*, 8 March 1924.

61 Ibid.

62 Department of State, Grant-Smith to the Secretary of State, no. 223, 1 March 1924, 875.032/7.

63 Ibid., Grant-Smith to the Secretary of State, 4 March 1924, 875.002/9.

64 *League of Nations – Official Journal,* Special Supplement, no. 23 (1924): 325.

65 A number of countries participated in the relief effort, including Great Britain, Italy, Spain, Sweden, Czechoslovakia, and Romania. Even Yugoslavia transported, without cost, maize purchased in that country.

66 *League of Nations – Official Journal* 5 (June 1924): 844.

67 Ibid.

68 For more details on Albania and the League, see chapter 5. In Albania's 1924 budget of some 15,000,000 gold francs, some 6,300,000 was allocated to the gendarmerie and the War Ministry, or over 40 per cent. See AQSH, F. 251, V. 1924, D. 395, f. 8, Council of Ministers' decision of 30 December 1924.

69 AQSH, F. 251, V. 1924, D. 401, f. 7.

70 Ibid., D. 395, f. 26.

71 Fischer, *King Zog*, p. 60; and Buda et al., *Historia*, p. 537.

72 *AQSH*, F. 251, V. 1924, D. 17, F. 23. 7 April 1924.

73 Department of State Decimal File, Record Group 59, 375.1123 – Coleman and De Long/15 (hereafter Coleman and De Long), telegram from Grant-Smith to the Secretary of State, 8 April 1924.

74 See the enclosed memorandum outlining a conversation between Mborja and the U.S. consul in Florence, Joseph Emerson Haven, in Department of State, Henry Fletcher to the Secretary of State, no. 159, 2 September 1924, 875.51/19.

75 At the time, the main assumption within the government was that the murders had been committed by foreign agents hoping to discredit Albania.

In London, Mehmet Konica argued that the government was 'convinced that the unprecedented crime was committed with a political aim, with the intention of discrediting the Albanian state in the eyes of the world' (*New York Times*, 8 April 1924). The prefect of Shkodër, A. Nepravishta, seemed to support the idea that the murders were the result of outside forces. In a dispatch of April 10 to the interior minister, he wrote that he had heard that the murder of the two Americans was organized by the Yugoslav military attaché in Tirana and carried out by two Yugoslav agents. He added that he strongly felt that another attack on a foreigner was planned by the Yugoslavs in order to create provocations to gain the right to occupy northern Albania (AQSH, MPB – Periudha i Zogut, V. 1924, D. 16, f. 2). Grant-Smith, however, seemed to change his mind on who perpetrated the crime. He suggested later that the Albanian government hoped to blame foreigners to shift the blame from itself and thus avoid paying a heavy indemnity (Department of State, Grant-Smith to the Secretary of State, 16 April 1924, 375.1123; Coleman and De Long/19).

76 Department of State, Trojan Kodding to Secretary of State, no. 244, 13 April 1924, 375.1123; Coleman and DeLong/51.

77 Joseph Swire has written that the incident was closed internationally after the government caught one suspect and killed two others near Kruje. See Swire, *Albania,* p. 428. The incident, however, remained open, and Noli's failure to solve the crime and convict Zogu was an important factor in the U.S. attitude toward him in the long run.

78 AQSH, F. 251, V. 1924, D. 17, f. 57.

79 Rustemi had returned to Tirana to deal with his request for a visa for entry into the United States. While walking in Tirana, Rustemi was shot, and although he returned fire, the assailant disappeared into the mountains. According to an eyewitness report, a policeman looked on indifferently. See Department of State, U. Grant-Smith to the Secretary of State, 24 April 1924, no. 245, 811.111/Avni Rustem.

80 In a telegram to Vatra, liberal deputy Ali Kelcyra informed Vatra of Rustemi's murder and claimed the assassin had relations with supporters of Esad Pasha Toptani (*Dielli,* 24 April 1924).

81 Albanian communist-era historiography accepts without question that Zogu was responsible for the murder of Rustemi. See Buda et al., *Historia,* p. 538.

82 Zogu, 'King Zog Tells His Story,' p. 20.

83 Noli, *Autobiografia,* p. 95.

84 Selim Shpuza noted that the immediate cause of the revolution was the death of Rustemi. See Shpuza, *Revolucioni Demokratike,* p. 5.

85 Department of State, Grant-Smith to the Secretary of State, no. 258, 14 May 1924, 875.00/142.
86 *Drita*, 26 April 1924.
87 Beli Dedi et al., *Dokumenta e Materiale Historike nga Lufta e Popullit Shqiptar per Lire e Demokraci* (Tirana, 1959), Doc. 124., f. 128
88 Shpuza, *Revolucioni Demokratike*, p. 22.
89 Ibid., p. 26.
90 *Politika*, 24 April 1924.
91 Dilo, *Ligjëron Fan Noli*, p. 79.
92 Communist-era figures suggested there were 10,000 in attendance. The Interior Ministry, based on reports from the prefect of Vlorë, put the figure at 5,000, which is probably more accurate. See AQSH, MPB – Periudha i Zogut, V. 1924, D. 9, f. 8. As well, it is doubtful that 44 members of the assembly went to Vlorë; a more reasonable figure, provided by the U.S. legation, was 26.
93 Tako, *Fan Noli në Fushën Politike*, pp. 135–6.
94 *Politika*, 3 May 1924.
95 See Department of State, Enclosure no. 1 in Grant-Smith to the Secretary of State, no. 258, 14 May 1924, 875.00/142.
96 For this point, I am grateful to Professor Sami Repishti.
97 *Drita*, 3 May 1924. The opposition declared that Ceno Bey was operating out of Krumë, the capital of the Kosovo prefecture, and using his position to undermine the traditional bastion of Kosovo irredentists.
98 Buda et al., *Historia*, p. 540. Article 127 states, among other things, that the 'defence of this statute is the right and obligation of the Albanian people.'
99 AQSH, MPB – Periudha i Zogut, V. 1924, D. 388, F. 9, 13 May 1924.
100 Dedi et al., *Dokumenta e Materiale Historike*, Doc. 127, p. 130.
101 Department of State, Grant-Smith to the Secretary of State, no. 252, 8 May 1924, 811.111/Avni Rustem.
102 AQSH, MPB – Periudha i Zogut, V. 1924, D. 9, f. 3.
103 Fahri Reshid, minister of education, and Koco Kota, minister of public works, also resigned, leaving only four Muslim members.
104 According to a report from Belgrade, armed strife resulted in the clash over the capital's location (*New York Times*, 11 May 1924).
105 The Shkodër prefect's report on 1 January 1924 made this clear and noted that the Ora e Maleve group enjoyed wide support among priests and large portions of the Catholic population (AQSH, MPB, V. 1924, D. 1, f. 9).
106 Department of State, Grant-Smith to the Secretary of State, no. 252, 8 May 1924, 811.111/Avni Rustemi.

107 Ibid., Grant-Smith to the Secretary of State, no. 262, 22 May 1924, 875.00/143.
108 Ibid., Grant-Smith to the Secretary of State, no. 284, 11 June 1924, 875.00/149.
109 Noli, *Autobiografia*, p. 85.
110 Korçë had a long history of conflict with Zogu, who had twice attempted to force his resignation as war minister in the fall of 1923 and succeeded in March 1924.
111 Department of State, Grant-Smith to the Secretary of State, 19 May 1924, 875.00/124
112 Ibid., Grant-Smith to the Secretary of State, no. 273, 31 May 1924, 875.00/178.
113 An amnesty for those who fled the parliament had been passed by the rump assembly on 3 June 1924.
114 AQSH, MPB – Periudha i Zogut, V. 1924, D. 3, f. 61.
115 Grant-Smith noted that Zogu 'shone as the only courageous leader among the reactionaries' (Department of State, Grant-Smith to the Secretary of State, no. 284, 11 June 1924, 875.00/149).
116 Regent Gjon Coba resigned on May 24, and Xhafer Ypi and Refik Topia resigned on May 27.

3. Fan Noli in Power

1 Department of State, Grant-Smith to the Secretary of State, no. 287, 16 June 1924, 875.00/151. The most recent Albanian source notes that killed and wounded numbered around 200. See Academy of Sciences of the Republic of Albania, *Historia e Popullit Shqiptare* (Tirana, 2002), p. 226.
2 Swire, *Albania,* p. 432.
3 Department of State, Grant-Smith to the Secretary of State, no. 287, 16 June 1924, 875.00/151. Communist historiography also accepts that Noli's 'revolution' was a relatively bloodless affair, but for the wrong reasons. As noted, historians interpreted the years in the aftermath of the Congress of Lushnjë until the Noli revolution as almost solely a struggle between feudalism and liberalism, and argue that Noli's triumph was easy because the mass of peasants and workers supported Noli's movement and 'feudal reactionaries' were simply without the support of the people. According to Selim Shpuza, himself a founder of the Bashkimi group, a key partici- pant in the events of June and later a pillar of the communist interpreta- tion, the anti-landlord component of Noli's group fulfilled the needs of Albanian society at that time and was therefore well received by

the people. This interpretation, which was adopted primarily for political reasons and out of the need to maintain the fiction of a 'bourgeois-democratic revolution,' neglects key factors. See Shpuza's article in Institute of History, *Revolucioni i Qershorit 1924 në Kujtimet e Bashkëkohësve* (Tirana, 1974), p. 244.

4 Logoreci, *The Albanians*, p. 55.

5 The interview was reprinted in *Dielli*, 4 November 1924.

6 Ibid.

7 Department of State, Grant-Smith to the Secretary of State, no. 287, 16 June 1924, 875.00/151.

8 *New York Times*, 12 June 1924.

9 It seems the revolutionaries also suggested that Curri should be named as one of the country's regents, although this idea was withdrawn in an attempt to pacify the Yugoslavs. See Department of State, Grant-Smith's dispatch to the Secretary of State, no. 296, 2 July 1924, 875.01/247. Grant-Smith obtained these details in a conversation on July 1 with Noli.

10 Ibid., Grant-Smith to the Secretary of State, no. 285, 13 June 1924, 875.00/150.

11 Since communist historians tried to gloss over the role of the military in the revolution as well as important regional cleavages, they tended to see Noli's cabinet as a coalition of only two groups: progressives were identified as Noli, Gurakuqi, Koculi, and Vinjau, who were in coalition with more moderate members like Delvina, Shala, and Qafëzezi. See Pollo and Puto, *History of Albania*, pp. 192–3; and, in Albanian, see Buda et al., *Historia*, p. 544.

12 For this point, I am indebted again to Professor Nasho Jorgaqi. It is also worth recalling that it was Peci who had pushed for Noli's selection as delegate to the League Assembly in 1920 in order to get him out of the country.

13 *The Times*, 9 June 1924.

14 Ibid., 7 June 1924.

15 Ibid., 13 June 1924.

16 *Politika*, 10 July 1924.

17 Ibid.

18 Swire, *Albania*, pp. 443–4. In Albanian historiography, no mention is made of the monarchist sympathies of some members of Noli's coalition. Swire also suggested that Kosovar leaders like Curri and Jusufi were monarchists, although this is not accurate. Both Gurakuqi and Vrioni were already on record as supporting a constitutional monarchy in the Assembly (*Gazeta e Korçës*, 1 April 1924). Lastly, Wied still did not consider himself out of the picture and as late as April 1924 declared his willingness to return (*Dielli*, 8 April 1924).

19 Department of State, Grant-Smith to the Secretary of State, no. 284, 11 June 1924, 875.00/149.
20 According to that article, at least three members of the Council must be in attendance.
21 This was a very loose interpretation of Article 51, which stated that in the event of death or incurable illness of a member of the Regency Council, parliament was to elect another. In the event parliament was not in session (to say nothing of having been illegally disbanded), the prime minister could temporarily assume the post.
22 Department of State, Grant-Smith to the Secretary of State, no. 355, 20 November 1924, 875.00/163.
23 AQSH, Fondi Personal – Fan Noli, F. 14, D. 89, f. 1, Programi i Kabinet.
24 Ibid. It is especially interesting that the cabinet program sent to the legation in London omitted point 2, which called for retribution against the members of the old regime. For that version, see AQSH, F. 251, V. 1924, D. 195, f. 2–4. Great Britain, and other powers, took great exception to the decision to take reprisals on the former government. Joseph Swire only identified nineteen points. See Swire, *Albania*, pp. 434–5.
25 AQSH, Fondi Personal – Fan Noli, F. 14, D. 89, f. 1.
26 Quoted in Pipa, 'Fan Noli as National and International Albanian Figure,' p. 248.
27 See Skendi, *Political Evolution*, p. 88.
28 Because of its dogmatic commitment to class warfare, the Bashkimi organization is the only group to emerge relatively unscathed in communist historiography. See Institute of Marxist-Leninist Studies at the Central Committee of the Party of Labour of Albania, *History of the Party of Labour of Albania*, 2nd edn (Tirana, 1982), pp. 15–18.
29 *Bashkimi*, 8 July 1924.
30 Ibid.
31 Ibid., 5 September 1924.
32 Ibid.
33 Swire, *Albania*, p. 444.
34 *Shqiptari i Amerikës*, 8 July 1924.
35 In a last bid to thwart an expected invasion by Zogu, the political court issued sentences on 12 December 1924, which were as follows: Zogu and Ceno Bey Kryeziu were found guilty as principal authors of fratricide and sentenced to death; Sh. Verlaci and M. Libohova were found guilty of being principal accomplices in fratricide and also condemned to death; I. Vrioni, A. Dibra, K. Kota, and M. Aranitasi were found guilty as accomplices in fratricide and were sentenced to perpetual expulsion (AQSH, MPB – Periudha e Nolit, V. 1924, D. 179, f. 26).

36 Fischer, 'Fan Noli and the Albanian Revolutions of 1924,' p. 152.

37 Miranda Vickers, *The Albanians: A Modern History* (London, 1995), p. 114.

38 Department of State, Trojan Kodding to the Secretary of State, no. 327, 20 September 1924, 875/01/253.

39 Ibid.

40 *Fletore Zyrtare,* 23 June 1924, p. 5.

41 Selim Shpuza, 'Lufta e Brendëshme Politike dhe Shoqërore në Shqipëri ne Qershor-Dhjetor 1924,' *in* Academy of Sciences of the People's Socialist Republic of Albania, *Çështje të Lëvizjes Demokratike,* p. 201.

42 AQSH, MPB – Periudha e Nolit, V. 1924, D. 796, f. 10.

43 Ibid., f. 7.

44 *Fletore Zyrtare,* 22 July 1924.

45 Shpuza, 'Lufta e Brendëshme,' pp. 200–1. Communist historiography argues that unfortunately Noli did not go far enough in destroying the remnants of the old regime.

46 Swire, *Albania,* p. 436.

47 *The Near East,* 25 September 1924, p. 2.

48 Ibid.

49 Department of State, Grant-Smith to the Secretary of State, no. 285, 13 June 1924, 875.00/150.

50 The interview was sent to the U.S. consulate general in Rome. See Department of State, enclosure no. 1 in Leon Dominian to the Secretary of State, 26 August 1924, 875.00/156.

51 *Shqiptari i Amerikës,* 5 July 1924.

52 *Bashkimi,* 23 September 1924.

53 Ibid., 26 September 1924.

54 *Politika,* 7 August 1924.

55 *Gazeta e Korçës,* 6 September 1924. The failure to take an even firmer stand against the country's 'feudals' has since been judged by communist-era historians as a key component of Noli's failure to consolidate his rule and carry through the revolutionary agenda. This position, again more a reflection of the need to justify the Albanian communists' imposition of violent class struggle after 1944, maintains that the liberal bey component of Noli's coalition blocked a thorough cleansing of all levels of government, and in not going far enough they left untouched many pro-Zogist or pro-feudal elements. See Shpuza, 'Lufta e Brendëshme,' p. 206.

56 *Dielli,* 31 July 1924.

57 See Shpuza, *Revolucioni Demokratike-Borgjez i Qershorit 1924 në Shqipëri;* and Buda et al., *Historia,* p. 552.

58 Shpuza, 'Lufta e Brendëshme,' p. 211.

59 Ibid.

60 AQSH, MPB – Periudha e Nolit, V. 1924, D. 179, f. 15.

61 Shpuza, 'Lufta e Brendëshme,' p. 212.

62 *Politika,* 25 September 1924. The paper argued that elections should be held no later than 1 January 1925 by direct voting, that all 'troublesome elements' should be eliminated, and that candidates should be able to read and write.

63 *Bashkimi,* 17 October 1924.

64 Ibid., 16 September 1924.

65 Ibid., 10 October 1924.

66 *Politika,* 2 October 1924.

67 Tako, *Fan Noli në Fushën Politike dhe Publicistike,* p. 146.

68 *Shekulli,* 12 November 1924.

69 Department of State, Grant-Smith to the Secretary of State, no. 345, 8 November 1924, 875.00/162.

70 Trojan Kodding to the Secretary of State, no. 327, 20 September 1924, 875.01/253.

71 Ibid.

72 Ibid.

73 Border incursions by both sides had become commonplace throughout the summer and fall. In September, however, a serious incursion took place that the Albanians considered to be a preparatory step for an eventual invasion. As well, final delimitation of Albanian borders was still pending, and it appeared to many that the Yugoslavs were preparing to take the disputed regions of Saint Naum and Vermosh by force. See chapter 4 for more details.

74 See Department of State, Trojan Kodding's dispatch to the Secretary of State, no. 323, 30 August 1924, 875.01/250.

75 Ibid. Kodding reported that all of the diplomatic representatives believed the position of Noli's cabinet to be 'untenable for any appreciable length of time.'

76 Tako, *Fan Noli në Fushën Politike dhe Publicistike,* p. 146.

77 In August 1924 representatives from all three religious affiliations met in Tirana to discuss a uniform school program. The Catholic representatives walked out after a call to do away with separate schools by Orthodox and Moslem representatives. See Department of State, Kodding to the Secretary of State, no. 310, 24 August 1924, 875.00/158.

78 See chapter 4 for details of Noli's attempt to internationalize the Kosovo problem at the League of Nations.

79 AQSH, MPB – Periudha e Nolit, V. 1924, D. 894, f. 7. There was to be one deputy for every 12,000 inhabitants.

80 *Politika,* 6 November 1924.

81 According to the plan, the bureaucracy was to be cut by some 30 per cent, and salaries were reduced by amounts ranging from 5 per cent for lower paid officials to 25 per cent for high-ranking officials. See Department of State, Kodding to the Secretary of State, no. 320, 24 August 1924, 875.00/158.

4. Albania's Neighbours – Yugoslavia and Greece

1 Paskal Milo, *Shqipëria dhe Jugosllavia* (Tirana, 1992), p. 235.

2 *New York Times,* 9 June 1924.

3 The telegram was sent on 17 June 1924.

4 Emine Arifi-Bakalli, 'Qeveria Demokratike e Fan Nolit dhe Qëndrimi i Mbreterisë SKS ndaj saj,' *Gjurmime Albanologjike* 11 (1981): 240.

5 Milo, *Shqipëria dhe Jugosllavia,* p. 236. Yugoslavia refused to recognize Noli's government.

6 See Puto, *Demokracia e Rrethuar,* p. 18; and Živko Avramovski, 'Qëndrimi i Anglisë ndaj Qeverise së Fan Nolit në Shqipëri ne Vitin 1924,' *Gjurminme Albanologjike* 2 (1972): 165.

7 Since the creation of an independent Albania, Belgrade's policy was shaped by the concept that Albania was a divided nation destined to be the site of a battle for power between the minority Christians and the majority Moslems, and that these contradictions within Albania would be the cause of perpetual instability. This was made abundantly clear during the crisis in Mirdita. See Puto, *Demokracia e Rrethuar,* p. 22.

8 Hasan Prishtina had invited both Gurakuqi and Noli to take part in his short-lived administration in 1921 – Gurakuqi as finance minister and Noli as foreign minister. See *Hasan Prishtina: Permbledhje Dokumentash, 1908–1934* (Tirana: General Directorate of the State Archives, 1982).

9 Harold Nicolson of the British Foreign Office believed that Zogu was the next Esad Pasha. See *DBFP,* series 1, vol. 22, no. 732, p. 799, footnote 2, where he made this assertion in a margin note.

10 Noli and Gurakuqi travelled with Bajram Curri and Hasan Prishtina. The Kosovo leaders intended to present a petition to the League and a list of crimes committed against the Albanian community by the Belgrade government. See AQSH, F. 251, V. 1924, D. 147, f.1.

11 *Politika,* 10 October 1924; AQSH, F. 251, V. 1924, D. 276, f. 18. The Albanian legation in Belgrade kept a close watch on trends in the Yugoslav press. It is also interesting to note that the Tirana government covered the costs of the Kosovar delegation, even though the Albanian treasury could barely find

the funds to send Noli and Gurakuqi to Geneva. The Kosovars also hoped to lobby in Paris and London, but the Albanian government was forced to turn down the request due to financial constraints. See AQSH, F. 251, V. 1924, D. 147, f. 1.

12 Ibid.

13 The Yugoslavs routinely alleged that Curri and Prishtina did not merely seek minority rights guarantees but instead the union of Kosovo with Albania. See Belgrade's *Politika*, 14 October 1924. While Curri and Prishtina did merely present a list of grievances to the League, the Yugoslavs were correct that the goal of the Kosovo Committee was the 'annexation to Albania of those territories which are predominantly Albanian.' See Department of State, U. Grant-Smith to the Secretary of State, no. 354, 19 November 1924, 875.01/256. Grant-Smith reported on a conversation with Curri.

14 AQSH, F. 251, V. 1924, D. 129, fl. 1–2.

15 Vuk Vinanver, 'Anglia dhe Pozita Ndërkombëtare e Shqipërisë Midis Dy Luftave Boterore,' *Gjurmime Albanologjike* 1 (1968): 202.

16 See Milo, *Shqipëria dhe Jugosllavia*, p. 242, and Puto, *Demokracia e Rrethuar*, pp. 20–5, for an assessment of the link between Yugoslav and Italian aims in Albania and the effect on Yugoslav policy.

17 This analysis was made in a report from Belgrade on 30 June 1924 (AQSH, F. 251, V. 1924, D. 257, F. 2–4).

18 The Albanian embassy in Belgrade reported on June 24 that Zogu had in fact arrived with 19 officers, 150 soldiers, 50 family members, and 60 civilians and other bureaucrats (AQSH, F. 251, V. 1924, D. 257, fl. 7).

19 *DBFP*, series 1, vol. 26, no. 175. p. 259.

20 *Gazeta e Korçës*, 8 July 1924.

21 Zogu, 'King Zog Tells His Story,' p. 21.

22 See Arifi-Bakalli, 'Qeveria Demokratike e Fan Nolit dhe Qëndrimi i Mbreterisë SKS ndaj saj,' p. 240.

23 *Bashkimi*, 15 July 1924.

24 Zogu even convinced Yugoslavia's Little Entente ally Czechoslovakia to withhold recognition and had promised economic concessions to the Czechs with his return. See Milo, *Shqipëria dhe Jugosllavia*, p. 243.

25 AQSH, F. 251, V. 1924, D. 283, F. 107.

26 Ibid., f. 122; and Milo, *Shqipëria dhe Jugosllavia*, p. 236.

27 Arifi-Bakalli, 'Qeveria Demokratike,' p. 245.

28 AQSH, F. 251, V. 1924, D. 133, f. 298.

29 Ibid., f. 237.

30 Ibid. This is a situation report from Kolonja to Foreign Minister Delvina on 21 August 1924.

31 AQSH, F. 251, V. 1924, D. 283, F. 143.

32 Ibid., f. 160. This was a situation report sent on 30 September 1924.

33 Ibid.

34 Noli had stated that Albania needed good relations with Yugoslavia if the state was to develop, prosper, and organize itself. See Milo, *Shqipëria dhe Jugosllavia,* p. 239.

35 AQSH, F. 251, V. 1924, D. 283, f. 160.

36 Ibid., f. 161.

37 Ibid.

38 See Department of State, H. Percival Dodge's confidential dispatch to the Secretary of State, no. 2458, 22 September 1924, 760h.75/53.

39 Ibid.

40 Ibid.

41 Ibid.

42 Albania had complained, both to Belgrade and the League of Nations, about the incursions of Montenegrin tribesman on three earlier occasions: 15 and 23 August and 2 September 1924. See Swire, *Albania,* p. 442.

43 Arifi-Bakalli, 'Qeveria Demokratike,' p. 250.

44 AQSH, F. 251, D. 63, F. 367. The letter was written in French, which meant that Kolonja was supposed to transmit it in its entirety to the Yugoslav authorities.

45 Ibid.

46 AQSH, F. 251, V. 1924, D. 63, F. 366.

47 Ibid., f. 340.

48 AQSH, F. 251, V. 1924, D. 265, f. 10–11.

49 Ibid., f. 12.

50 Ibid.

51 The denial was made in *Vreme* on September 28.

52 See *Vreme,* 28 September 1924. For the entire position of the Yugoslav government on the incursion, see *League of Nations – Official Journal* 5 (Oct. 1924): 1372–4.

53 AQSH, F. 251, V. 1924, D. 131, F. 467–468.

54 *League of Nations – Official Journal* 5 (Oct. 1924): 1373.

55 While at the League, Noli noted that frontier delimitation expenses had almost reached 1,000,000 gold francs and that continued delays 'would prevent the Albanian people from devoting themselves to the solution of their many internal problems.' See *League of Nations – Official Journal* 5 (Oct. 1924): 1336.

56 *DBFP,* series 1, vol. 26, no. 236, p. 352. The note was sent by the Foreign Office to Geneva on 2 October 1924.

57 Ibid., no. 232, p. 348, 30 September 1924. In another telegram to the Foreign Office on September 29, Eyres noted that the Albanian government 'admits that original raid was an incursion by Albanian raiders to steal cattle' (no. 237, p. 348).

58 For example, on September 2, the Korçë prefect complained that despite all Albania's efforts to maintain good relations, Yugoslavia continued to attempt to disturb the peace in Albania and that if such a policy continued, Albania should consider taking similar actions. See AQSH, MPB – Periudha e Nolit, D. 97, f. 143.

59 Arifi-Bakalli, 'Qeveria Demokratike,' p. 251.

60 The Yugoslavs later argued that the border had been fixed in an arbitrary manner and because of pressure from Austria-Hungary and Italy prior to the war. The Yugoslavs further argued that, based on previously unknown documents, the monastery had in fact originally been assigned to Yugoslavia. Owing to strategic, economic, historical, and ethnographic arguments, it should be returned to Yugoslavia. As well, there was considerable confusion over the wording of the 1913 border delimitation, which stated that Albanian territory went 'up to' the monastery and that 'up to,' according to the Yugoslavs, did not mean 'including.' The Council of Ambassadors asked the League Council to consider the whole issue in light of the fact that continued territorial disputes would endanger peace. See Swire, *Albania*, pp. 441–2.

61 AQSH, V. 1924, D. 131, f. 201.

62 AQSH, F. 251, V. 1924, F. 24–25. The Foreign Ministry also reported spontaneous demonstrations throughout the spring of 1924, in Shkodër, Elbasan, Pogradec, Permet, and Durrës, calling for support in Albania's territorial battles.

63 *DBFP*, series 1, vol. 26, no. 175, p. 258.

64 Great Britain, at the outset, supported the Albanian claim, while France, Greece, and Italy supported the Yugoslav claim. Great Britain, it appears, supported the Albanian position because of its reluctance to overturn a previous Conference of Ambassadors decision. See *League of Nations – Official Journal* 5 (Oct. 1924): 1370. As well, the position of the Great Powers was made clear in a letter from Mehmet Konica in which he noted that Britain would stand by the decision of 1922 (AQSH, F. 251, V. 1924, D. 64, F. 21). The letter was sent to Foreign Minister Illias Vrioni on 20 April 1924.

65 These arguments were laid out in a position statement from the Albanian delegation before the Delimitation Commission of the Frontiers of Albania, 2 June 1924 (AQSH, F. 251, V. 1924, D. 64, F. 125–127).

66 *Trgovinski Glasnik,* 27 September 1924; and AQSH, F. 251, V. 1924, D. 63, f. 369.

67 *DBFP,* series 1, vol. 26, no. 307, p. 464; see footnote 4. This document was dated on December 31 and thus after Zogu had returned to power. In a private letter, Lampson did not hide his support of the idea that Albania and Serbia settle this issue in order to avoid further conflict. In Lampson's opinion, Albania should turn the monastery over to the Serbs for future considerations.

68 On 6 August 1924 the Albanian War Ministry advised all relevant prefectures in Albania that based on good information, in the event the Yugoslavs could not gain Vermosh by diplomatic means, they were prepared to use force. The War Ministry suggested that urgent diplomatic action be taken, especially to inform the border commission of the aggressive intentions of the Yugoslavs. See AQSH, F. 251, V. 1924, D. 61, f. 307–308.

69 See Živko Avramovski, 'Kontribut Studimit te Çështijes se Marradhenieve Shqiptaro-Jugosllave Midis dy Luftave Boterore,' *Gjurmime Albanologjike* 2 (1968): 131–2.

70 See Milo, *Shqipëria dhe Jugosllavia,* pp. 300–3.

71 The diplomat was A.T. Aneriti, and he sent his memo to Rome from Durrës on 9 January 1925. See AQSH, F. 251, V. 1925, D. 105, f. 3–5. In the note, he suggested the agreement was made in August; this is unlikely since Pašić was not in power.

72 Ibid., f. 5.

73 Radić's attack on policy toward Albania was but a small fraction of his overall attack on the Serbian political establishment, especially the military, which provoked the resignation of the war minister, Hadžić, and led ultimately to the collapse of Davidović's government and the return of Pašić in November 1924. See Joseph Rothschild, *East Central Europe between the Two World Wars* (Seattle, 1974), pp. 222–3.

74 AQSH, F. 251, V. 1924, D. 287, F. 5. The declaration was translated from a Belgrade newspaper and forwarded by Ali Kolonja to the Albanian Foreign Ministry on October 6.

75 Ibid.

76 Ibid.

77 In an article of October 14 in *Samouprava,* the official paper of Pašić's Radical Party, Radić was attacked in the harshest of terms. His suggestion that Serbia had territorial ambitions against Albania 'flies in the face of successive Yugoslav government official declarations respecting the indepen-, dence of Albania,' and his project on the partition of Albania is a 'simple demagogic machination.' As to Albanian progressivism, the paper wondered

aloud if the looting and pillaging of South Serbia was an example of this progressivism or, rather, of Noli's relationship with thieves like Bajram Curri and Hasan Prishtina. See AQSH, F. 251, V. 1924, D. 287, f. 16–17.

78 Milo, *Shqipëria dhe Jugosllavia,* p. 310.

79 *New York Times,* 22 October 1924.

80 The telegram was sent to Belgrade on October 22 (AQSH, F. 251, V. 1924, D. 288, f. 19).

81 The note was sent on October 21 from Albania's permanent secretariat at the League (AQSH, F. 251, V. 1924, D. 287, f. 52).

82 I would like to thank my colleague Mark Biondich for providing me with this document from the Historical Archives of the City of Zagreb, Croatia (Povijesni Arhiv grada Zagreba, Fond Stjepan Radić i HSS, box 1, no. 197, letter from F. Noli to S. Radić).

83 For discussions on the legacy of this agreement, see Publications of the Permanent Court of International Justice at the Hague, Series C. No. 5-II, Fifth Ordinary Session. *Question of the Monastery of Saint Naoum,* p. 151.

84 For the full details of the arrangement, see Basil Kondis, *Greece and Albania, 1908–1914* (Thessaloniki, 1976), p. 131.

85 Pollo and Puto, *History of Albania,* pp. 158–9.

86 For the full details, see Basil Kondis, 'The Albanian Question at the Beginning of 1920 and the Greek-Albanian Protocol of Kapestitsa, May 28th, 1920,' *Balkan Studies* 20, no. 2 (1979): 411.

87 Publications of the Permanent Court of International Justice, *Question of the Monastery of Saint Naoum,* p. 142.

88 This argument has been put forth in a scholarly manner by Kondis in *Greece and Albania, 1908–1914.*

89 P.R. Magocsi, *Historical Atlas of East Central Europe* (Toronto, 1993), p. 144.

90 See Stavro Skendi, 'The Northern Epirus Question Reconsidered,' *Journal of Central European Affairs* 14, no. 11 (July 1954): 145. All Christians who were dependent on the Patriarchate of Constantinople were called Roum, that is,Greek.

91 For excellent details on the struggle for control over southern Albania, see Edith P. Stickney, *Southern Albania or Northern Epirus in European International Affairs, 1912–1923* (Stanford, 1926).

92 The original delegation consisted of Major Meinich (Norway), Colonel Schaeffer (Luxemburg), and M. Thesleff (Finland). The Finnish delegate was later replaced by Professor J. Sederholm, also of Finland (ibid., pp. 147–8).

93 Ibid., p. 149.

94 *League of Nations – Official Journal* 3 (March 1922): 263.

95 Ibid., p. 578.
96 Ibid.
97 Department of State, Joseph Emerson Haven, Report on Albania, 28 April 1919, 875.00/47.
98 Ibid.
99 Ibid.
100 Ibid.
101 *DBFP,* series 1, vol. 22, no. 617, p. 680. The report was sent from Durrës on 10 May 1921.
102 Ibid.
103 Ibid., no. 656, p. 726, 23 July 1921.
104 Ibid., no. 792. p. 852, 30 July 1921.
105 Ibid, no. 793, 6 July 1922, pp. 852–3.
106 *League of Nations – Official Journal* 4 (1923): 492.
107 See Kaliopi Naska, 'Kongresi Themeltar i Kishës Ortodokse Autoqefale në Berat' in Academy of Sciences of the Republic of Albania – Institute of History, *70 Vjet te Kishës Ortodokse Autoqefale Shqiptare* (Tirana, 1993), pp. 10–20.
108 Despite continued appeals from Orthodox leaders, it was only in 1937 that the Patriarchate finally recognized the Albanian Church's independence.
109 Naska, 'Kongresi Themeltar,' p. 10.
110 Department of State, Emerson Haven, Special Report on Albania, 28 April 1919, 875.00/47.
111 *League of Nations – Official Journal* 3 (March 1922): 263.
112 Ibid.
113 Ibid.
114 *League of Nations – Monthly Summary,* 1 July 1921, p. 44.
115 For an examination of the motives for Tellini's murder, see James Barros, *The Corfu Incident of 1923: Mussolini and the League of Nations* (Princeton, 1965), pp. 29–32.
116 AQSH, F. 251, V. 1924, D. 66, F. 338. The report out of the Foreign Ministry is undated.
117 Joseph Swire suggests that the assassination had been with the collusion of local Greek authorities, but that Greek higher authorities were not implicated. See Swire, *Albania,* p. 419.
118 AQSH, F. 251, V. 1924, D. 60, f. 15.
119 Ibid., f. 9. Verbal note from the Albanian Foreign Ministry to the Greek Legation in Durrës.
120 Ibid., f. 16.
121 Puto, *Demokracia e Rrethuar,* p. 121.

122 Letter from the Albanian Foreign Ministry to the Albanian legation in Athens, 19 May 1924 (AQSH, F. 251, V. 1924, D. 63, f. 167).
123 Puto, *Demokracia e Rrethuar*, p. 26.
124 Ibid.
125 AQSH, F. 251, V. 1924, D. 130, F. 4, Report of the Albanian legation dated 21 June 1924.
126 The Conference of Ambassadors sent the decision to the Albanian legation in Paris on 25 August 1924. See AQSH, F. 251, V. 1924, D. 130, f. 98.
127 Ibid., f. 88. The request for troops was signed by Noli on August 18.
128 *Bashkimi*, 30 July 1924.
129 AQSH, F. 251, V. 1924, D. 211, F. 15.
130 Ibid., f. 54.
131 AQSH, F. 251, V. 1924, D. 160, f. 1.
132 AQSH, MPB – Zyra Sekrete, V. 1924, D. 154, f. 1. The Interior Ministry asked local authorities to examine the activities of Greek teachers and 'take action in the interests of the State.'
133 AQSH, F. 251, V. 1924, D. 234, F. 6–8. The Greek legation sent this note on August 29.
134 Ibid., f. 2.
135 The letter is reprinted in its entirety in *League of Nations – Official Journal* 5 (Oct. 1924): 1635.
136 Ibid., p. 1355.
137 Ibid., p. 1374.
138 Ibid.
139 Ibid., p. 1375.
140 AQSH, F. 251, V. 1924, D. 131, F. 310.
141 AQSH, MPB – Peruidha i Nolit, V. 1924, D. 75, f. 3.
142 Ibid.
143 The interview is reprinted in Puto, *Demokracia e Rrethuar*, pp. 272–5.
144 Ibid., p. 274.
145 Ibid., p. 278. The interview was published on 18 September 1924.
146 Ibid., f. 281. The interview was published on 10 October 1924.
147 AQSH, F. 251, V. 1924, D. 216, F. 1.

5. Great Britain, Italy, and the United States

1 Only these three powers had well-defined policies in Albania in the early 1920s. France, which played only a minor role in the search for an oil concession, is also briefly discussed.
2 *The Times*, 4 September 1924.

3 See Andrew Ryan, *The Last of the Dragomans* (London, 1951), p. 314.

4 Upon his return to power in December 1924, Zogu appointed Stirling to help reorganize Albania's gendarmerie. See Fischer, *King Zog and the Struggle for Stability,* p. 102.

5 AQSH, F. 251, V. 1924, D. 17, f. 75–76.

6 D. 7, F. 226. Stirling responded on July 25 that he was ill and did not expect to be able to travel until the end of August. He requested that the minister wire his proposals.

7 Department of State, Trojan Kodding to the Secretary of State, no. 327, 20 September 1924, 875.01/253.

8 Ibid., Maxwell Blake to the Secretary of State on Albania and the League and political intrigue at Tirana, 5 September 1922, 875.01/235.

9 Ibid., American Consul in Trieste to the Secretary of State on the political situation in Albania, 875.00/74.

10 Živko Avramovski, 'Qëndrimi i Anglisë ndaj Qeverisë Fan Nolit në Shqipëri ne vitin 1924,' *Gjurmime Albanologjike* 2 (1972): 162.

11 *DBFP,* series 1, vol. 22, no. 609. p. 669.

12 'Bajraktar' is the Albanian word for tribal chief and commonly employed to describe Zogu.

13 Eyres (1856–1944) had been employed on a special assignment in Albania in 1916. He was an experienced officer in the Levant Consular Service and was sent to Durrës to help the Foreign Office shape its position on the Albanian question. In November 1921, Great Britain had recognized Albania, and in early 1922 Eyres was appointed as His Majesty's representative at Durrës. See *Who Was Who IV* (1941–1950), p. 370.

14 *DBFP,* series 1, vol. 22, no. 604. p. 658.

15 Ibid., no. 823. pp. 880–1.

16 Avramovski, 'Qëndrimi i Anglisë,' p. 164.

17 *DBFP,* series 1, vol. 26, no. 170. p. 249. See footnote no. 7.

18 Ibid.

19 AQSH, F. 251, V. 1924, D. 140, f. 13–14.

20 Konica, brother of Faik, had a distinguished career in Albanian politics. In 1912 he was a member of the Vlorë government and was later sent as a delegate to the Conference of Ambassadors in 1913. During the brief government of Prince Wied, he served as minister to Greece. He later proposed that Albanians organize a regiment under the command of Aubrey Herbert to fight as a unit of the British Army in the First World War. In 1922 he was named Albania's minister in London and was also accredited to Paris. See AQSH, Fondi Personal – Mehmet Konica, #441, D. 165.

21 AQSH, F. 251, V. 1924, D. 140, f. 10.

22 Ibid., f. 11.

23 Ibid., f. 15.

24 Ibid.

25 Ibid.

26 Shpuza, *Revolucioni Demokratike-Borgjez,* p. 33.

27 Department of State, Grant-Smith to the Secretary of State, no. 287, 16 June 1924, 875.00/151.

28 Eyres's position in the battle was also noted by U.S. minister Grant-Smith, who in a telegram of June 6 to the secretary of state noted that the British minister 'openly encouraged and supported the government and his protege' (Department of State, Grant-Smith to the Secretary of State, 6 June 1924, 875.00/136). Even the newspaper *Tirana* lauded Eyres, writing that he did 'not spare at all his moral assistance in protecting Albania from the dangers into which it has been plunged by some of its own sons who were, unknowingly, made the tools of our enemies' (*Tirana,* 6 June 1924).

29 AQSH, F. 251, V. 1924, D. 140, f. 16.

30 In a telegram of June 18 to Konica, Noli had made his concerns about Eyres clear, writing that he had proof that Eyres had encouraged the 'feudal' government to crush the revolution, and that he was not a suitable person for the development of good relations between Albania and Great Britain. See Puto, *Demokracia e Rrethuar,* p. 34.

31 AQSH, F. 251, V. 1924, D. 198, f. 10.

32 Ibid., f. 11.

33 Ibid., f. 17.

34 Ibid., f. 19.

35 *DBFP,* series 1, vol. 26, no. 188, pp. 281–2.

36 See Veniamin Toçi, *Ndërhyrja e kapitalit të huaj në Shqipëri dhe qëndrimi i qarqeve demokratike, 1921–1925* (Tirana, 1974); and Iljaz Fishta and Veniamin Toçi, *Gjendja Ekonomike e Shqipërisë në Vitet, 1912–1944* (Tirana, 1983).

37 Arben Puto, 'Mbi Marredheniet e Jashtëme te Qeverisë Demokratike te 1924-es,' in Institute of History and Language, *Mbi Lëvizjen Kombëtare dhe Demokratike Shqiptare në vitet 1918–1924* (Tirana, 1966), p. 230.

38 Zenel Hamiti, *Historiku i Vajgurit ne Shqipëri* (Tirana, 1966), p. 63.

39 AQSH, F. 251, V. 1924, D. 323, f. 15.

40 *DBFP,* series 1, vol. 22, no. 730. p. 796.

41 Ibid.

42 Ibid.

43 Ibid., no. 732. p. 799; Avramovski, 'Qëndrimi i Anglisë,' pp. 162–3.

44 AQSH, Fondi Personal – L. Gurakuqi, F. 34, D. 11, F. 2.

45 Ibid., f. 6.

46 *Ora e Maleve,* 22 September 1923.

47 APOC offered 13.5 per cent of production to the state, while Standard Oil was prepared to give 15 per cent. Lastly, APOC sought a sixty-year term to Standard Oil's fifty-year bid.

48 See Puto, *Demokracia e Rrethuar,* p. 29.

49 Villa was general secretary of the Foreign Ministry under Noli.

50 Parr was third secretary at Durrës and chargé d'affaires from June 15 until August 26.

51 *DBFP,* series 1, vol. 26, no. 170. p. 248.

52 British representatives had earlier identified such joint U.S.-Italian companies as a mere cloak for the interests of Standard Oil of the United States. See *DBFP,* series 1, vol. 22, 1921–2, no. 754, p. 819.

53 AQSH, F. 251, V. 1924, D. 324, f. 8. The letter was sent to Tirana on October 22.

54 Boshnjaku was an unofficial spokesman of Soviet interests in Albania.

55 *Politika,* 10 July 1924; AQSH, F. 263, V. 1924, D. 131, f. 22–23. It is true that Britain had defended part of the Greek position vis-à-vis southern Albania. However, Harry Eyres had argued in favour of the Albanian position. See *DBFP,* series 1, vol. 22, no. 731, pp. 797–8, and no. 650, pp. 726–7.

56 Ibid. It is interesting to note that the Italian legation in Vlorë picked up this article and passed it along to the legation in Durrës as an example of the partisan politics of England and Harry Eyres. See AQSH, F. 263, V. 1924, D. 131, f. 21.

57 AQSH, F. 251, V. 1925, D. 154, f. 105. This was an undated letter written to Pandele Evangheli, probably in early 1925.

58 AQSH, F. 251, V. 1924, D. 324, F. 1. The telegram was sent on July 16 and received in Tirana on the 17th.

59 Ibid., f. 2.

60 *DBFP,* series 1, vol. 26, no. 285. p. 432.

61 Ibid. Austen Chamberlain, as foreign secretary, in a margin note, agreed with Ninčić's statement.

62 Alan Cassels, *Mussolini's Early Diplomacy* (Princeton, 1970), p. 243.

63 AQSH, F. 251, V. 1924, D. 246, f. 5. The details of the meeting were sent from Rome on July 20.

64 Ibid., f. 6.

65 Ibid.

66 The interview took place in July, and the report was sent from Rome to Albania's Foreign Ministry on August 1st. See AQSH, F. 251, V. 1924, D. 246, f. 9.

67 Ibid.

68　Ibid. The notion that Noli's government had a short life expectancy came, according to Indelli, direct from Mussolini.

69　Ibid.

70　Ibid., f. 10.

71　Department of State, enclosure in U.S. embassy in Rome to the Secretary of State, no. 159, 3 September 1924, p. 3.

72　Ibid.

73　Ibid.

74　*Bashkimi,* 19 September 1924.

75　These statements were made in a report of September 20 from Rome for the Foreign Ministry. Mborja suggested that he had this information based on his own discussions with Italian officials. See AQSH, F. 251, D. 246, F. 21.

76　See Puto, *Demokracia e Rrethuar;* and Puto, 'Mbi Marredheniet e Jashtëme te Qeverisë Demokratike te 1924-es,' p. 232. Puto argued in both works that in refusing to recognize Noli's government the United States 'hid behind' a juridical position, but its attitude was really political.

77　Department of State, Division of Near Eastern Affairs to F.M. Dearing, 18 June 1921, 875.6363/9.

78　Ibid.

79　Department of State, enclosure in Ambassador Child in Rome to the Secretary of State, 22 May 1922, 875.00/76.

80　F.M. Dearing to the Secretary of Commerce, 13 July 1921, 875.6363/8.

81　Hoover to the Secretary of State, 25 April 1922, 875.6363/21.

82　Ibid.

83　Department of State, Maxwell Blake to the Secretary of State, 16 September 1922, 875.00/79.

84　Ibid.

85　Department of State, Sinclair Oil Exploration Company to the Secretary of State, 19 September 1922, 875.6363/29.

86　Ibid.

87　Department of State, Secretary of State to the Albanian Commissioner, 22 September 1922, 875.6363/29.

88　Ibid., Maxwell Blake to the Secretary of State, 26 October 1922, 875.6363/33.

89　This was the text of a telegram from Mr Soper in Albania to Sinclair Oil Company in New York. See Department of State, Maxwell Blake to the Secretary of State, 26 October 1922, 875.6363/33.

90　Ibid., Soper to Sinclair Oil; see Blake to Secretary of State, 29 October 1922, 875.6363/34.

91 Department of State, Division of Near Eastern Affairs to the Secretary of State, 16 November 1922, 875.6363/43.
92 Ibid.
93 Department of State, Hughes to the American Legation, 27 February 1923, 875.6363/49.
94 Ibid.
95 Department of State, memorandum from the Division of Near Eastern Affairs to the Secretary of State, 12 March 1923, 875.6363/72.
96 Ibid.
97 Department of State, Grant-Smith to the Secretary of State, 3 March 1923, 875.6363/57. Grant-Smith claimed to have the information from reliable official and unofficial sources.
98 Department of State, Division of Near Eastern Affairs, memorandum, 8 January 1923, 875.51A/14.
99 Ibid.
100 Department of State, Office of the Economic Advisor, memo to the Assistant Secretary, 30 January 1923, 875.51A/27.
101 AQSH, F. 251, V. 1923, D. 230, f. 96.
102 Ibid., f. 98.
103 Department of State, Merrit-Swift to the Secretary of State, 13 September 1923, 875.00/97.
104 Ibid.
105 On 16 April 1924, Mr E.S. Sheffield of Standard Oil had asked Grant-Smith to 'make the strongest proper representations to the Albanian government to have the proposals referred to the Albanian parliament at the earliest possible moment' (AQSH, F. 251, V. 1924, D. 323 f. 40).
106 Ibid., f. 36.
107 Department of State, Grant-Smith to the Secretary of State, 27 March 1924, 875.6363/145. Charges and counter-charges of bribery were rife in this period. U.S. officials speculated that Zogu had received 30,000 pounds in the fall of 1923, while other sources suggested that the U.S. interests were subsidizing an unnamed Albanian paper in hopes of influencing public opinion. See Department of State, report of the U.S. Vice-Consul in Salonika on the economic situation in Albania, 27 February 1924, 875.50/10.
108 Department of State, Grant-Smith to the Secretary of State, 22 June 1924, 875.01/244.
109 Ibid., Grant-Smith to the Secretary of State, 19 June 1924, 875.00/10.
110 Ibid. In a telegram of June 25 to Hughes, Grant-Smith wrote that it had largely been through the intermediary of the Nationalists 'while in

opposition that the efforts of Ahmet Bey Zogu to disregard American rights to equal opportunity were thwarted' (Grant-Smith to the Secretary of State, no. 292, 25 June 1924, 875.01/246).

111 Department of State, Grant-Smith to the Secretary of State, no. 296, 2 July 1924, 875.01/247.

112 Ibid.

113 Department of State, Hughes to Grant-Smith, 23 June 1924, 875.01/243.

114 Ibid., Hughes to Grant-Smith, 25 June 1924, 875.01/244.

115 The United States eventually applied the same standard to Noli's government that was adopted toward Bolshevik Russia. Noli's regime remained unrecognized because it was a 'regime functioning in a country as the government thereof which has attained its control by force and in opposition to a local constitution in the absence of ample evidence that the change has been in fact supported by the people' (Department of State, Office of the Solicitor, memo, 3 October 1924, 875.00/157).

116 Department of State, Grant-Smith to the Secretary of State, no. 285, 13 June 1924, 875.00/150.

117 AQSH, F. 251, D. 17, V. 1924, f. 207.

118 Department of State, Grant-Smith to the Secretary of State, no. 288, 19 June 1924, Coleman and De Long, 385.1123/c and d/79.

119 In a telegram of September 16, the U.S. legation advised the State Department that 'at no time since the minister's [Grant-Smith was on leave] departure have conditions been so changed as to justify on my part reopening the question of recognition' (Department of State, Trojan Kodding to the Secretary of State, 16 September 1924, 875.00/157).

120 Department of State, Grant-Smith to the Secretary of State, no. 340, 27 October 1924, Coleman and De Long, 375.1123/c and d/98.

121 Ibid., enclosure no. 1, p. 3, in Grant-Smith to the Secretary of State, no. 377, 2 January 1925, 376.1123/Coleman and De Long/114. The enclosure offers a translation of the court's verdict.

122 Ibid. The court claimed to have secret documents from the Interior Ministry. I was unable to locate any such documents. It is worth noting that the court also concluded that the murder was undertaken with the aid of Yugoslavia.

123 As the verdict of the trial was delivered on December 14, Berati's visit was well timed.

124 Department of State, enclosure no. 1 in Grant-Smith to the Secretary of State, no. 264, 13 December 1924, 375.1123/Coleman and De Long/111.

125 Ibid.

126 Department of State, Office of the Solicitor to the Secretary of State, 9 January 1925, 375.1123/Coleman and De Long/117.

127 Ibid. This conclusion was also reached by the Division of Near Eastern Affairs.

128 Ibid. This report was necessary so as to decide the U.S. position on Zogu's seizure of power on 24 December 1924.

129 Department of State, enclosure no. 1, p. 7, in Haven to the Secretary of State, no. 226, 6 October 1924, 875.00/161.

130 Ibid., p. 6.

131 Ibid.

132 Ibid., p. 8.

133 See all the articles in Institute of History and Language, *Mbi Lëvizjen Kombëtare dhe Demokratike Shqiptare në vitet 1918–1924* (Tirana, 1966).

134 The idea that Noli favoured an 'Albania for the Albanians' approach crept into the historiography merely to satisfy the agenda pursued by communist party leader Enver Hoxha. For details on communist foreign policy, see Elez Biberaj, *Albania: A Socialist Maverick* (Boulder, 1990).

135 Živko Avramovski suggested that during his September trip to the League, Noli met with both French prime minister Herriot and British prime minister MacDonald. It appears that only after these meetings did Noli understand the link between elections and recognition. See Avramovski, 'Qëndrimi i Anglisë,' p. 177.

6. The League of Nations and the Soviet Union

1 *League of Nations – Official Journal,* Records of the Fourth Assembly, Supplement no.13, p. 207.

2 Ibid., p. 208.

3 Ibid.

4 Since 1920, Albania has fought any trends aimed at allowing different regions greater control in decision-making. Politicians felt that such forms of government would encourage separatist movements, especially among the Greek population in the south. As well, in the north it would also encourage Yugoslav meddling, especially in the aftermath of the Mirdita uprising in 1921.

5 *League of Nations – Official Journal* 5 (1924): 727–8. The foreigner he was referring to was Colonel Stirling.

6 On 1 March 1924 the Albanian representative in Geneva had been informed that many deputies, as well as the finance minister, were insisting on the denunciation of Hunger's contract. The representative, Benoit Blinishti, was asked to gauge the impression such a move would have on the League. See AQSH, F. 251, V. 1924, D. 425, f. 1.

7 In a letter to the League, Benoit Blinishti had noted that his salary and expenses were nearly 100,000 gold francs and that the sum 'constituted a

heavy charge upon the modest budget of Albania. This sacrifice was only made in the expectation of an improvement in the country's financial and economic position. Not a single reform, however, has been carried out in the past year, nor has a single serious measure been taken for the economic reconstruction of the country.' See *League of Nations – Official Journal* 5 (June 1924): 843.

8 Department of State, Grant-Smith to the Secretary of State on the termination of Hunger's contract, 4 March 1924, 875.51A/42.

9 *League of Nations – Official Journal* 5 (May 1924): 762–3.

10 Ibid., January 1924, p. 165.

11 Article 22 stipulated that 'the financial advisor's engagement shall be valid for a period of five years, but may, after the first year, be terminated at three months' notice by either of the parties' (AQSH, F. 251, V. 1924, D. 7, F. 216–216).

12 Ibid.

13 Ibid., f. 221–222.

14 AQSH, F. 251, V. 1924, D. 236, f. 18.

15 In a League session of June 17, ostensibly held to discuss the question of Saint Naum and Vermosh, the League secretary noted 'the new government of Albania will doubtless wish to devote its attention to the question of the cancellation of Mr. Hunger's contract' (AQSH, F. 251, V. 1924, D. 131, F. 81).

16 AQSH, F. 251, V. 1924, D. 164, f. 13–15. According to the correspondence, Harry Eyres had sent the message to the Foreign Office on behalf of the president of the Council, who apparently could not obtain telegraphic facilities. The Foreign Office then advised its delegation in Geneva, which passed on the request to the Albanian permanent secretary to the League, B. Blinishti.

17 AQSH, F. 251, V. 1924, D. 141, F. 1.

18 Ibid., D. 7, F. 273–74.

19 The *New York Times* reprinted the speech in its entirety and called it the 'most talked of, and certainly the most picturesque, speech of the session' (*New York Times*, 5 October 1924).

20 *League of Nations – Official Journal*, Special Supplement no, 23. 1924, pp. 100–2.

21 Ibid., p. 101.

22 For this point, I am grateful to Professor Nasho Jorgaqi of the University of Tirana.

23 *League of Nations – Official Journal*, Special Supplement no. 23, 1924, p. 41.

24 Logoreci, *The Albanians*, p. 55.

25 The main defender of this interpretation has been Arben Puto. See his
   Demokracia e Rrethuar and 'Sur les rélations extérieures du gouvernement
   démocratique de 1924 en Albanie,' *Studia Albanica* 2 (1964): 29–45. For
   the official communist viewpoint, see Institute of Marxist-Leninist Studies,
   History of the Party of Labour of Albania, 2nd edn (Tirana, 1982), pp. 15–18.
   See also Valentina Duka, *Historia e Shqiperise* (Tirana, 2007).
26 AQSH, F. 251, V. 1923, D. 210, f. 18–19.
27 Ibid., D. 198, f. 2.
28 Ibid.
29 Ibid., f. 4–5.
30 Ibid., f. 6–7.
31 Ibid., f. 9.
32 Ibid., V. 1924, D. 296, f. 3.
33 The Council of Ministers met on 28 June 1924, and the order was made
   official on July 3 (AQSH, F. 251, V. 1924, D. 297, f. 2). Communist-inspired
   works on Soviet-Albanian relations neglect to mention the sentence in the
   decision that makes reference to the confiscation of property.
34 AQSH, F. 251, V. 1924, D. 296, f. 3.
35 Ibid., f. 17.
36 Ibid.
37 Ibid., f. 23.
38 *Journal de Geneve,* 22 October 1924; and AQSH, F. 251, V. 1924, D. 298, f. 4.
39 Miles Lampson noted that he had nothing to confirm this report and felt
   that the activity on the Albanian border with Serbia had been 'pure ban-
   ditry' with 'no political organization' (*DBFP,* series 1, vol. 26, enclosure no.
   281, p. 427).
40 AQSH, F. 251, V. 1924, D. 262, f. 1.
41 *Morning Post,* 27 November 1924.
42 AQSH, F. 251, V. 1924, D. 296, f. 36.
43 Ibid., f. 34.
44 *DBFP,* series 1, vol. 26, no. 287, p. 438.
45 Ibid., pp. 437–8.
46 AQSH, F. 251, V. 1924, D. 296, f. 43.
47 Ibid., f. 49.
48 Ibid., F. 56.
49 According to Arben Puto, the early December démarche to the Soviet
   embassy in Rome had arrived late in Moscow and received no attention. It
   is doubtful, however, that Soviet diplomatic correspondence was so poor
   that the many attempts made by the Albanian government were simply not
   received. What is more likely is that the Soviets tried to impose a *fait accompli*

on both Albania and the outside world. See Puto, *Demokracia e Rrethuar,* p. 50.

50 Bushati was a nephew of Gurakuqi who had obtained his post after the purge of some of Albania's key legations abroad. Professor Sami Repishti pointed this out to me.

51 AQSH, F. 251, V. 1924, D. 296, f. 51–52.

52 See Grigory Bessedovsky, *Revelations of a Soviet Diplomat* (Westport, 1971 [1931]), p. 29.

53 AQSH, F. 251, V. 1924, D. 296, f: 27. This telegram is neither dated nor signed, but the context suggests that it was sent in the aftermath of Bushati's news that visas had been given to a Soviet delegation.

54 Reshat Kellici, *Me Djemtë e Bashkimit* (Tirana, 1965), p. 110.

55 AQSH, F. 251, V. 1924, D. 295, F. 1.

56 Ibid., f. 10.

57 Ibid., f. 11.

58 *Times,* 30 December 1924.

59 Ibid., 7 January 1925.

60 Shpuza, *Revolucioni Demokratiko-Borgjez,* p. 14.

61 The role of Boshnjaku has not been fully assessed. Owing to a later quarrel with Enver Hoxha, any references to Boshnjaku disappeared. Boshnjaku's grandson, Kosta, pointed this out to me in Tirana in 1991.

62 Department of State, telegram from Grant-Smith to the Secretary of State, no. 218, 6 February 1924, 875.032/6.

63 The one remaining member of the country's Regency Council, Sotir Peci, was opposed to the move *(DBFP,* series 1, vol. 26, no. 287, 11 December 1924; see footnote no. 9).

64 *Times,* 11 December 1924.

65 *DBFP,* series 1, vol. 26, no. 287. p. 437.

66 Avramovski, 'Qëndrimi i Anglisë,' p. 178

7. Traitor One Day, Patriot the Next

1 Puto, *Demokracia e Rrethuar,* p. 225.

2 The Yugoslavs helped to spread disinformation on Zogu's movements with the aim of confusing Albanian political circles. On November 17, the Belgrade *Politika* published an article stating that Zogu had left for France. Subsequently the Albanian press published the same information. However, Zogu in fact never left Yugoslavia. See *Bashkimi,* 18 and 22 November 1924.

3 Kolonja was paying an unnamed woman who was on 'intimate terms' with Zogu. Kolonja's only problem was the simple fact that he lacked the necessary funds to keep the woman happy. See his telegram of December 3 to the Foreign Ministry (AQSH, F. 251, V. 1924, D. 257, f. 148).

4 Ibid.

5 Ibid., f. 149.

6 AQSH, F. 251, V. 1924, D. 275, f. 151, 3 December 1924.

7 Ibid.

8 Internal memo, Foreign Affairs Ministry, AQSH, F. 251, V. 1924, D. 257, f. 149.

9 *Bashkimi,* 9 December 1924.

10 Swire, *Albania,* p. 45.

11 AQSH, F. 251, V. 1924, D. 257, f. 175, 14 December 1924.

12 Ibid., f. 194, memo to foreign legations, 18 December 1924. The note stated that twenty-three soldiers were captured and that three were Serb regulars. The presence of Serb soldiers and weapons, the Foreign Ministry argued, constituted 'brilliant proof that the frontier troubles are fomented by the Serb government.'

13 In the memo, the Albanians also suggested that refugee Bulgarians and Macedonians, dressed in Albanian costumes, joined regular Serb forces in the frontier attack. Owing to the situation, the Albanian government was forced to declare general mobilization and sent an appeal to the Great Powers and the League to intervene with Belgrade to end this 'grave menace to peace in the Balkans' (Albanian Information Bureau communiqué, 19 December 1924, AQSH, V. 251, V. 1924, D. 264, f. 77).

14 In a telegram of December 16 to the relevant foreign representatives in Albania, the Albanian Information Bureau made this point clear, noting that the commander of the frontier in Kosovo stated that the initial attack was by Serb regular troops, who were later replaced by irregular troops (AQSH, F. 251, V. 1924, D. 257, f. 187).

15 After receiving an official complaint from the Albanian representative in Greece, the Greek government issued assurances that it would maintain strict neutrality (AQSH, F. 251, V. 1924, D. 264, f. 108).

16 The initiative for the meeting came from the Italian side, and Yugoslav foreign minister Ninčić arrived on December 10 in Rome, ostensibly to take part in League of Nations discussions. In the aftermath of discussions, Mussolini and Ninčić issued a statement on December 13 that they would not interfere in Albanian internal affairs. See Puto, *Demokracia e Rrethuar,* p. 219.

17 Arifi-Bakalli, 'Qeveria Demokratike,' p. 256.
18 In a memo of December 11 to the Foreign Ministry, Konica wrote that Britain would make a démarche to the Yugoslav government (AQSH, F. 251, V. 1924, D. 257, f. 170).
19 Telegram of December 12 from Belgrade, AQSH, F. 251, V. 1924, D. 257, f. 173.
20 AQSH, F. 251, V. 1924, D. 265, f. 123.
21 Ibid., f. 125.
22 Ibid., f. 124.
23 Department of State, Dodge to the Secretary of State, 18 December 1924, 875.00/166.
24 *DBFP*, series 1, vol. 26, no. 300, p. 452.
25 Department of State, aide-memoire to the U.S. Secretary of State from the U.S. legation of the Kingdom of Serbs, Croats and Slovenes, 20 December 1924, 875.00/172.
26 See the discussion between Branko Lazarević of the Albanian Section of the Yugoslav Foreign Ministry and Percival Dodge, in Department of State, Dodge to the Secretary of State, no. 2510, 16 December 1924, 875.00/174.
27 Ibid.
28 Ibid.
29 'Monthly Summary,' *League of Nations – Official Journal* 4.12 (Dec. 1924): 283. Both articles called for international arbitration.
30 *League of Nations – Official Journal* 6.5 (May 1925): 640.
31 Ibid., p. 641.
32 Albanian Information Bureau. AQSH, F. 251, V. 1924, D. 264, f. 76.
33 Ibid., f. 80.
34 Proclamation of the prime minister, AQSH, Fundi Personal – Fan Noli, F. 14, D. 89, f. 2.
35 Ibid.
36 *Bashkimi*, 20 December 1924.
37 According to a telegram of December 23 from London, Mehmet Konica advised the Foreign Ministry that the Italian government had semi-officially informed the British government that they would not demand a mandate (AQSH, F. 251, V. 1924, D. 255, f. 12).
38 Ibid., f. 14.
39 Ibid., f. 7, 15 December 1924.
40 Ibid., f. 8.
41 Ibid., f. 10, 20 December 1924.
42 On December 13, Mborja was authorized to approach the Italian government with a view to obtaining arms (AQSH, F. 251, V. 1924, D. 251, f. 6). On

December 16, Mborja was informed that the minister of war had authorized
a Mr Kodeli to sign a contract with Mr Stamati for munitions. The Foreign
Ministry also advised Mborja that he was to take a special interest in this and
accelerate the shipments (ibid., f. 2).
43 Ibid., f. 5.
44 Ibid., f. 1,
45 Ibid.
46 Ibid., f. 7.
47 AQSH, F. 251, V. 1924, D. 255, f. 13.
48 On December 26 the Albanian legation in Athens announced that government
troops had fortified a line along the Shkumbin River and that a provisional
capital had been established in Vlorë (AQSH, F. 251, V. 1924, D. 209, f. 3).
49 *New York Times,* 27 December 1924.
50 *The Times,* 30 December 1924.
51 Ibid.
52 *Dielli,* 6 January 1925.
53 *DBFP,* series 1, vol. 26, no. 310, p. 471.
54 AQSH, F. 251, V. 1924, D. 264, f. 130.
55 Ibid.
56 Department of State, U. Grant-Smith to the Secretary of State, no. 373, 26
December 1924, 875.00/177.
57 Ibid.
58 *League of Nations – Official Journal* 6.5 (May 1925): 642.
59 *DBFP,* series 1, vol. 27, no. 3. p. 6.
60 Ibid., vol. 26, no. 308, p. 466.
61 Puto, *Demokracia e Rrethuar,* p. 239.
62 See Fischer, *King Zog,* p. 88.
63 Ibid.
64 Puto, *Demokracia.,* p. 40.
65 Department of State, Hughes to U. Grant-Smith, 10 January
1925, 875.01/258.
66 Ibid., Hughes to U. Grant-Smith, 20 January 1925, 875.01/260.
67 A new trial was convened on 9 April 1925. The court exonerated Zogu,
convicted seven people, and declared the motive to be robbery. See
Department of State, 375.1123/Coleman and De Long/128.
68 Three key leaders, Bajram Curri, Hasan Prishtina, and Luigi Gurakuqi, were
all assassinated. Curri and Gurakuqi were murdered in 1925, while Prishtina
was shot in Salonika in 1933. Albanian communist historiography maintains
Zogu undertook the murders with the aid of Yugoslav agents. See Buda
et al., *Fjalori Enciklopedik,* pp. 145, 328, and 867–8.

69 Noli, *Autobiografia*, p. 87.
70 This is the main conclusion of Bernd Fischer in *King Zog and the Struggle for Stability in Albania.* Joseph Swire, in *Albania: The Rise of a Kingdom,* also credited Zogu with the key role in nation building. It would be fair to say that Zogu did manage to unify the country from an administrative point of view, but judging from Albania's experience during the Second World War and under communist rule, the interwar period did little to alleviate the main religious and regional obstacles to unity.
71 Noli, *Autobiografia*, p. 86.

8. Conclusion

1 Noli, *Autobiografia*, p. 86. In communist historiography, the party line was that the 'destruction of democratic government and the June Revolution was directly the result of foreign intervention; the combined action took shape as an international conspiracy' (Puto, *Demokracia e Rrethuar,* p. 254).
2 Quoted in Owen Pearson, *Albania and King Zog: Independence, Republic and Monarchy* (London, 2004), p. 240.

Bibliography

Manuscripts

Albania

Arkivi Qendror i Shtetit i Shqipërisë (State Central Archives of Albania,
Tirana, Albania; *Abbreviation:* AQSH)

PERSONAL RECORDS

Luigj Gurakuqi
Faik Konica
Mehmet Konica
Kosovo Committee
Fan S. Noli
Hasan Prishtina
Avni Rustemi
Ahmet Bey Zogu

GOVERNMENT RECORDS

Ministria e Jashteme, 1921–1925 – Fundi 251 (Foreign Ministry)
Ministria e Brendshme, 1923–1925 (Interior Ministry; *Abbreviation:* MPB)
    Periudha e Zogu (Period of Zogu)
    Periudha e Nolit (Period of Noli)

United States

Department of State Decimal File, Record Group 59, 375.1123 – Coleman and De Long. National Archives, Washington, DC. (*Abbreviation:* Coleman and De Long)

General Record of the Department of State, Record Group 59 – Visa Division – Visa Case Files, 1924–1932. National Archives, Washington, DC. (*Abbreviation:* Department of State)

Records of the Department of State Relating to the Internal Affairs of Albania, 1910–1944. Record Group 59, National Archives Microfilm Publication M1211, 16 rolls. National Archives, Washington DC.

Published Documents

Albania: Fletore Zyrtare (Official Gazette)

Documents on British Foreign Policy, 1919–1939. First Series. London: Her Majesty's Stationery Office, 1946 – (*Abbreviation: DBFP*)

Documents Relating to the Advisory Opinion No. 9. The Hague: Publications of the Permanent Court of International Justice, Series C, No. 5-II, Fifth Ordinary Session, 4 September 1924.

Hasan Prishtina: Permbledhje Dokumentash, 1908–1934. Tirana: General Directorate of the State Archives, 1982.

The League of Nations – Monthly Review. Geneva: Publications of the League of Nations, 1920–5.

The League of Nations – Official Journal. Geneva: Publications of the League of Nations, 1920–5.

The League of Nations – Special Supplements. Geneva: Publications of the League of Nations, 1920–5.

Question of the Monastery of Saint Naoum. Leyden: A.W. Sijthoff's Publishing Co., 1924.

Newspapers

Albanian

Aferimi
Bashkimi (Vlorë)
Dielli (Boston)
Drita (Gjirokastër)
Gazeta e Korçës (Korçë)
Ora e Maleve (Shkodër)

Politika (Vlorë)
Shekulli (Organ of the National Democratic Party)
Shqipëria e Re (Romania)
Shqiptari i Amerikës (Korçë)
Zëri i Popullit (Tirana)

English

Chicago Tribune
The Independent
The Near East
New York Times
The Times (London)

Secondary Literature

Academy of Sciences of the People's Socialist Republic of Albania. *Çështje të Lëvizjes Demokratike dhe Revolucionare Shqiptare në Vitet 1921–1924.* Tirana: Institute of History, 1977.
Academy of Sciences of the Republic of Albania, *Historia e Popullit Shqiptare.* Tirana: Toena, 2002.
Academy of Sciences of the Republic of Albania – Institute of History, *70 Vjet të Kishes Ortodokse Autoqefale Shqiptare.* Publication of the Symposium, Tirana, 19 September 1992.
Agani, Hilmi. 'Revolucioni i Qershorit 1924.' *Rilindja*, 13 July 1974, pp. 12–13.
Arifi-Bakalli, Ermine. 'Qeveria Demokratike e Fan Nolit dhe Qëndrimi i Mbreterisë SKS ndaj saj.' *Gjurmime Albanologjike* 11 (1981): 239–60.
Avramovski, Živko. 'Battling and Bargaining over Kosovo and Albania during the First World War.' In *Kosovo Past and Present.* Ed. Gordana Filopović. Belgrade: Review of International Affairs, 1989. 75–90.
– 'Qëndrimi i Anglisë ndaj Qeverise së Fan Nolit në Shqipëri ne Vitin 1924.' *Gjurmime Albanologjike* 2 (1972): 161–83.
– 'Kontribut Studimit te Çështijes se Marradhenieve Shqiptaro-Jugosllave Midis dy Luftave Boterore.' *Gjurmime Albanologjike* 2 (1968): 121–60.
– 'Kontribut Studimit te Historise së Shqipërisë ne Perioden Midis dy Luftave Boterore.' *Gjurmime Albanologjike* 2 (1968): 121–62.
Baerlein, Henry. 1922. *Southern Albania: Under the Acroceraunian Mountains.* Chicago: Argonaut Inc., 1968.
Banac, Ivo. *The National Question in Yugoslavia: Origins, History, Politics.* Ithaca and London: Cornell University Press, 1984.

Barros, James. *The Corfu Incident of 1923: Mussolini and the League of Nations.* Princeton: Princeton University Press, 1965.

Bessedovsky, Grigory. 1931. *Revelations of a Soviet Diplomat.* Westport, CT: Hyperion Press, 1971.

Biberaj, Elez. 'Kosova: The Balkan Powder Keg.' *Conflict Studies* 258 (Feb. 1993): 1–26.

– *Albania: A Socialist Maverick.* Boulder, CO: Westview Press, 1990.

Buda, Aleks, et al. *Fjalori Enciklopedik Shqiptar.* Tirana: Academy of Sciences of the People's Socialist Republic of Albania, 1985.

– *Historia e Shqipërisë.* Tirana: Institute of History and Language, 1965.

Burks, R.V. *The Dynamics of Communism in Eastern Europe.* Princeton: Princeton University Press, 1961.

Cassels, Alan. *Mussolini's Early Diplomacy.* Princeton: Princeton University Press, 1970.

Dedi, Beli, et al. *Dokumenta e Materiale Historike nga Lufta e Popullit Shqiptar per Liri e Demokraci, 1917–1941.* Tirana: State Archives of the People's Republic of Albania, 1959.

Dilo, Lefter L., collector. *Ligjëron Fan Noli.* Tirana: Ismail Mal'Osmani, 1944.

Djordjevic, Dimitrije, and Stephen Fischer-Galati. *The Balkan Revolutionary Tradition.* New York: Columbia University Press, 1981.

Dragnich, Alex N., and Slavko Todorovich. *The Saga of Kosovo: Focus on Serbian-Albanian Relations.* Boulder, CO: East European Monographs (distributed by Columbia University Press), 1984.

Duka, Valentina. *Historia e Shqipërisë.* Tirana: Kristalina – KH, 2007.

Durham, M.E. (Edith). *High Albania.* London: Virago, 1985.

Elsie, Robert. *Historical Dictionary of Albania.* 2nd edn. Toronto: Scarecrow Press, 2010.

Federal Writers' Project of the Works Progress Administration of Massachusetts. *The Albanian Struggle in the Old World and New.* Boston: The Writer, Inc., 1939.

Fischer, Bernd J. 'Fan Noli and the Albanian Revolutions of 1924.' *East European Quarterly* 22 (June 1988): 147–58.

– *King Zog and the Struggle for Stability in Albania.* Boulder, CO: East European Monographs (distributed by Columbia University Press), 1984.

Fishta, Iljaz, and V. Toçi. *Gjendja Ekonomike e Shqipërisë në Vitet 1912–1944.* Tirana: 8 Nentori, 1983.

Fitzherbert, Margaret. *The Man Who Was Greenmantle: Biography of Aubrey Herbert.* London: John Murray, 1983.

Frasheri, Kristo. *The History of Albania.* Tirana: 9 Nentori, 1964.

Funder Burk, David. 'Anglo-Albanian Relations, 1920–1939.' *Revue des Etudes Sud-est Européennes* 13 (1975): 117–25.

Gage, Nicholas. 'The Forgotten Minority in the Balkans: The Greeks of Northern Epirus.' *Mediterranean Quarterly* 4.3 (Summer 1993): 10–29.

Grothusen, Klaus-Detlev, ed. *Handbook on South Eastern Europe: Albania.* Vol. 7. Gottingen: Vandenhoeck and Ruprecht, 1993.

Hall, Derek. *Albania and the Albanians.* London: Pinter, 1994.

Hamiti, Zenel. *Historiku i Vajgurit ne Shqipëri.* Tirana: Naim Frasheri, 1966.

Hasluck, Margaret. *The Unwritten Law in Albania.* London: Cambridge University Press, 1954.

Heathcote, Dudley. *My Wanderings in the Balkans.* London: Hutchinson and Company, 1925.

Heaton-Armstrong, Duncan. *A Six Month Kingdom: Albania, 1914.* London: I.B. Tauris, 2005.

Hutchings, Raymond. *Historical Dictionary of Albania.* London: Scarecrow Press, 1996.

Institute of History. *Revolucioni i Qershorit 1924 në Kujtimet e Bashkëkohëve.* Tirana: 8 Nentori, 1974.

Institute of History and Language. *Mbi Lëvizjen Kombëtare dhe Demokratike Shqiptare në vitet 1918–1924.* Tirana: Insitute of History, 1966.

Institute of Marxist-Leninist Studies at the Central Committee of the Party of Labour of Albania. *History of the Party of Labour of Albania.* 2nd edn. Tirana: 8 Nëntori, 1982.

Janku, Virgil. 'Veprimet Luftarake dje Ushtria Shqiptare në Revolucioni Demokratike-Borgjez të Qershorit 1924.' *Studime Historike* 1 (1985): 51–67.

Jelavich, Barbara. *History of the Balkans.* 2 vols. Cambridge: Cambridge University Press, 1983.

Jorgaqi, Nasho. *Jeta e Fan Nolit.* Tirana: Ombra GVG, 2005.

– *Udhëtim me Fan Nolin.* Tirana: Dituria, 1994.

Kastrati, Jup. *Faik Konica.* New York: Gjonlekaj, 1995.

Kellici, Reshat. *Me Djemtë e Bashkimit.* Tirana: Naim Frasheri, 1965.

Kodra, Masar. *Fan Noli: Në Rrjedhat Politike të Shoqërisë Shqiptare, 1905–1945.* Prishtina: Rilindja, 1989.

Kondis, Basil. 'The Albanian Question at the Beginning of 1920 and the Greek-Albanian Protocol of Kapestitsa, May 28th, 1920.' *Balkan Studies* 20.2 (1979): 393–417.

– *Greece and Albania, 1908–1914.* Thessaloniki: Institute for Balkan Studies, 1976.

Kondis, Basil, and Eleftheria Manda, eds. *The Greek Minority in Albania: A Documentary Record, 1921–1993.* Thessaloniki: Institute for Balkan Studies, 1994.

Konica, Faik. *Albania: The Rockgarden of Southeastern Europe.* Boston: Vatra, 1957.

Kontos, Joan Fultz. *Red Cross – Black Eagle: A Biography of Albania's American School.* Boulder, CO: East European Monographs (distributed by Columbia University Press), 1981.

Kourvetaris, Yorgos A., and Betty A. Dobratz. *A Profile of Modern Greece in Search of Identity.* Oxford: Clarendon Press, 1987.

Logoreci, Anton. *The Albanians: Europe's Forgotten Survivors.* London: Victor Gollancz, 1977.

Lukacs, John A. *The Great Powers and Eastern Europe.* New York: American Book Company, 1953.

Magocsi, Paul R. *Historical Atlas of Central Europe.* Toronto: University of Toronto Press, 2002.

– *Historical Atlas of East Central Europe.* Toronto: University of Toronto Press, 1993.

Malcolm, Noel. *Kosovo: A Short History.* London: Macmillan, 1998.

Michalopoulos, Dimitris. 'The Moslems of Chamuria and the Exchange of Populations between Greece and Turkey.' *Balkan Studies* 27.2 (1986): 303–13.

Milo, Paskal. *Shqipëria dhe Jugosllavia.* Tirana: Enciklopedike, 1992.

– 'Marredheniet Shquptare – Jugosllae ne vitet 1922–1924.' *Studime Historike* 1.1 (1990): 107–29.

Naska, Kaliopa, 'Kongresi Themeltar i Kishes Ortodokse Autoqefale në Berat,' In Academy of Sciences of the Republic of Albania – Institute of History, 70 *Vjet te Kishës Ortodokse Autoqefale Shqiptare.* Tirana, 1993. 10–20.

Noli, Fan, *Autobiografia.* Prishtina: Rilindja, 1968.

_ ed., and comp. *Fiftieth Anniversary Albanian Orthodox Church in America, 1908– 1958.* Boston: Albanian Orthodox Church, 1960.

Pano, Nicholas C. 'Konica and the Albanian Community in the United States.' Conference paper delivered at the Vatra-sponsored symposium on Konica at Fordham University, New York, 22 April 1995.

– 'The Albanian Cultural Revolution.' *Problems of Communism* 23.4 (July-Aug. 1974): 44–57.

– *The People's Socialist Republic of Albania.* Baltimore: Johns Hopkins University Press, 1968.

Pearson, Owen. *Albania and King Zog: Independence, Republic and Monarchy.* London: The Centre for Albanian Studies in association with I.B. Tauris, 2004.

Pipa, Arshi. *The Politics of Language in Socialist Albania.* Boulder, CO: East European Monographs (distributed by Columbia University Press), 1989.

– 'Fan Noli as National and International Albanian Figure.' *Sudost Forschungen* 43 (1984): 241–70.

Pollo, Stefanaq, and Arben Puto. *The History of Albania: From Its Origins to the Present Day.* London: Routledge and Kegan Paul, 1981.

Puto, Arben. *Demokracia e Rrethuar.* Tirana: 8 Nëntori, 1990.

– 'La Question du statut international de l'Albanie devant la Société des Nations et la Conférence des Ambassadeurs.' *Studia Albanica* 2 (1965): 19–44.

– 'Disa Probleme Juridike të Paverësisë Shqiptare.' *Studime Historike* 1 (1965): 1–29.

– 'Çeshtja e njohjes ndërkombëtare te Qeverisë Democratike të 1924-es.' *Studime Historike* 1 (1964): 5–34.

– 'Sur les rélations extérieures du gouvernment démocratique de 1924 en Albanie.' *Studia Albanica* 2 (1964): 29–45.

Qosja, Rexhep. 'Fan S. Noli (1882–1965).' *Gjurmime Albanologjike.* 1 (1969): 196–238.

Rossos, Andrew. *Russia and the Balkans: Inter-Balkan Rivalries and Russian Foreign Policy, 1908–1914.* Toronto: University of Toronto Press, 1981.

Rothschild, Joseph. *East Central Europe between the Two World Wars.* Seattle: University of Washington Press, 1974.

Roucek, Joseph S. *Balkan Politics: International Relations in No Man's Land.* Stanford: Stanford University Press, 1948.

Ryan, Andrew Ryan. *The Last of the Dragomans.* London: Geoffrey Bles, 1951.

Selenica, T. *Shqipria e Illustruar.* Tirana: Ministry of the Interior, 1928.

– *Shqipria më 1927.* Tirana: Ministry of the Interior, 1928.

– *Shqipria më 1923.* Tirana: Ministry of the Interior, 1923.

Shpuza, Selim. *Revolucioni Demokratike-Borgjez i Qershorit 1924 në Shqipëri.* Tirana: Ministry of Education and Culture, 1959.

Sjoberg, Orjan. *Rural Change and Development in Albania.* Boulder, CO.: Westview Press, 1991.

Skendi, Stavro. *The Albanian National Awakening, 1978–1912.* Princeton: Princeton University Press, 1967.

– ed. *Albania.* New York: Praegar, 1958.

– 'Albanian Political Thought and Revolutionary Activity, 1881–1912.' *Sudost Forschungen* 13 (1954): 1–40.

– 'The Northern Epirus Question Reconsidered.' *Journal of Central European Affairs* 14.2 (July 1954): 143–53.

– *The Political Evolution of Albania.* Mimeographed Series, No. 19, 8 March 1954. New York: Mid-European Studies Center, 1954.

Statuti i Shoqnis 'Bashkimi.' Tirana, 1924.

Stavrianos, Leften S. *The Balkans since 1453.* New York: Rinehart and Company, Inc., 1958.

Stefanovic, Djordje. 'Seeing the Albanians through Serbian Eyes: The Inventors of the Tradition of Intolerance and Their Critics, 1804–1939.' *European History Quarterly* 35.3 (July 2005): 465–92.

Stickney, Edith P. *Southern Albania or Northern Epirus in European International Affairs, 1912–1923*. Stanford: Stanford University Press, 1926.

Story, Somerville, ed. *The Memoirs of Ismail Kemal Bey*. New York: E.P. Dutton and Co., 1920.

Sugar, Peter F., and Ivo Lederer, eds. *Nationalism in Eastern Europe*. Seattle: University of Washington Press, 1969.

Sulzberger, Cyrus Leo. *A Long Row of Candles*. Toronto: Macmillan, 1969.

Swire, Joseph. *Albania: The Rise of a Kingdom*. New York: Arno Press, 1971.

Tako, Piro. *Fan Nolin në Fushën Politike dhe Publicistike*. Tirana: Nëntori, 1975.

Thernstrom, Stephan, ed. *Harvard Encyclopedia of American Ethnic Groups*. Cambridge: Harvard University Press, 1980.

Toçi, Veniamin. *Ndërhyrja e kapitalit të huaj në Shqipëri dhe qëndrimi i qarqeve demokratike, 1921–1925*. Tirana: Naim Frasheri, 1974.

– 'Qeveria fan S. Nolit dhe Kapitali i huaj ne Shqipëri.' *Probleme Ekonomike* 4 (1974).

Tomes, Jason. *King Zog: Self Made Monarch of Albania*. Stroud: Sutton, 2003.

Verteniku, Hilmi. 'Problemi i Asamblesë Kushtetuese dhe Zgjedhjet e vitet 1923.' *Studime Historike* 4 (1968): 111–43.

Vickers, Miranda. *The Albanians: A Modern History*. London: I.B. Tauris, 1995.

Vinanver, Vuk, 'Anglia dhe Pozita Ndërkombëtare e Shqipërisë Midis dy Luftave Boterore.' *Gjurmime Albanoligjike* 1 (1968): 185–238.

Who Was Who III (1929–1940). London: Adam and Charles Black, 1941.

Winnifrith, T.G. *Badlands – Borderlands: A History of Northern Epirus / Southern Albania*. London: Duckworth, 2002.

Wolff, Robert Lee. *The Balkans in Our Time*. Cambridge: Harvard University Press, 1974.

Ylli, Kahreman, 'La révolution de juin 1924.' *Studia Albanica* 2 (1964): 17–28.

Zapantis, Andrew L. *Greek-Soviet Relations, 1917–1941*. Boulder, CO: East European Monographs (distributed by Columbia University Press), 1982.

Zog, Ahmed. 'King Zog Tells His Story.' Unpublished manuscript, Tirana, 1932. Available on-line at http://www.albanianhistory.net/texts20_1/AH1933.html

Index